THE ART
of
SELF-SUPERVISION

Studying the link between self-reflection and self-care

LAURIE PONSFORD-HILL

The Art of Self-Supervision
Copyright © 2018 by Laurie Ponsford-Hill

All rights reserved. No part of this publication may be reproduced, distributed, or transmitted in any form or by any means, including photocopying, recording, or other electronic or mechanical methods, without the prior written permission of the author, except in the case of brief quotations embodied in critical reviews and certain other non-commercial uses permitted by copyright law.

Tellwell Talent
www.tellwell.ca

ISBN
978-0-2288-0629-5 (Hardcover)
978-0-2288-0628-8 (Paperback)
978-0-2288-0630-1 (eBook)

TABLE OF CONTENTS

ABSTRACT IX
DEDICATION XI
ACKNOWLEDGEMENTS XIII
INTRODUCTION XV
    Research Question and Purpose xx

CHAPTER ONE: LITERATURE REVIEW. 1
    Nature of the Self 1
        Self of the modernist and postmodernist. 5
        Self-construction 9
        Self-construction through art 14
    Healing through Art Therapy 16
    Self-Study as Self-Care and the Art Therapist 24
        Art as self-exploration. 27
    The Self-Portrait 30
        The use of self-portraiture as meaning-making 35
        Self-Portraiture as self-reflection 38
    Self-Reflection. 41
        Art as therapy 46
        Art and lived-experience 52
        Dialoguing with images 55
        Visual journals and responsive writing 57
    Arts-Based Assessments in Art Therapy 59
        Draw A Person (D-A-P) 60
        Kinetic-House-Tree-Person (K-H-T-P) 60
        The objective approach 61
        Symbols of the self 63
    Research Implications 76

CHAPTER TWO: METHOD 77
    Research Paradigm 78
    Methodology. 82
        Phenomenology. 82
        Arts-based research. 86
    Methods. 88
        Participants. 89
        The data collection procedure. 92
        Data analysis. 95
        Reflexivity. 96
        Credibility, dependability and trustworthiness. 97
    Ethical Considerations 99

CHAPTER THREE: RESULTS 101
    Analysis of Data 101
    Thematic Analysis 103
        Self-awareness though symbolism of environment. 103
        Symbolism expressed through use of media.. 109
        Self-awareness through emotional, spiritual and bodily-awareness. . . . 121
        Construction of self through word in art. 129
        Self-awareness through engagement with the inner-child. 139
        Self-awareness through transformation. 150
        Self-awareness of professional self-identity. 159
        Self-awareness through self-care. 174
        Self-awareness of hope and appreciation.. 183
    Summary. 188

CHAPTER FOUR: DISCUSSION 189
    Evaluation of process. 189
    Discussion of Findings 194
        Feeling and thinking through self-portraiture and reflection. 194
        The true self through self-portraiture and reflection. 198
        Self-care as a professional responsibility. 200
        Self-portraiture for art therapists 202

 Implications 205

 Limitations 206

 Conclusion 207

 Recommendations for Further Study 207

CHAPTER FIVE: PERSONAL AND THEOLOGICAL REFLECTIONS . . 209

EPILOGUE. 219

REFERENCES 221

APPENDIX A: ADVERTISEMENT. 237

APPENDIX B: WEEKLY REFLECTION PROCESS. 239

APPENDIX C: QUESTIONS FOR THE TELEPHONE SCRIPT 241

LIST OF TABLES

Table 1: Constructivism Compared with Existentialism.................. 23

Table 2: Approach to Picture Interpretation and Symbols of Self........... 66

Table 3: Meanings of Colour 70

Table 4: Six Stages of Development.................................... 72

Table 5: Descriptive List of Participants by Category and Number 91

Table 6: Frequencies and Percentages of Essential Themes............... 102

LIST OF TABLES

Figure 1. Self-Portraits by Linda 105

Figure 2. Self-Portraits by Laura 110

Figure 3. Self-Portraits by Salina 114

Figure 4. Self-Portraits by Sade 123

Figure 5. Self-Portraits by Tracey 131

Figure 6. Self-Portraits by Alice 134

Figure 7. Self-Portraits by Justin 140

Figure 8. Self-Portraits by Sandy 147

Figure 9. Self-Portraits by Penny 152

Figure 10. Self-Portraits by Mary 157

Figure 11. Self-Portraits by Sally 162

Figure 12. Self-Portraits by Bessie 166

Figure 13. Self-Portraits by Karen 176

Figure 14. Self-Portraits by Megan 181

Figure 15. Self-Portraits by Nike 185

Figure 16. Self-Portraits by Laurie 214

LIST OF ABBREVIATIONS

CATA   Canadian Art Therapy Association

D-A-P   Draw A Person Test

K-H-T-P   Kinetic-House-Tree-Person

OATA   Ontario Art Therapy Association

ABSTRACT

This phenomenological, arts-based study examined the experiences of 15 art therapists using five-minute, full-bodied self-portraiture with 55 minutes of self-reflective journaling once a week for four weeks at the end of each work week. The therapists determined the location for this practice. Subsequently, the four artworks, as a serial, were explored with each participant in a one-hour telephone or Skype interview to understand their lived experience through art, and its signs, and symbols. This process enabled the therapists to act as witness to their respective self/selves, deepening their insights and connections about self. Eight themes about the self surfaced, including self-awareness through: symbolism of environment; emotional, spiritual and bodily awareness; construction of self through word in art; engagement with inner-child; transformation; awareness of professional self; self-care; and awareness of hope and appreciation. The results, confirmed with each participant, found that their self-portraits, using simple materials such as photocopy paper and markers, resulted in images which visually captured the artist's actual experience, in ways that words could not. The subsequent reflections concerning the images resulted in rich descriptions that facilitated their respective self-assessments, and in turn, their future directionality. The results also affirmed the importance of self-care for the art therapist through the creation of art, as a means for maintaining their inner artistic drive and desire, and balance and well-being and as a means for self-supervision.

DEDICATION

This project is dedicated to my fellow arts therapists and particularly those art therapists who willingly gave their time, and shared their artwork and stories to me. Their delightful combination of courage, humour, wisdom and inspiration is reflected through their portraits, and will be with me always . . . through exhibitions and publications to come.

ACKNOWLEDGEMENTS

I begin by thanking all my art teachers and professors I have encountered along the way for being the inspiration for this project and for all the clients that I have had the privilege to serve at the private practice where I have worked since graduation. I would also like to thank all the students that I have had the pleasure of supervising for their kind advice, enthusiasm and support.

Acknowledgements and thanks go to my advisor, Dr. Kristine Lund. During the many years of this project Professor Lund's clear vision provided a foundation for continued effort to see this project through to fruition. I would like to acknowledge Dr. Olena Darewych for her ideas for this project, combined with the creative knowledge and experience in arts-based research methods taking me into unthought-of areas of expertise and development. I would also like to thank my committee members Dr. Marshall Fine and Dr. Allen Jorgenson for their insights and enthusiasm. I would like to thank my external, Kelvin Ramirez from Lesley University for his participation and observations. I also thank my professor/retired committee member Dr. Nancy Riedel Bowers, for her ongoing belief in this project and in me. I would also like to acknowledge my supervisor, Patricia Berendsen, who has been a big inspiration for my continued progression.

I thank my husband, Brian for all his support and encouragement during this time. To my children, Roland and Emerald, I apologise for the time commitment this project took, the continued pile of books, articles and the like that started to encroach all the tabletops of the house and for understanding my ongoing commitment to this project. To my son Roland and editor Susan McBroom, I say a special thank you.

INTRODUCTION

I began the exploration of self-portraiture and its implications while obtaining a Fine Art undergraduate degree, and later when attending the advanced degree program at the Vancouver Art Therapy Institute. I was interested in learning how to surface meaning about identity through self-portraits. My journey began by exploring photographers who specifically examined the use of self-portraiture, such as Arnulf Rainer and Cindy Sherman. Arnulf Rainer drew over photographs of himself to reflect psychological states on a "drive to self-transcendence through self-abnegation" (Hoy, 1987, p. 73). Cindy Sherman photographed her multiple self, depicting her self-portraits as "archetypes active within contemporary culture" (Hoy, 1987, p. 91). The depiction of various psychological states within the self-portrait appealed to my interest in pursuing art therapy. Subsequently, I was particularly influenced by Natalie Rogers who was electronically interviewed by Tony Merry (1997), a psychology professor at the University of East London. Natalie Rogers, the daughter of the founder of client-centred therapy, Carl Rogers, discussed her own life journey, noting that writing about her life is part of her own therapy. She observed that writing about herself led to her decision to combine person-centred philosophy with the creative arts process.

Rogers defined the person-centred expressive therapist, as one using artistic expression as a healing strategy to promote self-exploration and understanding. At the core of humanistic, expressive arts therapy is faith in the individual's ability to find appropriate self-direction. Rogers believed that if the psychological climate is empathic, honest and caring, this will occur. She described this phenomenon using her experience of expressing sad or angry feelings through dance, noting that in the presence of an empathic, non-judgemental witness, her feelings and perceptions would shift dramatically. She observed that, after the dance movement, her visual artwork became expressive, spontaneous and revealing. When she followed visual art-making with free writing, she was able to plunge deeper into previously guarded feelings and thoughts. One expressive art form stimulated and nurtured another, invoking deeper and more profoundly meaningful revelation of her inner truths. At the same time, Rogers was aware that inner healing had taken place.

I was also inspired by Brown (2008) and Allen (1992) who illuminated the need for art therapists to continue their art work and engage in the self-reflection that artistic activity inspires, while carrying on their therapy practice. Discussing her research findings, Brown (2008) stated that it is imperative for art therapists to nurture their own creativity during professional practice, noting that failure to do so can lead to caregiver burnout. She underscored Aliaga's (2003) and Allen's (1992) opinions that burnout, stress, career drift and clinification[1] result when the art therapist neglects to engage in regular art making. Noting that art therapists differ from other therapists by using creative processes to engage with clients, Brown (2008) agrees with McNiff's (1998) observation that art therapists feel pressured to develop a medically modelled image aligned with those of more clinical therapists, rather than reflecting their own artistic personae.

Brown's (2008) research addressed the frequency with which creative arts therapists experience care-giver burnout, noting that they often become aware of this when making art outside the workplace. She listed many of the benefits of maintaining an active art practice, including a sense of wholeness and completion, increased commitment, greater spiritual depth, achieving balance, enrichment and transformation, as well as finding tranquility in chaos. By contrast, art therapists who did not engage in art-making outside the workplace experienced a sense of depletion and disconnection. Brown (2008) noted the need for more research into the effects, on art therapists, of suspending their own artistic activities, and the ways in which this affects

---

[1] Clinification refers here to the process whereby art therapists minimize their use of art in therapy and adopt the methods and techniques of other therapies.

their clients. Her research findings and her insistence on the need for further investigation undergird this study with its focus on the importance of art-making for the therapist's sense of completion, connection and self-care.

Finally, Cameron (2007) influenced this journey. She examined the factors discouraging art therapists from engaging in self-nurturing and self-reflective practice, observing that the artist is likely to avoid artist dates, and suggesting that this is caused by resistance and fear of self-intimacy. Noting that avoidance is common in difficult relationships, she believes that, in such instances, the therapist wishes to avoid self-disclosure because it will involve acknowledging and expressing possibly hurtful information. She adds that, despite its inherent challenges, self-disclosure brings true intimacy within a relationship, stating,

> In order to have a real relationship with our creativity, we must take the time and care to cultivate it. Our creativity will use this time to confront us, to confide in us, to bond with us, and to plan. (Cameron, 2007, p. 35).

Further, Cameron (2007) believed that engaging in creativity is a spiritual experience and designed her intervention to enable the individual to recognize, nurture, and protect his/her inner artist. Understanding that participation, in an art practice, allows the individual to move beyond pain and creative constriction, her process of creative recovery incorporates two basic tools. She terms the first tool "the morning pages" (p. 513), described as a regular engagement in longhand, stream-of-consciousness writing. The second tool is called the "artist date" (p. 513) and requires the individual to nurture creative consciousness by devoting a specific amount of time to be engaged in artistic practice. Contending that art-making is the work of the inner "creative child" (p. 4), Cameron (2007) states that spending time in solitude with the artist-child is essential to self-nurturing for the artist. She explains that, since art therapy is based on the creation of art, it is necessary for the art therapist to consecrate time in the company of the artist-child in a place of solitude, to engage in creative, self-nurturing behaviours. Her therapeutic strategy helps therapists reconnect with their creative inspiration, by regularly engaging in two different modes of reflective practice, namely, writing and creating artwork.

My personal experiences, as a clinician and as an art therapist, affirm the importance for members of the helping professions to monitor and maintain their well-being. Catherine Hyland Moon (2002) reminded me that the art therapy profession has slowly evolved to its contemporary form with the acknowledgement that the therapist is a mental health professional. She underscored the usefulness of artistic expression as a therapeutic strategy enabling clients to access their deepest levels of self-awareness and self–actualization. The art therapist is aware that the creative process is both more profound and significant to the individual than what is actually created. Making the assumptions that a therapist's professional responsibility incorporates ensuring his/her own mental wellness, and that art therapy seeks to heal, improve or restore personal well-being, I concluded it would be valuable to examine the effectiveness of weekly self-portraiture in promoting the self-awareness and professional effectiveness of art therapists. As a result, this study was designed to obtain insight from the experience of other art therapists regularly using a specific creative intervention as a means of self-reflection and self-supervision. By requiring study participants to reflect on the "self", I believed it was possible to obtain information concerning whether this specific art intervention increased the individual therapist's understanding of their self-concept.

Prior to proceeding, three particular personal experiences occurred which are relevant to this research. First during a trip to Toronto, I visited the Art Gallery of Ontario where Suzy Lake, my fine arts mentor at the University of Guelph, was holding retrospective show culminating years of photography. In her forward to *Introducing Suzy Lake,* Gevinson (2014) cites the *Oxford English Dictionary's* definition, in 2013, of the selfie as "a photograph that one has taken of oneself, typically with a smart phone or webcam and uploaded to a social media website" (p. 13). I observed that Suzy Lake took selfies for more than forty years, creating many series of images exploring personal identity and performance. Gevinson quotes Lake as saying, "What is really important is that the awareness of all of this becomes a constructive thing so that we're not victims by our own hands. It is empowering to understand and overcome these gestures. Self-awareness is self-empowering" (p. 13). Uhlyarik (2014) quotes Lake addressing the manner in which aging changes our perceptions of ourselves and observing that viewing her own work over time has enabled her to feel "her true self in her true space in her true rhythm" (p. 173).

As I walked through the gallery of Lake's work, I engaged in a retrospective reflection on my artistic pursuits. I was reminded of my first opportunity to create a hand drawn selfie in high school, when assigned to draw a self-portrait while looking in a mirror. No matter how hard I tried, I always drew one eyebrow raised higher than the other, depicting a questioning attitude. I would see a placid face reflected in the mirror yet could not control the pencil to draw what I saw. Interestingly, the photographic selfies, taken during undergraduate work with Suzy Lake, resulted in similar observations and insights. Remembering that my interest in exploring self-portraiture had started long ago, I realized that, until developing this project, I had postponed this investigative journey.

The second experience concerned my use of self-portraiture with clients to enable self-reflection. Subsequently, I conducted an examination of the engagement of several clients using self-portraiture in therapy and published an article entitled, *Art and Psychotherapy* (Hill, 2014). The results noted that clients' self-portraits indicated that they had engaged in considerable self-reflection and that the process allowed them to connect with themselves on physical, emotional, psychological and spiritual levels. This led to greater self-awareness, permitting clients to experiment with new ways of being, and to move towards transformation. These observations led the researcher to examine the possible effects of self-portraiture on the internal and external experience of art therapists.

The third event was my decision to engage in the same self-reflective process required of the participants. I was initially aware of my avoidance for engaging in the self-portrait process and scheduling precious time each week to engage in the ritual practice. For example,

> As I load my files and paperwork into my rolling briefcase; there hadn't been enough time during the day to answer the flood of emails and complete evaluations, professional development plans or to process through receipts. I reflect on my day and then my week and wonder, where did the time go? Although the work day was active, and the hours seemed to fly by, I have found the pace and demands of being a therapist at some points

overwhelming. I head home after my day knowing that I have to find time in the evening to complete these still undone tasks. (Hill, personal reflection journal, June 17, 2014)

From this experience, I realized how easy it is to fill the day with client sessions. It is harder to manage the demands of the necessary paperwork, and more difficult still, to consecrate adequate time for self-reflection and engagement in the creative process. Nevertheless, I chose to do so.

Research Question and Purpose

The primary research question for this study was: what is the art therapist's lived-experience of drawing a full-bodied self-portrait each week for four weeks?

Projective drawing assessment is a tool used by art therapists with clients to generate an image and facilitate the client reflection of their perception of the lived experience. The assumption is that this self-portrait reflects elements of a client's perception of conflict, body image, relationships, self-awareness, self-concept, and self-image (Allen, 1995; Furth, 1988; Glaister, 1996; B. L. Moon, 1995; Nunez, 2009).

Historically, the projective drawing assessment tool was used for psychological assessment predominantly with children. The psychologist would give their clients a simple drawing test using 8.5x11 inch drawing paper and pencil with a rating scale (Kroon, 1999). With the evolution of the profession of art therapy, the self-portrait has been implemented as a psychological assessment with a wide range of client's experiencing an array of issues (Gilroy et al., 2012; LeClerc, 2006; Manchover, 1980; Miller, 2014). More recently, some art therapists have included the use of coloured pencils, markers, pastels, and/or larger paper (Darewych, 2014; Kroon, 1999).

The current study was devised to address the use of the self-portrait as a self-reflective tool for art therapists. The goal of this study was to contribute to a better understanding of self-portraiture as a process of self-reflection, and as a strategy, whereby art therapists can increase self-understanding and address the self-care responsibility mandated by their profession. The approach was influenced by the work of Cameron (2007) and offers art therapists a methodology that mirrors its philosophy and practice. The study was designed for its ease of administration and brevity for the practicing art therapist. The intent was for the art therapist to easily incorporate and integrate self-portraiture and self-reflection within his/her practice as a means of self-supervision.

There were three primary reasons that led to this research question and approach. The first, as previously mentioned, concerned my interest in the use of self-portraiture, as a means for helping professionals maintain well-being, and explore self. The second reason surfaced as I read the literature about the tendency of art therapists to experience career drift and clinification. I believed that integrating self-portraiture and self-reflection would minimize both. Third, there are very few phenomenological studies which investigate the use of full-body self-portraiture in art therapy. Furthermore, I was unable to find published evidence of phenomenological studies focused on art therapists and their regular use of full-body self-portraiture for self-reflection.

Chapter One reviews the literature concerning the many aspects of the self and the literature related to self-reflection using self-portraiture in art therapy. The review offers a discussion about: the nature of self; healing through art therapy; self-care and the art therapist; the self-portrait; self-reflection; and arts-based assessments in art therapy. The review offers information found to further investigate and explore the therapeutic needs of the self of the therapist and the therapeutic potential of the self-portrait.

Chapter Two discusses the methodological framework for this qualitative study which was descriptive phenomenological, arts-based research. The study used The Descriptive Phenomenological Psychological Method created by Amedeo P. Giorgi (1997), to examine lived-experience with each art therapist. Also, because the basis of the lived-experience is in the creation of art, arts-based research was the means of inquiry for examining the multiple ways of seeing and multiple ways in which experience can be constructed (Finlay, 1994). This chapter offers an overview of qualitative research and the research paradigm or the set of underlying beliefs and assumptions that guided this research; identifies the methodology and methods used to answer the research question, including participant selection, informed consent, data collection and analysis, credibility, dependability and trustworthiness, and reflexivity; and reviews the ethical considerations and procedures followed throughout this research.

Chapter Three presents the self-portraitures and reflections of the fifteen Art Therapists. Additional insights come to light as the therapists review their respective portraits side-by-side with me. It is important that I have purposefully avoided providing any detail regarding the backgrounds of the Art Therapists to insure anonymity. All participants' names have been replaced with pseudonyms.

Chapter Four discusses the overarching findings and implications that surfaced from this research; points out some of the limitations of this research; and provides some recommendations for further research. Finally, Chapter Five presents some of my self-portraits with my personal and theological reflections concerning this research.

The present study is unique in its focus on the art therapist's sense of self while experiencing life and work. In the act of creating a self-portrait, the artist is exploring themselves, in effect looking within to do their self-research, by exploring an image of their internal and external reality (Cederbaum, 2009). The self-portraits that were created by the therapists provided both insights for the participant's and answered the research question. It is my intent that this study adds to the body of knowledge of an arts-based self-reflective intervention for art therapists to explore their lived-experience, influence self-care practice, as a means of self-supervision and influence institutional change to include continued practice of self-care.

CHAPTER ONE
LITERATURE REVIEW

This chapter reviews the literature about the development and exploration of self, and the use of self-portraiture and reflection in art therapy. The purpose of this review was to inform the conduct and analysis of this inquiry and is organized to discuss: the nature of the self; healing resources of art therapy; an overview of the self-portrait; self-reflection; arts-based assessments in art therapy; and the implications for the research process and analysis. The self is first explored, as the basis of the self-of the self-portrait.

Nature of the Self

For the purposes of this research project, the self is understood to comprise those elements of the personality which make one person different from any other. Self may be parallel to the essence of an individual's being. The characteristics of an individual's self are known as his/her identity. The identity is composed of internal mental images, or constructs, that create that individual's self-image (Santrock, 2011). The different elements that compose the self-image are exposed in a self-portrait. This section reviews those different elements and begins with what makes up the psyche (Freud, 2010), the connection of mind and body (Orbach, 2009), the self as subject and as object as self-experience (Kohut, 1971), the difference of true self and false self (Winnicott, 1965), and the acquisition of self-knowledge (Baumeister & Bushman, 2001).

Identity is defined as "the condition or fact of being a specific person or thing; individuality" (Coles Concise English Dictionary, 1978, p. 374).

The elements that make up identity include essential character traits and those qualities that are fundamental to the individual's sense of well-being. It follows that every individual has an internal mental picture of who they are; an internal self-portrait of an inward reflection of outward appearance. The internal mental images depict who the individual is in the current moment and contain images of their past and future selves (Glaister, 1996; Hanes, 2007; Smith, 2008). The past, present and future selves intertwine and coalesce into a belief system about self that makes up everyone's self-concept – providing the answer to the question, "Who am I?" (Berger & Luckman, 1966).

At the beginning of the twentieth century, Sigmund Freud developed psychoanalysis to deconstruct and understand the individual psyche. Freud (2010) postulated a theory of the elements comprising the psyche of the self that became the cornerstone of future researchers' understanding. He (2010) identified the ego, id and superego as the three fundamental components of the self, indicating that they are all present in the individual's mind at birth, and noting that they constitute an individual's personality. According to Freudian (2010) theory, the ego is the part of the psyche that mediates between the id and the demands of the individual's environment. The id is an impulsive, subconscious part of the self that seeks pleasure and avoids pain. The superego works to incorporate the socio-cultural values and morals of the community in which the individual lives. When the ego fails to hold the id's selfish and impulsive needs in check, the superego floods the individual's consciousness with feelings of guilt. The superego contains the ego-ideal, an imagined vision of the individual's ideal-self-image of how they ought to look and behave when at their best.

Freud (2010) contended that the greater part of what constitutes the self, and the way its components function, was either preconscious or subconscious. He believed that preconscious and subconscious information were not consciously available to the individual in the present moment but had the potential to be called into consciousness. Perceptions and ideas which could not become conscious and were therefore, not available to introspection, were termed unconscious. He also identified transference, as an element of unconscious behavior in which an individual redirects emotion from past experience to another person.

Orbach (2009) observes that Freud was captivated by the relationship between mind and body, examining physical symptoms for which there was no medical explanation and drawing links between mind and body experience. He said, "From there [Feud] drew links between what individuals had experienced, their construction and memory of what had happened and how they made sense of that experience in the light of their unconscious longings and conflicts" (p. 9). This research project was intended to do just that; allow the participants to draw links between their lived-experience and their construction and memory over four weeks through self-reflection on their portraits.

Orbach (2009) describes the effects of embodiment upon the individual's sense of self, discussing the impact of conflict within the mind upon the body, and emphasizing that both identity and the physical body are shaped and formed with reference to our visual world. The self and self-identification are reflected in: who it is we are on the inside; how we look on the outside; and how we are perceived by others. We are both the subject and object of lived-experience (Orbach, 2009).

Building upon the work of Freud's psychoanalytic theory, Kohut (1971) developed the modern psychoanalytic theory of self-psychology. He postulates that the individual self is both the subject, who lives through experience, and the object of that experience. Kohut (1971) suggests that while self-representations, or self-schemas, reside within the individual's id, ego and superego, contradictory conscious and preconscious self-representations can also exist within him/her. He identifies a developmental stage through which the individual develops from autoerotism (instinctual satisfaction) to narcissism (self-love), describing it as a time of fragmented self. Narcissism tends to be used as a pejorative term, however each individual needs to have a sense of love for self to positively love or help others. Kohut (1971) indicates that this time of fragmentation develops into the stage of the cohesive self, in which the individual's increased physical and mental self-experience is cohesive, in space, and has continuity over time. This sense of cohesiveness might also be termed authenticity (McNiff, 2007; B. L. Moon, 1997; Winnicott, 1965). Authenticity can be described as an individual having the sense that they are the same on the outside as on the inside.

Kohut's (1971) theory suggests that when the cohesive self is firmly established, the individual can experience overall enjoyment of the diverse components making up self. He observes that the different internal elements that comprise the self, function in relation to both the individual's body and their mind, so that when cohesiveness is firmly established, they experience enjoyment "because [they] feel secure that these body parts and their functions belong to a firmly established total self" (p. 118). What is happening within the psyche and the feelings of the body or soma are therefore important to the individual's sense of cohesiveness or feeling 'whole', all of which are fundamental to a sense of well-being. Kohut (1971) adds that, when the cohesiveness of the self-experience has been strengthened, the cohesiveness and continuity of the self "leads to not only a subjective feeling of well-being but secondarily also to an improvement in the functioning of the ego" (p. 120).

He also attributes increased working efficiency to cohesiveness, stating that an absence of cohesiveness results in a fragmentation of the self that can be identified by "chronic work disturbances" (Kohut, 1971, p. 120). This statement is important to this research, since the assumption is that the weekly self-portrait provides a means to explore the self-experience by the therapist. In turn, this could provide the opportunity for: strengthening self-experience and increasing cohesiveness, continuity and a sense of well-being for the therapist, which could increase work efficacy.

Winnicott (1965) offers another view of self-cohesiveness and authenticity. He coined the terms true self and false self, defining the true self as a sense of self based on an experience of authenticity whereby the individual perceives that the inner and outer selves are aligned and real. By contrast, the individual experiences having a false self when they do not feel alive and present a mere façade of authenticity. Winnicott (1965) suggests that appropriate parenting provides the infant with an accurate mirror of his/her experiences, and as a result, the child feels a sense of pleasure at being alive, inhabiting a reality that encourages continued true self growth. When parenting fails to mirror the infant's experience, the child develops a sense of false self, necessitating the development of a façade or hiding internal emptiness behind a pretended real self on the outside. This could imply that being able to provide a mirror for oneself of one's lived-experience could encourage continued true self-growth, and increased self-knowledge of reality.

Baumeister and Bushman (2001) contend that the self is made up of three different elements which they name: self-knowledge; the interpersonal self; and the agent self (p. 59). They suggest that self-knowledge, or self-concept, refers to the way the individual knows and experiences self. The authors indicate that an individual's self-knowledge is composed of self-awareness, self-esteem and self-deception, identifying the looking glass self as the individual's vision of how he/she appears to others, which can either be accepted or rejected (p. 69). The agent self is the part of the self that makes decisions for healthy living. Enhanced self-knowledge means that an individual needs to be able to see themselves clearly to be their own self-agent.

Thus, the self is composed of conscious and unconscious elements (Freud, 2010), which can be fragmented and false (Kohut, 1971) or cohesive and true (Winnicott, 1965). The false or true nature of self cannot be overlooked, as it is the foundation of the individual's self-image or self-representation. Because the false self is not cohesive, dis-integration or loss of the central-self can occur. Alternatively, the true or cohesive self incorporates all the different parts of self, resulting in the individual's sense of personal well-being (Kohut, 1971), which enables the agent self to make healthy personal and professional choices (Baumeister & Bushman, 2010). One way to understand the agent self is to consider the modernist and post-modernist influences on the nature of self.

Self of the modernist and postmodernist

Because individuals interpret themselves differently according to their view of the world, a discussion follows about the modern and post-modern view of self. I compare the phenomenological concept of the person as self-interpreting with the modern Cartesian view. The modern view of self, as a distinct individual having a core way of being, has been replaced with the post-modern view of self, in which everyone has many "selves".

Modernism declares that knowledge is power, and it is important to know one's true or authentic self. By the late nineteenth century, debates within the disciplines of physiology, psychology and philosophy, and scientific findings, indicated that the evidence of bodily senses were unreliable (Otero-Pailos, 2010). This inspired a change from the modernist to postmodernist perspective regarding the self, and significantly affected the way individuals viewed themselves, their work and their roles in society. What was once premised on establishing an authentic self became the need to change self, based upon experience, context and the need to be a different self.

Cresswell (2011) suggests that the individual contains different kinds of selves which give rise to a dynamic self that depends upon self-experience and context. This suggests that the individual's self is made up of elements that are based on individual experience which can shift and change depending upon the individual's current context. This combined capacity results in the formation of different selves and different identities, each based upon the individual's lived-experience. This had important implications in regard to the interpretation of the self through the serial self-portrait.

According to Otero-Pailos (2010), Husserl (1859-1938) was instrumental in the development of phenomenology with its emphasis on the nature of and relationship between experience and consciousness, melding intellectual and body experience together (p. 253). "Husserl transposed this discourse of attention from the empirical to the transcendental" (p. 253). Otero-Pailos (2010) makes the important clarification that the idea of individuality is a modern construct whereas postmodernism contends that there are many different selves, more than one way of being, and that individuals are made of up many parts.

Cresswell (2011) indicates that the postmodern, social constructivist view of the self is socially constructed and changeable. Gemin (1999) concurs contending that the self is not static, observing that a post-modern mindset permits theorists to suggest that the self develops in multiple ways. These include understanding that self-creative processes are not only directed outwardly to worldly objects and events, but also inwardly, challenging the limits of experience and self-identity. This implies that, by creating a serial self-portrait and reflecting upon it, the creator has an opportunity to become aware of and reflect upon their respective selves. The interpretation of the self-portrait becomes flexible based on the frame of reference. This new perspective affords the creator an awareness that the nature of self is fundamentally dynamic. This dynamism can influence the way in which therapists practice.

Loven (2003) discusses the paradigm shift from the modern to the post-modern era, addressing many of the changes this involved in terms of work, family and education. His research findings indicate that, from a post-modern viewpoint, counseling should be oriented "more towards the whole person and his or her life projects." (p. 123), thereby encouraging clients to become proactive in the construction of their lives. This suggestion is based upon the postmodernist opinion that the individual constructs his/her life based on ever-changing situations and experiences that require them to make changes in what they expect of self. Creation and re-creation then becomes fundamental to an individual's way of being in the world. Individuals, from this perspective, can continually design their reality based upon lived-experience.

Gemin (1999) suggests that, through the process of creativity and post-modern reflection, identifying the different experiential frames of reference is of primary significance to the individual. The author adds that the individual then integrates the differentiated frames of reference into the id, noting the roles of irony, paradox, double meanings, and contradictions of experience implicated in this task. He suggests that a creative interplay between order and disorder results, during which the self is understood to be either a work in progress or fractured. He also observes that in the creative process there is a pendulum-swing between lived-experience and any material, such as language, that allows the experience to be integrated. These ideas make a significant contribution to understanding the processes involved in self-reflection.

Writing about the art and science of caring, Leonard (1994) summarizes the differences between the modern Cartesian view of the person and Heidegger's phenomenological perspective. From a Cartesian viewpoint, the self is the subject, passively viewing the external world as object. The self is understood to possess a body and to hold cognitive representations of the world, while meaning is grounded in the individual's actions. Leonard (1994) identifies the paradigm shift, from Cartesian to phenomenological perspectives, as a movement from speculation about being, to speculation about what being means to the individual. Lived-experience becomes meaning-making.

For a phenomenological theorist, meaning is derived through personal experiences, relationships and language. These meaningful elements center on the individual's relationship to their environment. Leonard (1994) observes that this perspective incorporates understanding that things meaningful to one individual may qualitatively differ from those of another person. Furthermore, differences in individual situations result in individuals addressing qualitatively different concerns. Leonard concludes that to understand a person's world and meanings requires studying the individual in a holistic context. She says,

> It matters to the clinician what meaning a pregnant woman's anxiety has because by understanding the world and meanings of the pregnant woman, the clinician is far more able to determine whether to intervene to help the woman to see new possibilities in her situation that will have meaning for her given her world. (p. 51)

A phenomenological perspective views everyone as self-interpreting, with the meaningful elements of the self, having emerged from each individual's background. The everyday lived-experience of the embodied self is taken for granted. When something happens to the body, the individual develops insight. Leonard (1994) describes this phenomenon, as follows, "one approaches illness as a rupture in the patient's ability to negotiate the world" (p. 53). She suggests that a practice to encourage self-interpretation, that brings experiences that might otherwise be taken for granted into consciousness, enables the individual self to gain insight about the context of these experiences. Self-interpretation becomes key.

Heidegger's phenomenological view envisages a person being-in-time as directional and relational. Leonard (1994), in describing Heidegger, adds that a person is studied within the context of their having-been-ness. Leonard (1994) contends that being, in both the past and future, is care, stating "Care, in Heidegger's sense, is having our being be an issue for us" (p. 54). This implies that an individual's overview of self does not distinguish past, present and future. The self understands all periods of time to be interrelated, so that the past, present and future experiences are equally significant and important. Koskela (2012) describes the modern understanding of truth as an individual's subjective way of being in the world as both "truth and untruth" (p. 116). To show oneself is self-manifestation. Things are uncovered to someone in many ways, and even in ways that they are not. Koskela (2012) in his description of Heidegger's view suggests that unconcealment is an event in which truth of ones being in the world is uncovered into a unity manifesting a discourse "driven by human needs and human interests"

(p. 121). Truth is seen as a clearing in which understanding of being or essence can prevail while incompatible possibilities are concealed (p. 124).

This literature underscores the importance of having research participants identify their respective frame of reference during their creative process. This encourages them to be aware of their creative interplay, which Gemin (1999) suggests is between order and disorder, and regarding the self as a work in progress or fractured. From a post-modern perspective, as individuals move from one context to another they construct their lives (Loven, 2003). Different kinds of selves are influenced by an individual's environmental context, culture, experiences and relationships (Cresswell, 2011). Within everyone, the identity of the self is engaged in a continual process of negotiating between the self and the individual's psycho-social and environmental context. When an individual looks in the mirror or creates, and then examines, a self-portrait, their image may reveal different aspects of self, depending on the context.

Self-construction

Self-concept develops and gives rise to identity as part of the construction of the larger self. For purposes of this research, self-concept is defined as "an idea of the self constructed from the beliefs one holds about oneself and the responses of others" (Oxford English Dictionary, Retrieved May 2017). While self is defined as "the identity, character or essential qualities of a person" (Coles Concise English Dictionary, 1978, p. 679), self-image is defined as "one's concept of oneself and one's identity, worth, abilities, etc." (p. 680). The act of looking in a mirror or creating and examining a self-portrait provides access to the individual's sense of both self-concept and identity by depicting what can be seen, and what resides within the subconscious. Here two theories of the self are explored; existential and authentic, and social self-construction.

Argyle (2009) defines the existential self as the awareness by an individual of their authentic self; that which makes an individual separate and consistent. However, Argyle (2009) suggests that the individual's sense of self in social encounters affects their self-image because of the feedback they obtain from the reactions of others. Argyle (2009) emphasizes the importance of this socially-based feedback, noting that it constructs the framework upon which identity develops. As such, the ever-evolving construction of the self depends upon the feedback the individual receives from the outside world. This determines the individual's way in which they see themselves and as well how satisfied they are with themselves.

To investigate whether satisfaction with life is an indicator of personal adjustment, Palacios, Echaniz, Fernandez, and Ortiz de Barron (2015) explored the relationships between personal self-concept and satisfaction with life. They note that the ways in which one sees oneself, physically, academically, professionally, socially and privately, comprise an individual's self-concept. Their study addresses the four following dimensions of self-concept. The first dimension is self-fulfillment or whether individuals have achieved their life goals. The second dimension is autonomy which concerns whether individuals feel self-sufficient in their ability to make their own decisions, and understand themselves to be equal, yet different, from others. The third-dimension addresses honesty or whether individuals see themselves as being trustworthy and honourable. The final dimension of self-concept concerns the ways in which individuals evaluate their emotional regulation. Concluding that satisfaction with life is an indicator of personal adjustment, the authors contend that personal adjustment "reflects the extent to which people value their life positively and feels satisfied with what they have achieved in it" (p. 56). They indicate that the way the individual sees self has an impact on their self-image, self-concept and sense of identity.

Santrock (2011) suggests that, "identity refers to our self-portraits that develop over a life time and are made up of many components, including negations and affirmations of various roles and characteristics" (p. 317), not all of which are conscious to the individual. Berger and Luckmann (1966) add, "Only a small part of the totality of human experiences is retained in consciousness" (p. 67). They suggest that experiences settle, like sediment, into memorable entities, adding that, unless intra-subjective sedimentation happens, individuals cannot make sense of their biographies of knowledge. Berger and Luckmann (1966) observe that experiences shared with others who have similar biographies become incorporated into common knowledge. They note that shared experiences are transmitted from one generation to the next by a linguistic sign system, adding that the sign system can also be transmitted, through physical objects and actions which serve as objective means to integrate new experiences into the existing knowledge base, affirming that reality is constructed, not just individually but in a social context. An art object such as the self-portrait can serve as a means to integrate new experience.

Berger and Luckmann (1966) conclude that the sociology of knowledge concerns itself with the social construction of reality. The development of the self takes place in an inter-relationship with the individual's environment and therefore, the nature of the self is socially determined. As previously mentioned, Berger and Luckmann (1966) suggest that individuals create themselves, noting that this does not take place in solitude, but is a social enterprise. The existence, within the individual's consciousness, of the generalized other, enables the individual's acknowledged self-identity to attain stability and continuity. The authors state that self-identification occurs when a "symmetrical relationship is established between objective and subjective reality", and when what is "real on the outside corresponds to what is real within" (p. 133). Interpretation of experience leads to authenticity.

The authors contend that there are both primary and secondary socialization processes. They identify primary socialization as the starting point of internalization, when the individual's interpretation of an objective event is experienced as expressing meaning and becomes subjectively meaningful to the individual. In secondary socialization, an internalized reality of the objective event and its previously established subjective meaning is already present because of primary socialization. The previously established meaning of the event stands in the way of making further additions to previous information, blocking the individual's opportunity to acquire new internalizations.

The foregoing description implies that the individual's experience of any reality, that takes place after primary socialization, is artificially modified by the process of secondary socialization. Berger and Luckmann (1966) explain that, for new realities to augment realities that have already been internalized through primary socialization, the new realities need to be "brought home" (p. 143) in a vivid, relevant, and interesting way that connects them to the knowledge already internalized by primary socialization. The new knowledge must be interesting enough for the individual to move away from the primary internalizations and accept the new "artificial internalizations" (p. 143). When this occurs, the new realities become newly acquired knowledge, augmenting the individual's self-concept. This insight is important to the construction of self, as the individual self-reflects. For example, connections can be made vivid with an art object, such as a self-portrait, allowing new insight to be adopted into new behavior.

Rogers (1959) believes that self-concept is composed of self-image, self-esteem and the ideal-self. He defines self-image as the individual's view of self that does not necessarily reflect reality, and notes that it is comprised of several elements. The first element comprises the observable, physical appearance of the individual. A second element concerns how the individual perceives their performance in social roles. Personality traits comprise another category of elements and include the individual's descriptions of how they perceive themselves. Rogers defines the ideal self as the person an individual would like to be, and states that congruency exists when the ideal self and the actual experience of an individual are consistent. If there is inconsistency between an individual's self-image and their ideal self, the incongruence negatively affects the individual's sense of self-worth and self-esteem. This observation is relevant to this research, given that an individual's sense of self is based on the individual's image of self which may or may not be congruent.

For Berger and Luckmann (1966), identity represents the objective reality within which the individual is situated in society. In a community where there is a simple division of labour and minimal distribution of knowledge, everyone's identity would be easily recognizable, both objectively and subjectively. The authors observe that, as the distribution of knowledge becomes more complex, discrepancies occur in which hidden depths can be discovered within the self. A rupture can occur between the individual's visible conduct and 'invisible' self-identification when a discrepancy occurs between appearance and reality in the individual's self-understanding. Discovering the existence of such discrepancies is a crucial element in the process of increasing self-understanding. Clarifying whether realities are conscious or visible, and whether they are unconscious or invisible, appears to be essential for strengthening cohesiveness within the self. The true self can only be revealed when self-understanding is achieved, by unearthing and exploring the differences between what is only appearance, and what is reality for the self. When one thinks of appearance, one thinks of the body. What an individual looks like on the outside and resulting bodily experience.

As previously noted, the self is composed of both psyche and body (Berger & Luckmann, 1996; Freud, 2010; Leonard, 1994; Orbach, 2009; Ostero-Pailos, 2010). According to Berger and Luckmann (1966), because everyone is a body and has a body, they experience self as an entity that is not identical with the body. They state, "In other words, man's experience of himself always hovers between being and having a body" (p. 50). Given that having a body is an important component of identity, an exploration of the body's role in self-reflection should be incorporated in any attempt to increase self-knowledge. The question of who an individual is can only be answered by incorporating both the internal and the external experiences that make up the self.

Berger and Luckmann (1966) state that "individualism" prompts the individual to ask, "Who am I?" (p. 167), noting that this question would not arise in a society with minimal knowledge. Only when individuals encounter others with hidden selves, do they reflect and ask, "Who am I?" (p. 167). The authors suggest that this question is the result of a "mirror effect" (p. 171) that motivates the individual to ask self the questions they ask others and apply what they experience from others to self. Berger and Luckmann (1966) suggest that "The individual continues to experience himself as an organism, apart from and sometimes set against the socially derived objectifications of himself" (p. 183), contending that this dialectic can be a struggle between a higher social identity-related self and a "lower" (p. 183) pre-social or anti-social self. I suggest that the back and forth movement of the mirror effect parallels the back and forth movement required to explore the self within the context of the creation, dialectic, and reflection about the self, especially for the art therapist. The construction of the self is in relation to others and this relationship with self develops over a life time.

The self has been examined as both socially constructed and comprising many different selves. Identity is: formed in relationship; comprised of symbols, roles and activities that are either validated or invalidated by others; and reflected in an individual's construction of self (Berger & Luckman, 1966). Introspection is an important means by which the individual gains self-knowledge, and the feedback that the individual obtains from others can either support or challenge their internal sense of self (Baumeister & Bushman, 2010). When the internal sense of self is consistent with self-experience and the individual's ideal self, they experience a sense of congruency

(Rogers, 1959). Authenticity results when congruency is achieved (Rogers, 1959). To work intentionally toward increased congruency to become more conscious, and more purposeful (Rogers, 1959), an individual must be able to learn from, and respond to, the demands of their immediate temporal context at any given time. The ability to learn and adapt simultaneously increases with experience.

Self-construction through art

As children, we begin to draw to communicate our experience and make sense of the world. We begin to construct ourselves through art. This section explores how, as adults, we continue to construct ourselves and make sense of the world, and how that process of self-construction is undergirded through art.

Cederboum (2009) discusses that the ego is the 'I' of the conscious part of the mind of both internal and external activity, while the self is made up of the inner subconscious part of the psyche. She describes that, with the use of the artistic process, the supervising eye of the superego is removed so that what was once subconscious can become conscious, allowing the individual the ability to begin to self-explore. The use of art allows the individual to attain the insight needed to clearly see the self.

Lowenfeld and Brittain (1975) observe that drawings provide good indications of growth, by depicting the individual's gradual progression from an egocentric point of view to awareness of self as part of a larger environment. They suggest that a positive self-concept ameliorates the individual's ability to learn, adding that drawings essentially contain representations of the self and its feelings. The authors discuss Machover (1949), who observed that individuals project their own personalities into their drawings of the self. From the drawings, the individual can reflect on both internal and external dynamics.

Lowenfeld and Brittain (1975) suggest that the act of self-portraiture reflects one's ability to face oneself. They add that this activity may reveal developmental delays, noting that identifying such delays could greatly facilitate therapeutic changes in self-concept. One explanation for not using self-portraiture, as a tool for assessing developmental delays, is that most of us discontinue drawing between the ages of 12 and 17. Another reason might be that the artist associates drawing with an idealised time in the past or with a difficult time, in which the individual remains stuck (de Botton & Armstrong, 2014).

Adults also bring their child self along with them into adulthood. As Erikson (1980) points out, adults need to be creative, to generate, and to struggle against stagnation (p. 166). Dewdney and Nicholas (2011) add,

> Although adults develop qualities of the self and have different qualities and abilities from when they were children, they still have a child self. This child does not fade away with time, but rather plays a powerful role in the formation of the adult self. (p. xvi)

This describes the artist's need to generate as well as to integrate experience. Adult ego development makes psychosocial gains through intimate engagement in activities such as parenting. Erikson (1980) makes the important observation that such activities combine both ego-related and social aspects of the personality; they not only generate experiences, but also provide the opportunity to integrate experience with values accrued over the individual's lifetime. Being able to integrate experience is an important aspect of both personal and professional development.

Discussing "professional identities", Erikson (1980) describes the individual's developmental need for "opportunities for ego functions in spheres free from conflict" (p. 166), noting the professional responsibility of the therapist to include social, organizational and cultural conditions in their therapeutic analysis of the client's situation. It is pertinent to note that this responsibility also applies when the therapist and client are the same individual. The adult's primary need is to identify, address and work through personal issues to see self clearly and understand where they fit within the larger environmental context (Erikson, 1980). This challenge adds extra responsibilities to the art therapist's roster of efforts to maintain their professional identity. He/she must be able to create and integrate their personal experience while simultaneously working through the experiences generated by their ever-evolving, professional identity.

This section explored the importance of how an individual construct the self throughout the various stages of development and lived experiences

(Berger & Luckmann, 1966; Erikson, 1997; Gemin, 1999; Lowenfeld & Brittain, 1975). The goal of the adult is to gain competency by being able to integrate experience (Berger & Luckmann, 1966; Erikson, 1980; Gemin, 1999; B. L. Moon, 1995). The use of art can facilitate the process of bringing forth that which was unconscious to consciousness to explore both internal and external dynamics at play (Cameron, 2007; Cederboum, 2009; Lowenfeld & Brittain, 1975).

Healing through Art Therapy

Art therapy encourages individuals to express and understand emotions, resolve issues and improve self-awareness. To express one's self artistically can aid in the healing process by surfacing meaning. Through art there is an opportunity to connect with the unconscious which can foster increased self-awareness. Through this connection lived experience can be explored, including both positive and negative effects enabling the opportunity for healing. As explored by Stuckey and Nobel (2010), art helps to: express experience; explore meanings of past, present and future; integrate situations and illness into the life story; and give meaning and contribute to maintenance or reconstruction of positive identity (p. 258). This is the fundamental purpose of art therapy.

> Art therapy is a mental health profession in which clients, facilitated by the art therapist, use art media, the creative process, and the resulting artwork to explore their feelings, reconcile emotional conflicts, foster self-awareness, manage behavior and addictions, develop social skills, improve reality orientation, reduce anxiety, and increase self-esteem (American Art Therapy Association, 2013, p. 1).

The discipline uniquely combines two modalities; art-making and therapy. Ulman (2001) considers both components to be essential for the client's exploration of their inner and outer worlds. The goal of art therapy is for healing to occur (American Art Therapy Association, 2013; Merry, 1997). The process of art therapy facilitates the individual's self-awareness regarding their current functioning and sense of well-being. Greater understanding of their emotional experience can help identify the need to: modify specific behaviors; develop skills; improve his/her reality orientation; reduce anxiety; and/or increase self-esteem. It follows that, when art therapists seek to explore their own inner and outer worlds, combining spontaneous art expression with an examination of their own interpretation of this experience could be efficacious.

Farrar, Stopa and Turner (2015) conducted a study using art therapy with individuals with high body dissatisfaction. Their findings suggest that the therapeutic use of imagery improves aspects of the working self, increases body satisfaction and results in an improved positive effect on self-image. The authors conclude that negative and positive self-images have different effects on self-esteem and, in some cases, on self-concept. Noting that images may represent different "working selves" (p. 12), the researchers recommend further studies using imagery techniques to investigate restoring and/or building a client's positive self-image.

Ball (2002) observes and identifies the change processes occurring in art therapy, describing a significant moment, in a session, when an art therapist's empathic intervention facilitated a re-focusing of the child-client's behavior and creative process. Prior to that moment, Ball (2002) indicates that the therapist and client frequently shift between art-making and engagement in their relationship. The pattern of their interaction suggests that client and therapist take on clearly-defined roles while working together, allowing the creative process to unfold. Ball (2002) identifies the turning point in therapy, as the moment when an emerging focus on the self can be recognized, noting that art serves to shift the client's focus from external to internal variables. By extrapolation from Ball's (2002) observations, the internal shifting of focus involved in the creative self-reflection process can aid the individual's efforts to focus on their self and create self-change.

Ball (2002) contends that the mystery of change emerges because of emotion-related aspects of the therapeutic experience, and from the ways in which therapist and client mutually influence each other. She concurs with Kohut (1984) and Winnicott (1953), whose work addresses the phenomenon of mirroring attunement, or resonance, and misattunement, or dissonance. Ball (2002) observes that either a sense of gratification or a sense of frustration, when experienced within a trusting relationship, motivates the individual to engage in further self-development.

Wright (2009) envisions the artist as an adaptive mother, manipulating materials to repair the negative effects of early deficits in mirroring attunement. He suggests that 'adaptive mothering' occurs when the artist creates their own self-containing forms/images. Given that the artist creates self-containing artwork, it may be inferred that when a relationship develops between the artist and their artwork, within the safety of a trusting relationship, it can challenge/motivate the artist in the direction of further self-development. As the artist develops self, they incorporate the changes they experience into new or modified self-containing images/forms. In the same way, an art therapist engaging in creative self-reflection can create their own self-containing artwork.

Spiegel, Severino and Morrison, (2000) support Kohut, (1971) who suggests that the goal of maturation is to differentiate within an empathic relationship. Spiegel et al. (2000) contend that, in mutual gaze transactions, empathic attunement exists when the caregiver's facial expressions stimulate and amplify the positive affect and joy which the child desires and celebrates. They suggest that the experience of attunement reactivates memories of past experiences. They add that these memories serve as model behaviors for the individual in new interpersonal encounters, and result in his/her maturation as a self. In self-reflective self-portraiture practice, the art therapist could amplify the positive affect that results from engaging with their creative self, thereby enabling empathic attunement with the 'other' to facilitate maturation. Addressing ways to promote this process, Ball (2002) concurs with Rogers' suggestion (as cited in Merry, 1997) that an empathic, honest and caring climate facilitates an internal shift of focus that enables the individual engaging with art to recall past experiences and to gain a different perception of those experiences, enabling insight and change (p. 85).

Misattunement diminishes joy. Spiegel et al. (2000) suggest that it can be an experience of shame during which the self is experienced as "deficient, helpless, confused, exposed, and passive, and at the same time is experiencing the shaming other as if inside the self" (p. 25). Misattunement leads to patterns of connectedness based on fear, undermining the individual's attainment of self-intelligence in social engagement. It seems reasonable to assume, on the basis of Spiegel et al. (2000) and Ulman's (2001) arguments, that a client's engagement with shame experiences could hinder their empathic attunement with the self in art therapy, and thus support the need to include both art and therapy.

C. H. Moon (2002) describes the responsibility of the witness, and the act of bearing witness, "to see (or sense) for oneself, to take note of, and then to attest to what has been observed through reflecting back" (p. 201). She suggests that bearing witness is helpful in: establishing the therapeutic alliance; offering ongoing support; empathizing to achieve greater understanding; and offering the client a means to increase his/her self-awareness (p. 214). When a therapist bears witness, the client is aware of being seen and understood. When it is directed toward their healing, this can foster insight, growth, change and self-improvement (C.H. Moon, 2002). The author discusses using portraiture as a vehicle to provide a direct way to witness another. She explains that her portrait of a client not only bears witness to their behavior, but can also feel their feelings, being with them in the moment. C. H. Moon (2002) contends that this enables the client to feel acknowledged, and can clarify their perceptions, as the empathic connections between therapist and client are strengthened. Observation of the other provides a witnessing that fosters the therapeutic alliance.

Art therapist Bruce L. Moon (1995) coined the term "canvas mirror" to describe the observation that everything an individual creates, partly reflects who the artist is in art therapy. He notes that an individual who continually neglects the use of their imagination will gradually lose the ability to do so, just as neglecting to speak a second language results in the loss of that ability. The mirror is both in the artwork and in the therapeutic engagement to "see" the self clearly. Schaverien (1995) indicates that both an inward-looking and an outward-looking-gaze are part of the therapeutic process, describing the phenomenon as countertransference. Regarding the artwork, the therapist's countertransference comprises aesthetic appreciation; their eye travels around the created image and the therapist is affected by the aesthetic qualities of what they see. The therapist then looks inward to relate their experience of the artwork to the therapeutic relationship. Regarding the gaze of the client, Schaverien (1995) describes the process of transference taking place as the client forms a picture of the therapist, who is seen as both the other and the client's unconscious. The client experiences being observed in this transference process.

It is interesting to note that the word 'gaze' can be used as either a noun or a verb, "to look intently and steadily; stare as in wonder" (Coles Concise English Dictionary, 1997, p. 312). One can experience the gaze of another, or gaze into another's eyes. To gaze connotes more than simply to look, suggesting that the one who gazes is in awe of, or fascinated by something that holds their interest for a long time because they recognize it as beautiful. To gaze is to contemplate; to self-reflect. To gaze off into the distance indicates that one is lost in imagination. To gaze into another's eyes is an attempt to see into the person within; to see into the soul of the other.

According to Schaverien (1995), the gaze of the artist lies behind the image: it is present, and yet cannot be seen. She notes that when an art object (created by the artist) becomes the object of transference, the artist may experience countertransference with their own image. The author calls the art object a magical investment, as it evokes deeper elements of the unconscious, and becomes a powerful vehicle for transference and countertransference. Schaverien points out that the therapist/viewer cannot help but actively attempt to identify with the artist's position, and the viewer's gaze into the picture is instrumental in deepening the relationship between artist and therapist, as well as deepening the artist's relationship to self.

Tuber (2008), who examined the work of Winnicott (1958; 1967), adds that, in therapy, the identification of true and false selves is a catalyst to understanding an individual's quality of life on personal, professional and societal levels. He suggests that therapeutic mirroring serves as an intervention enabling the client to feel real and find their true sense of self. Tuber (2008) describes this intervention as, "a direct and vivid endorsement for empathy as the prime vehicle for interpersonal and therapeutic growth" (p. 82). He (2008) notes that Winnicott identifies authenticity and originality, as the hallmarks of mental health because they are essential for the individual's ability to: form connections; be attuned to others; and be in solitude with the self. The ability to be in solitude provides the individual with a safe place in which to feel secure and relax.

Machover (1949) contends that personality develops through movement, thinking and feeling. She says, "The body, or the self, is the most intimate point of reference in any activity" (p. 5). She suggests that the false self is an overdevelopment of certain parts of the self which can be revealed in drawings, noting, "In a significant portion of cases, drawings do permit accurate judgements covering the subject's emotional and psychosexual maturity, his anxiety, guilt, aggression, and a host of other traits" (p. 23). A false self creates a falsified sense of the individual's inner and outer self, including a false sense of one's own body. This results in a dissonant identification with the false body which prevents the individual from achieving a sense of authenticity.

Machover (1949) also contends that therapy must encourage true self growth by identifying the pathological and graphic traits of the false body, so that a range of authentic body feelings can emerge. The process whereby individual focuses, from within and without self, necessitates their conversation with the critical self, and movement between, and among, the body-self, the intellectual-self, the emotional-self and the contextual environment of the self. Self-reflection allows the individual to practice mindfulness on the self and about the self (B. L. Moon, 1997). In this reflective state, spiritual awareness and meaning-making occur (B. L. Moon, 1997). B. L. Moon (1995) suggests that the goal of therapy is to enable the client to understand the depths of their existence. He states, "The primary work of the visual image is engaging the client in a creative struggle with the ultimate concerns of human existence" (p. 7). The goal is not to save the client from self, but rather to help the client accurately see self and experience who they really are. This process enables the client to acknowledge their experience, to move beyond it (B. L. Moon, 1995). By sharing their story in a creative endeavor, the individual gains a clearer perspective of their experiences, and can determine their meaning and purpose in creation, including how they want their story to unfold.

Levine (2005) indicates that individuals seek therapy because they have experienced dis-integration; a feeling that they have "lost their central self around which the personality coheres" (p. 21). The author contends that dis-integration necessarily promotes the development of the self by breaking down the "false unity of narcissistic self-identification" (p. 21), noting that although the former stable identity has been lost, the individual dislikes change and clings to the image of the former self. He adds that the restored self is different from the initial identity, describing it as "a movement towards wholeness and unity" (p. 23). Accordingly, the goal for the individual in therapy and/or self-reflection is to identify authentic body feelings and progress to the re-integration of the central self from which the authentic self can emerge.

In their examination of art and therapy, de Botton and Armstrong (2014) describe self-esteem as an individual's subjective emotional evaluation of self and their worth in the world. They observe that by fostering self-compassion, by acknowledging what is good and strong, as well as what is weak, they can self-appreciate and recognize their positive features. The authors describe art as a process of appreciation, stating, "Art is a resource that can lead us to a more accurate assessment of what is valuable by working against habit and inviting us to recalibrate what we admire or love" (p. 59). They contend that art has the power to honour qualities and issues that can evade the viewer, and the power to teach the viewer to be more just towards self as they make the best of their circumstances, relationships, profession, experiences of aging and frustrated ambitions.

Klugman (1997) discusses the existentialist and constructivist models of subjectivity, examining the way clinicians make meaning of client's subjective experience (see Table 1). He describes the contrast between these views of the self, suggesting that either viewpoint might be useful. He observes that constructivism challenges the belief that an individual can know the self and the world in a way that transcends context. For this reason, therapy can explore the way in which the client's experiential world has been assembled, allowing change to occur, because of that awareness. Existentialism dictates that what is within constitutes authenticity, suggesting that within our authentic self we can discover "true subjectivity and the direct experience of the self" (p. 308). He suggests that these theories can work together in phases.

Table 1

Constructivism Compared with Existentialism

Constructivism	**Existentialism**
Focuses on the many different selves incorporated in the process of being, accompanied by systematic doubt about theories regarding the nature of the self.	Suggests that anxiety and uncertainty of being center on concerns regarding death, meaninglessness, isolation and freedom.
Understands that reality is a construction of the person experiencing the reality. The self is a narrative; personal identity is a partly invented story.	Emphasizes the first-person, subjective, mental and emotional state; experience over reflection; existence before essence; inwardness of being and being in the moment.
The self is a construction with local characteristics, a socially constructed set of functions, attributes and beliefs, and is witness to any self-experience.	The self is an entity with universal features, a substance of being, a universal given, a free and given being, an entity and is present in the moment without reflection.
Self-awareness moves from problem-dominated stories to preferred stories of possible ways of experiencing reality and the self.	The self has the potential for actualization, peak experience, self-realization and higher stages of development.
A person is consciousness and participates in the construction of his/her own reality which is only known through inter-subjectivity.	A person is an objectively knowable subject.
The client is a reflector, an observer of the self who has been.	The client is an experiencer of the self in the now. Man is a being with aspirations, hopes and God-like qualities.

Note. Adapted from Existentialism and Constructivism: A Bi-polar Model of Subjectivity by D. Klugman (1997), in the *Clinical Social Work Journal,* (25)3, pp. 297-313. Copyright 1997 by Springer.

This literature suggests that healing can occur through art therapy, as a means of reflecting (C. H. Moon, 2002). The mirroring process, through both transference and countertransference can deepen relationship (Ball, 2002; Sheverien, 1995; Wright, 2009). Further, therapeutic mirroring can start a dialogue that can facilitate the process of change (Ball, 2002; Tuber, 2008), and can highlight attunement or misattunement (Kohut, 1971; Shaverien 1995; Spiegel, et al., 2000; Winnicott, 1953). When an artist creates self-containing forms, such as a self-portrait, the artist could affect early deficits in mirroring attunement, and strengthen the positive aspects of self (Wright, 2009). Self-reflective practice or the critical conversation with self can foster meaning-making and self-compassion (Machover, 1949) offering the opportunity to accurately see the self and facilitate an internal shift in focus (Rogers, 1959).

The next section examines the importance of self-care for the art therapist.

Self-Study as Self-Care and the Art Therapist

Important to the work of the therapist is a continued self-study process; one that lends itself to taking care of the self. Boy and Pine (1980) discuss how an important counselling goal for the counsellor is to be authentic. To avoid counsellor burnout the authors, discuss the need for counsellors to be committed to a specific counselling theory, to engage in self-assessment in order to care for the counsellor's inner core, so that "when understood, permits a higher level of commitment and effectiveness" (p. 163), which encourages role renewal. Everyone has a way in which they care for themselves, such as listening to music, or going for a walk. It provides a means to tend to the self to manage stress, emotions, and body and mind fatigue.

The art therapist is often the 'witness' to client experiences and the process they take to work through their issues. The art therapist also needs this process to be an agent self. This means incorporating self-study within their practice, with an emphasis on art. C. H. Moon (2002) defines "self-study" (p. 57) as an attempt to know more about the self within the context of efforts to achieve authenticity and describes her engagement with her own art-making as a means of self-study. She describes the ethic of care as demonstrated by commitment to: the acquisition of knowledge through engagement in ongoing learning; sustained immersion in the arts; and insistence on maintaining disciplined practice. For this enquiry, self-care is linked to: self-study as a means to attune to the self of the therapist; ongoing self-witnessing to increase self-awareness; and continual engagement with the arts as disciplined practice for self-supervision.

Gilroy (2004) found that there "can never be enough time paid to art practice and how the making and looking in and out of art therapy is theorized and positioned in relation to the art therapist's identity" (p. 69). Gilroy (2004) assumes that an art therapist's professional effectiveness is limited, if their identity is primarily associated with the clinical setting. It seems reasonable to hypothesize that the art therapist, who becomes increasingly clinified, will become dissatisfied with their therapeutic work when it fails to express their artistic nature and orientation, which originally led them to the practice of art therapy. Gilroy (2004) adds that when the therapist's identity is associated with making, looking and thinking about art, this focus further informs broadening of their gaze, expanding the scope and scale of the therapist's professional perceptiveness.

Gilroy (1992) investigates art therapists' occupational motivation and interest in art; tracking their art-making and personal journeys to the point of their admission into post-graduate art therapy education and work. Her research addresses the assumption that art therapy training increased the student's self-awareness and capacity for honest reflection. Gilroy (2004) also notes that many art therapy students reported that the rigorous demands of training effectively diminished their own art practice and observes that this "appeared to have potential serious consequences for maintaining the uniqueness of the discipline" (p. 69). She recognizes that art therapists' struggle to continue art-making is directly related to the demands of their clinical work, most of which has nothing to do with art.

Gilroy (2004) also notes that factors, such as the availability of adequate space for painting, often restricts the use of media within the practice. When space is limited, it is easier and more convenient to use portable, basic media such as pencils and markers. Gilroy (2004) observes that by neglecting to provide an adequate environment for art-making, educational and therapeutic institutions subtly imply that talking is more important than art-making.

Brown (2008) discusses similar findings when describing the work of Marsha Aliaga (2003) and Pat Allen (1992), both of whom theorize that "clinification" can be one of the consequences for the art therapist who does not engage in regular art making. As previously mentioned, Allen (1992) defines clinification as "a dual developmental process whereby the art therapist gradually takes on the skills and characteristics of other clinicians, while at the same time his/her investment in, and practice of, art skills decline" (as cited in Brown, 2008, p. 22). It seems reasonable to suggest that, to continue utilizing the creative and imaginative aspects of the profession, all art therapists need to maintain their engagement with art.

The increasing need for postmodern therapeutic approaches has prompted increasing interest in the self of the therapist. This research assumes that this also applies to art therapists. Lum (2002) suggests creative ways to externalize the internal processes of therapists seeking to "heal themselves to be therapeutically congruent" by resolving problematic personal issues (p. 181). The author describes the therapists' goal of facilitating personal awareness as becoming, "aware of inner process[es], accepting of what is, knowing one's self, and to be able to reflect upon oneself in order to develop awareness" (p. 182).

Lum (2002) questioned a number of therapists regarding the eight areas (i.e., (spiritual, interactional, contextual, nutritional, intellectual, emotional, physical and sensory elements) described in model of the self, as defined by Satir Banmen, Gerber, and Gomari (1991), and about issues of balance and care. He observed that maintaining health and wellness was important for therapists who must cope with stress and the risk of burnout, noting that compassion fatigue can only be offset when the therapist consistently maintains self-care, self-esteem, awareness of self and awareness of the perceptions they have regarding their world. Allen (1995), Lum (2002) and C. H. Moon (1995) concur with Satir et al. (1991) who envision therapy as a spiritual experience.

Bruce L. Moon (1995) suggests that the artist's goal is two-fold. First, the artist seeks to create an artwork that is an expression of self and an expression of the soul. Second, the artist wishes to acknowledge, experience and observe their feelings; becoming more self-aware. Moon notes that this two-fold objective results in artwork that should be viewed both from the artist's perspective and their environmental context. He (1997) adds that the work represents the essence of the artist's day and what has shaped him/her. The creation of art is an act of love, like birth, full of emotion, imagination and conflict. Bruce L. Moon contends that, although the process of self-restoration leads to the awareness of being alone, "The process of making art is a metaphor for life itself, in that as the artist works the artist has absolute power to change the image. It can be reworked if and when the artist decides to change" (p. 85).

As an existentialist, B. L. Moon (1997) says, "Authentic life demands contemplation" (p. 54), observing that increasing congruence leads to authentic relationships, satisfying work and greater personal meaning. Hocoy (2007) observes that contemplation provides an opportunity to gain new insight and question self-knowledge. That which is inaccessible to conscious awareness may be brought into light "through careful and continuous observation through meditation, personal therapy, journals, artwork, dreams, reveries" (p. 29).

From a constructivist perspective, Brown (2008) notes that, as the self is ever evolving, reflective work takes persistent practice. She observes that life flows in a continuous movement of change; preferences, repertoires and aesthetics change, and so do the images and symbols that speak to art therapists. She adds that, when art therapists become stuck in repetitive patterns, it is difficult for them to help others "break theirs" (p. 202). The therapist needs to engage his/her self with the continuously changing nature of life over time. Otherwise, as life inexorably moves on and the therapist's workload increases, their ability to engage with and manage the self will decrease. It is axiomatic that, without self-monitoring and engagement with the self, the art therapist's self-care declines, with a concomitant decrease in their imaginative and artistic abilities.

The development of an art therapist begins with introspection. Their practice brings increased demands which can interfere with introspection and the practice of using art with clients and self. Self-study is an important means of self-care (C. H. Moon, 2002), healing (Satir et al., 1992) and maintaining occupational motivation (Gilroy, 2004). The challenge is committing the time for art-making and reflection.

Art as self-exploration

Building on the importance of self-care, this section explores the benefits of using art as a means for self-exploration.

Malchiodi (2007) and C. H. Moon (2002) observe that art-making promotes self-understanding and self-awareness and is a useful means for the art therapist to maintain authenticity. In her discussion of the self-portrait, Malchiodi (2007) refers to the self-portrait of an art therapist, Don Jones, as an example of a portrait that precisely captures the essence of "drawing from within" (p. 4). She underscores the importance of setting the stage, describing this as a significant part of the creative process when making art for self-exploration. When art is used for self-exploration, the art: reveals conflictual, difficult and/or ineffectual elements in the artist's life; identifies positive themes in the artist's story; indicates growth, improvements in self-understanding and self-appreciation; and increases meaning in the lived experience.

Janson (1986) states that in the visual arts, "We might say that a work of art must be a tangible thing shaped by human hands" (p. 11). Like Bruce L. Moon (1995; 1997) and Jennifer A. Moon (1999), Janson (1986) indicates that "The creative process consists of a long series of leaps of the artist's imagination and his attempts to give them form by shaping the material accordingly" (p. 11). Bruce L. Moon (1997) observes that the mastery of process and media are as important to the artistic process as the use of imagination and creativity, and links mastery to self-discipline and self-regard. Rogers (1959) indicates that self-discipline and self-regard are necessary for the therapist to be in a therapeutic relationship with self. For purposes of this research, self-discipline refers to being in control of oneself, while self-regard relates to self-esteem and consideration of one's own interests. Self-reflection is the act of thinking on experience with careful consideration and practicing self-reflection requires the individual to observe and/or be mindful of experience (B. L. Moon, 1997; Rogers, 1959). Art provides a means for self-discipline and is important to the maintenance of art within therapy for the art therapist.

Allen (1995) describes art as a means of self-knowing and spiritual fulfillment, contending that, when making an image, the artist first addresses their relationship with self. Discussing her therapeutic work with images, the author notes that artwork helps both client and therapist to be more aware, enabling them to learn the lessons inherent in any relationship.

Allen (1992), Backos (1997), Ball (2002), McNiff (1998), and B. L. Moon (1997) make significant comments regarding the therapist's specific techniques and tasks, which include maintaining therapeutic presence, tracking evidence of the therapeutic experience in relationship to the art-making, and fostering the art itself. In this research, art-making was designed to facilitate self-reflection through the interaction between the art therapist and their art. This encounter between artist and the mirror can provide a witnessing and an investigative activity where the artist looks within self and contemplates what is behind the mirror.

Ulman (2001) conducted further investigations into the nature of art therapy and the role of the art therapist. She contends that, in art therapy, the process is as important as the product. The author suggests that, within the art-making process, the self creates form, to more fully understand, or grasp, some aspect of reality, adding that both the subject of a self-portrait and the resulting object (the self-portrait itself) are essential. Ulman (2001) defines the processes involved in art therapy as "designed to assist favourable changes in personality or in living that will outlast the session itself" (p. 25), noting that they serve as "a means to discover both the self and the world, and to establish a relation between the two" (p. 26).

In *Canetti and Nietzsche: Theories of Humour in Die Blenung*, Harriet Murphy (1997) uses the vernacular phrase, "the eyes and the body are the window to your soul" (p. 155). This expresses the popular belief that the eyes and the body show not only what lies within a person, but also reflects this revelation back to the person who is looking from within. For example, one of B. L. Moon's (1995) clients described her pictures as windows to her soul. The client had experienced a loss of imagination and loss of meaning in her life. She described the process of change that occurred while working with art, as saving her from her withered existence and restoring her soul. In another example, B. L. Moon (1997) speaks of a former art student who had become successful yet found himself distressed by the lack of meaning in his life. When he contacted the author for help, B. L. Moon (1997) suggested, "when in crisis make art" (p. 99). The former student replied that he had no time, and struggled with the idea of making art. When he eventually drew his self-portrait, he was so surprised and upset by his creation that he begged B. L. Moon for the name of a therapist to address what he saw in his self-portrait. The self-portrait served as a mirror, allowing the artist to clearly see what he had previously avoided.

Schön (1983) describes reflective practice as a semi-structured, self-regulated process, noting that it is practicable for professionals in a variety of disciplines. He observes that the goal of self-reflection is to enhance the individual's ability to make informed and balanced decisions, adding that this is particularly important for the practicing professional. He believes that the creation and maintenance of a virtual world, such as a sketch pad, can open a reflective conversation about issues relevant to the artist. The conversation facilitates making discoveries and promotes further self-reflection on the individual's intuitive responses; it is both a method of inquiry and an intervention. Self-reflection is a valuable way for professionals to explore their experiences.

The act of creation brings the unknown onto the page enabling the art therapist to bring forth self to engage with their reality (B. L. Moon, 1997; C. H. Moon 2002; Ulman, 2001). The art therapist has the essential knowledge to liberate feeling, create new self-awareness and expose deep unconscious content, even when these elements are interpreted by and for themselves through their art (Allen, 1995; B. L. Moon, 1997; C. H. Moon, 2002). The therapist looks within to understand experiences, and the subsequent countertransference with their image evokes deeper elements of the unconscious (Shaverien, 1995). Professionals need a way to make informed and balanced decisions, and self-reflective practice provides a valuable means for the professional to explore their lived-experience (Schön, 1983). The art therapist is in a unique position to engage in self-exploration through art, as the profession is based on aesthetic exploration.

The Self-Portrait

This section offers an overview of the previous research using self-portraits as a method, and the different elements that comprise the self-portrait.

Recent literature reveals an increasing amount of evidence concerning art therapy research. Allen (1992), Brown (2008), and B. L. Moon (1997) discuss the strengths and stressors of art therapists, and Glaister (1996), Hanes (2007), and Smith (2008) suggest the usefulness of self-portraiture in helping clients connect with past and present aspects of themselves. Bryce-Smith (1992) offers an historical view of the self-portrait in western culture. Chilvers (2003), Platzman (2001), and Schilkraut (1999) suggest that the self-portrait offers the opportunity to: heighten self-awareness; construct identity; and discover different aspects of self. Carr and Hancock

(2016) explored the role portrait therapy plays in helping people living with life-threatening and chronic illnesses to explore and heal childhood trauma. Carr (2015) explored resolving self-identity disruption using portrait therapy as an art therapy intervention in her doctoral dissertation and book *Portrait Therapy* (2017) on the subject. Becerra (2018) studied the emotional and physiological impact of creating self-portraits using mandalas and human figure drawings and found that the process of drawing generally reduced state anxiety and pulse rate.

Kenworthy (1995) suggests that the act of creating the self-portrait and reflecting on the image are an expression of self; revealing internal and external hidden entities and interrelatedness. Morin, Pradat-Diehl, Robain, Bensalah, and Perrigot (2003) examine the physical body of the self-portrait indicating that erect self-portraits with the absence of facial features, lack of clothes, and/or hands could indicate a sudden handicap such as a brain lesion or speech disorder. Backos (1997) studies the use of self-portraits with rape survivors, and finds self-portraits are an effective modality for improving body image. Further, several articles have been written concerning the use of the self-portrait with health conditions, such as: chemotherapy (Koufer, Arbel, & Barak, 2004); head and neck cancer (Gilbert, Lydiatt, Aita, Robbins, McNeilly, & Desmarais, 2016); transitioning in motherhood (Scotti, 2016); narcissism (Thompson, 2013); personality disorder (Thorne, 2016); stroke (Morin et al., 2003); and memory dysfunction (Hendrixson, 1986). The general conclusion of these studies is that the self-portrait provides deep insight into self-image, physical and emotional issues that were previously hidden or difficult to express verbally.

Several studies (Craddick, 1963; Nasinovskaya, 2008; Welkener & Magolda, 2014) have been conducted with students engaged in the creation of a self-portrait. For example, Welkener and Magolda (2014) conducted a study using self-portraits, free writing and interviews to identify student's meaning-making, self, relationships and knowledge. The authors surmise that "Perhaps it is the element of freedom afforded students in the self-portrait creation process that enables deep insight into their developmental journeys" (p. 580) and suggest that additional research is needed. Craddick (1963) compared the Draw a Person (D-A-P) test with drawing a self-portrait to compare actual body image to figure drawings. The authors found that, with respect to size, sex of figure and placement on page, the Machover (1949) hypothesis was supported (p. 288). Nasinovskaya (2008) found that the self-portrait can be a means of symbolic portraying to overcome crisis. Esteban-Guitart, Montreal-Bosch, Perera, and Bastiani (2017) compared and contrasted self-portraits through the geographical representations and verbal explanations made by university students.

Art historian and Professor of Fine Arts at New York University, H.W. Janson, (1986) describes the imagination as the connector of the conscious and subconscious which holds together personality, intellect and spirituality. Janson (1986) contends that it is the imagination that allows the conception of possibilities in the future and provides an opportunity for understanding the past. Cederboum (2009), in her dissertation, explores the creation of her self-portraits suggesting that it provides a means of encounter between the ego and the self which strengthens knowledge and meaning, leading to growth and development.

Janson (1986) suggests that through self-portraiture, the image captures not only the likeness of the artist, "but also the soul of a sitter" (p. 20). Jensen (2004) furthers this discussion indicating that Plato believed that humans long for union with the Divine, and that God "is the source of the reflected beauty that we see" (p. 7). She adds,

> progression lies first in the attraction of the object for the observer, next in the relationship that emerges between the two, and finally in the recognition that both attraction and relationship are dependent upon the ultimate source of beauty itself. Beauty is not the goal or highest reality; its' source the Good is. (p. 8)

Jensen summarizes St. Augustine's opinion that the observer of divine creation not only begins to love the beautiful object but is inspired to change; beginning to imitate the beautiful; becoming good and responding to the Divine with gratitude. She suggests that the act of seeing leaves an imprint on the viewer that changes them, adding that, "Each creation is a spiritual exercise, strengthening or honing us in particular ways, making us more and more into what we shall become and how we understand ourselves in relation to the rest of the created world" (p. 10).

Jensen suggests that self-awareness begins with the creative act of self-exploration noting that the artist's whole body engages in the act of observation and the expression of ideas through visual images. She observes that "in fact, the theological basis for this way of knowing is the Incarnation" (p. 12), describing the process whereby God became human; whereby what was not seen could then be seen, felt and experienced. This revelation enables the artist to transcend their current place of being, allowing them to change into the person they long to be in God's eyes.

Jensen observes that the information to create an image originates from outside the self. Findigart (2013, March 13) agrees with Jensen, stating, "An artistic creation is the realization of the creator's mind contents into the level of a visual display, and is therefore a narrowed form of Creation. There cannot be a Creation without complete spiritual awareness to the created" (p. 3). He contends that incoming data resonates with something already in our minds or memories, even if we are unaware of it. We make connections between things we have always known and those things we see, hear, or otherwise experience with our senses. From a Christian perspective, the incoming data are not random. Jensen (2004) suggests that we encounter and engage with the divine through our imagination stating, "the inspiration is a Gift of the Spirit" (p. 14), and therefore "is a type of spiritual formation" (p. 16). It is worth noting here, that the artist engages their imagination to bring a self-portrait into existence (B. L. Moon, 1997).

Bruce L. Moon (1995) observes that the self-portrait reflects the artist's self-concept and identity. It depicts who the artist is, serving as the artist's statement, "This is who I am" (Berger & Luckman, 1966). The self-portrait depicts the mental image and beliefs the individual holds of self, including their character, strengths and weaknesses (Allen, 1992; B. L. Moon, 1995). This image also contains and reflects the feedback and responses from others. Bruce L. Moon (1995) suggests that attending to the details of life's canvas requires "imaginal restoration", and that to do this work the individual must learn to be still. Stilling the mind with active stimulation through art permits the therapist to direct attention towards self. This engages their use of the conscious while enabling their imagination to flourish and allowing the unconscious to emerge. Janson (1986) describes that, by using imagination in response to personality, intellect and spirituality enables private artistic statements to be understood; even if only at an intuitive level.

Bruce L. Moon (1995) likens beginning a work of art to initiating a long look in a mirror. He (1995) observes that the mirror reveals the reflection of who the artist is inside. Moon describes the artist coming to a decision; making a conscious choice about which part, or aspect of self to reveal. It is very difficult for the artist to decide what is safe to expose. Cederboum (2009) describes the process of engagement with the mirror, as the adult ego having the opportunity for a renewed encounter with the artwork which provides its own language. It is important to take these observations into consideration when exploring the lived-experience of the participants, in this research.

Bruce L. Moon (1995) discusses the existence of themes in the creative process, observing that they contain feelings, conflicts of past, present, and future, what is hidden, feared, and/or longed for, all of which reveals the artist's soul. The symbol of self permits the artist to look from the outside, to what is on the inside, and create a self-portrait that reflects "a growing sum of who I am" (p. 139); portraying a reflection of who the artist is, was, or wishes to be (B. L. Moon, 1995). By looking directly into the symbol of the self, the artist creates a specific interaction with their identity.

Cardinal (2014) suggests that many factors, including an individual's upbringing, continually shape the self, concurring with Herwig who states, "The self is a multidimensional psychological construct reflecting experience of mental being and physical existence" (p. 5). Cardinal (2014) identifies two specific elements within the individual: the psychological, that which is within and below the surface; and the physical being, that which is without and can be seen. Her conceptualization implies that a created self-image can take any form, and serves, not only as a reflection of what is happening within its creator, but also as a reflection of their physical self in that particular moment (Cardinal, 2014). It is important to remember that such reflections do not remain static, but continuously change (Cardinal, 2014; B. L. Moon, 1997). For an artist to be able to change their artwork, whether it is a self-portrait, indicates the artist's life can change (B. L. Moon, 1997). When an artist changes an image, it signifies that they do not have to remain stuck in any one situation and are empowered to change if they choose.

Although several studies have been conducted on the use of self-portraiture, none were found that specifically concerned art therapists using self-portraiture for self-reflection. The studies that have been conducted

found that face and eyes, and the process of creation reflects the Cre.
and the soul that lies within. The study of the face and eyes reveals inner
meaning and were found to be spiritual in nature (Findigart, 2013, March
13; Jensen, 2004; B. L. Moon, 1995). An individual has many different
aspects of self, with no two faces alike (Cederbaum, 2009). These faces are
reflected in the mirror, or through the creation of a self-portrait (B. L. Moon,
1995) revealing: beliefs; the soul; the past, present, future; and what is or
wished for (B. L. Moon, 1995). The self-portrait facilitates making meaning
through self-reflection.

The use of self-portraiture as meaning-making

A self-portrait is defined as a drawing created by the artist of self. It can be
made by copying one's reflection in a mirror, or by imagining the self and
drawing the image that comes to mind. Although the self-portrait differs
from a photographic selfie, they both depict the way the artist sees self in
the world. For example, when we look in a mirror, we wish to confirm that
we look the way we want to appear. The mirror provides us with a reflection
with which we internally resonate and/or reveals what we wish to show or
conceal. Making art is an act of creation, as is drawing a self-portrait. From
a theological perspective, the self-portrait reveals God within the artist's
soul. This section explores self-portraiture as mean-making.

The artistic creative process begins with the selection of raw material
which does may or may not contain meaning. The resulting art can make
and/or reveal meaning. Creation, as related in the Bible, describes God's
revealing of God's identity. As God reveals God's self in all Creation, the
artist reveals self and provides the viewer with an opportunity to engage
in wonder on the creation. The connection between God and humanity is
denoted by the Imago Dei, or Image of God derived from, "So God created
man in his own image" (Genesis 1:27, New King James Version). The artist
takes material created by God and transforms it, revealing aspects of reality
that humans overlook or may take for granted. Creation simultaneously
reveals both nature and human nature, as the artist uses imagination to
unearth meaning of life.

Benz (2005) describes God's image to man's image as based on the symbol
of the mirror and as such there is discontinuity between archetype and

Here the symbol of the mirror is not prime, but rather that [por]trayal' in man [sic] through procreation and birth" (Benz, [...]od actualizes himself in his highest form in his image as [ma]n [sic]. The soul is attuned to God and is coloured by God. [Benz stat]es "This 'self-portrait' is an internal impulse of self-portrayal of God, who starts anew in each human being and in each human being strives toward his perfection, toward his complete realization" (p. 232). In being united with God, participates in the work of God and take's part in God's creative activity revealing the soul and this contact awakens a new creative activity as co-worker of God (p. 234). The simple act of sensory perception of the viewer, the object and the focus of the mind, triggers the act of self-recognition, revealing understanding and discovers the self as the Imago Dei.

A self-portrait identifies the vulnerability and pain of being human, thereby compelling the artist to experience compassion and appreciate the "other's" need for care. Allen (1995) describes the process with her self-portraiture which surfaced feelings of being tired. She observes that, although it was designed to depict different strands of her psyche, the self-portrait showed her, "tattered and torn, reflecting difficulties in her new job" (p. 183). She observes that perceiving the other within enlarges the client's view of self when they witness self, as depicted in the portrait. She adds that the image represents the paradox of what is and what might be. Allen (1995) likens the image to a mirror which reflects distortions and the incomplete ego-self. It serves to cultivate access to self; opening the way to self-awareness. The process of self-portraiture can promote insight or conscious knowing that is a prelude to change and transformation.

Nunez (2009) explores the use of self-portraiture as a tool for self-therapy, noting that photography adds another dimension. Nunez (2009) describes each self-portrait as a non-verbal dialogue which enables the artist to live through their different personae. She notes that while the camera focuses on the external, the non-verbal dialogue focuses on interiority or the ability to express true essence. She describes the self-portrait experience, as an autobiographical project that exposes underlying issues, feelings and emotions, and provides an opportunity to understand meaning.

Nunez (2009) observes that every self-portrait is a form of performance that includes an inner dialogue involving self-perception, self-questioning and judgement, adding that the performance necessitates stepping out of oneself, and imagining oneself as someone else. Nunez (2009) views self-portraiture as a powerful tool, capable of uniting both inner and outer images to discover the real self. The self-portrait surfaces what might otherwise remain hidden, providing the artist with an opportunity to: know and accept self; perceive what the self is missing and what might be needed; and what hidden desires need expression.

Discussing the benefits of serial self-portrait drawing, Glaister (1996) observes that it enables the identification of changes occurring throughout the therapeutic process and provides a visual record of progress. For example, an individual portrait identifies the self at a specific moment in time, while a series of self-portraits can depict change over time. The author, a nurse, used serial self-portraiture as a therapeutic strategy with survivors of sexual abuse. To create a baseline, Glaister (1996) required them to use paper and crayons and draw self-portraits of themselves as children, and then a second self-portrait depicting themselves now. She also required clients to draw self-portraits at approximately six-month intervals or whenever a significant change occurred. As each self-portrait was completed, she displayed it alongside the client's previous self-portraits, and initiated a discussion of the client's feelings, themes and patterns, referring to changes or differences depicted in the series of portraits (Glaister, 1996). She observed that serial portraits could: facilitate awareness and increase understanding of the client's sense of self; and help clients recognize boundaries and various other aspects of self-identity. Nunez' (2009) experience with serial self-portraiture indicates that it facilitates the expression and development of self.

Alter-Muri (2007) notes that, although self-portraiture is not often used as a tool by art therapists, it has great potential as an introspective strategy to: facilitate self-acceptance; overcome and transform life experiences; and as a means of self-reflection. She suggests that "When therapists use self-portraits as a therapeutic intervention, they enrich their understanding of the ways that artists have been able to overcome and transform their life experiences" (p. 331). This suggests that art therapists could utilize self-portraiture themselves as a therapeutic intervention to transform their own life experiences.

Alter-Muri (2007) also notes the importance of introducing self-portraiture at the correct time during the therapeutic process, suggesting that if a client is asked to draw a self-portrait too soon in treatment, it can cause them to misrepresent a self-image or to regress. He indicates that, in some instances, self-portraiture may not be a healing strategy, and could increase negative thinking, repetitive patterns, feelings of despair, and obsessive thoughts about the self. There are certain clinical populations who are unable at a specific time to face the self. Alter-Muri (2007) states that "self-portraiture can be contraindicated as a therapeutic tool for clients who have a tendency to obsess on their thoughts and limitations" (p. 331). This tendency of obsession when engaging in self-portraiture can arguably be "accentuating" Vincent Van Gogh's "downward spiral" into his "manic depressive illness" (p. 331). In addition, the use of self-portraiture as a therapeutic process for clients with suicidal tendencies can further act as a hindrance to inner healing especially "if the self-portraiture process is introduced before the mid-point in the therapeutic relationship" (p. 338). This suggests that the client must be ready for what might be exposed. It seems reasonable that the therapist also needs to be ready to engage with his/her self.

This section explored the use of self-portraiture, as meaning-making for: looking in the mirror to explore the incomplete ego-self (Allen, 1995); re-creating the self (Glaister, 1996); transforming life experiences (Alter-Muri, 2007); and questioning the self (Nunez, 2009). While creating a self-portrait is not difficult or time-consuming, nor does it involve the use of complicated media, it is important for the therapist to commit the time and be prepared for what might be exposed about self. The following section addresses self-portraiture in terms of self-reflection.

Self-Portraiture as self-reflection

To create a portrait requires the individual to focus on self; to capture, in the moment, their lived-experience. The portrait is, therefore, a "snapshot" of a moment in time (Glaister, 1996). In contemporary post-modern terms, the portrait is a means for surfacing the many selves through self-reflection (Cresswell, 2011; Gemin, 1999; Loven, 2003; Orbach, 2009).

Rogers (1959) described awareness or consciousness as the symbolic representation of experience, stating. "In general self-experience is the raw material of which the organized self-concept is formed" (p. 200). The self-concept refers to an individual's view of self, looking from the outside in. The subjective back and forth movement of looking from the outside inward reflects the objective back and forth movement involved in the creation of a portrait. Berger and Luckmann (1966), in a similar discussion of the "mirror effect" (p. 171), observe that the individual moves back and forth between viewing self and others. Observing differences between the self and others motivates the individual to ask the self about others, and apply what they experience with others, to self, ascertaining who they most resemble. Berger and Luckmanns' (1966) observations regarding mirroring are similar to the back and forth movement of the artist engaged in self-portraiture. In this instance, the artist moves between the mirror and the canvas seeking the resemblance between the reflected and the created images of self (Shaverien, 1990).

Art critic, Laura Cumming (2010) suggests that the self has pure relationship with form. Creating a self-portrait offers the artist an opportunity to reveal both visible and invisible elements of the self, including the status of the individual's development in self-growth. She contends that the best self-portraits are created in older age, as they depict some consummation of the process of self-realization and/or self-fulfillment. They outline a more all-encompassing, contemporary understanding of the self.

In her master's thesis, Fiona Smith (2008) observes that an individual's face is linked closely to their identity and inner states, suggesting that, for this reason, self-portraiture may quickly bring issues regarding the individual's sense of self to the surface. In general, we tend to read a great deal into the faces of other individuals when we encounter them, and we make assumptions based upon what we intuit, describing this as what we see. It is important to remember, however, that the human personality is like an iceberg, with much hidden beneath the surface. Assessments such as projective drawings have been designed to reveal these hidden personality traits.

Machover (1949) notes that the projective methods of drawing the human figure "repeatedly uncovered deep and perhaps unconscious determinants of self-expression which could not be made manifest in direct communication" (p. 4). She suggests that the figure drawn and the personality of the individual, who is doing the drawing, are linked to the representation of the individual's body image. The identity of the individual and their body image has developed because of personal experience, and therefore, the figure drawn "provides a vehicle for the expression of one's body needs and conflicts" (p. 5). Kohut (1971) concurs, noting that, "The work of the artist is unconsciously recognized as unalterably bound up with the personality of its creator" (p. 310).

Discussing individuals with minimal satisfaction with their body image, Farrar, Stopa and Turner (2015) examine the impact of positive and negative imagery on aspects of the working self. They describe the working self as incorporating implicit and explicit self-esteem and self-concept clarity. Their research suggests that "images may represent different working selves" (p. 12). Defining the "working self" as the individual's current, long-term self who has been created to achieve goals, the authors found that when an individual holds a negative self-image their self-concept is diminished. "Imagery techniques which promote positive self-images improve aspects of the working self, body satisfaction and affect" (p. 8).

Hanes' (2007) contends that self-portraits can provide true-to-life representations of diseased aspects of the self, enabling the client to confront their pathology. Hanes, building on the work of Schaverein (1990), examines the creation of spontaneous frontal portraits. He observes that the creation of full frontal portrait indicates that an individual is ready to contend with reality, and to face truths that may alter their self-image. Thus, the individual who positions self directly, in a full-frontal position, is confronting the other within. This is an important consideration about self-reflection, specifically for the art therapist viewing and reflecting on their self-portrait. Essentially, the therapist is consciously and purposefully engaging self in a therapeutic sense.

Weiser (2008) studied personal snapshots and family albums, describing the snapshot, as a type of self-portrait; "a kind of mirror with memory" (p. 1), suggesting that such photographs are self-portraits of the photographer even when they are not in the image. Although her research focuses on technology and the use of photos in therapy with clients, Weiser (2008) makes interesting observations regarding the relationship between the insights generated by viewing photos and meaning-making. She notes that the details evoked by the snapshot during the process of looking at it ". . . spontaneously create the meaning that they [clients] think is coming from that photo itself" (p. 1). She adds, "Clients' photos are tangible symbolic constructs and metaphorical objects, silently offering the 'inner insight' about things that are less consciously-evident or verbally accessible" (p. 2).

This section explored how the self-portrait can: facilitate meaning-making as symbolic representation (Rogers, 1959; Weiser, 2008); reveal the reality of self and the surrounding world (Dalley, Rifkind, & Terry, 1993; Hammer, 1967; Hanes, 2007); identify self-growth, self-realization and self-fulfillment (Cumming, 2010); and surface conflict (Machover, 1949), disease (Hanes, 2007) and other issues (Shaverien, 1990). The literature suggests that the creation of self-images provide the individual with opportunities to reveal their true self (Winnicott, 1965), thereby increasing their sense of cohesiveness as they work towards self-love (Kohut, 1971). The next section explores the nature and value of self-reflection.

Self-Reflection

The term self-reflection may be understood, as the experience of gazing within, and describing the individual's ability to introspectively engage with the self. It is believed that the practice of self-reflection can enable the individual to: increase self-knowledge; be more aware of their way of being in the world; understand how others perceive them; and use self-knowledge effectively for themselves and with others. It involves: making meaning of past, present and/or future events; questioning and observing self to learn and grow; increasing understanding of insights and feelings; and determining future directions. Self-reflection requires commitment and ritual practice. For purposes of this work, self-reflection occurs through art and journaling.

Jensen (2004) links the description of creation in Genesis with repetition to ritualistic practice, and with the repetition implicated in living a spiritual and creative life. She contends that participation in artistic practice teaches the individual to discover and celebrate the artistic activity for itself, and for no other reason than to delight in the discoveries that propel him/her forward. She observes,

> By making their ideas visible, artists actually see them in a new way . . . and if these images or ideas are kept inside, rattling around in our brains . . ., we would become terribly anxious or profoundly depressed. Once we begin to externalize them, we see things we had missed or overlooked – and so the clamour starts all over again, and we realize there is still more to know, to learn, to express. The work of Creation is never done. (p. 18)

Steindle-Rast (1999) agrees with Jensen, observing that, "wakeful attention makes us aware of facts we had overlooked in a more superficial contact with reality; the fact for instance that in a real sense we become that to which we give ourselves, all our senses" (p. 42). B. L. Moon (1995) contends that, for meaning to be found within relationship, the individual must suffer the risk of being known, and makes the important observation that purpose can be realized only within the process of self-reflection. She (1995) believes that because the self-reflecting artist is aware of their power to make choices, they can choose to leave issues as they are revealed, accept them for what they are, or rework them into what they long for.

Baumeister and Bushman (2001) contend that individuals create a looking glass self to develop a ready response to how others might judge them. The authors identify introspection, social comparisons and self-perception, as the three sequential ways in which the self acquires self-knowledge. Individuals aspire to gain in self-knowledge in order to learn about their good qualities (introspection). They also desire to have their good qualities acknowledged by others. The reinforcement of the individual's preconceived impressions of self and the feedback obtained from others (social comparisons) serve to verify or invalidate the individual view of self (self-perception) in self-reflection. Baumeister and Bushman (2001) suggest that the individual gains self-knowledge, by obtaining access to and information about, what his/her inner self is thinking and feeling about their experiences. They note a significant limitation. They observe that, through introspection, the individual can gain self-knowledge only about issues which are accessible to consciousness, while the subconscious remains a mystery, from which self-knowledge cannot be gleaned (p. 74).

Jensen (2004) cites the words of the Apostle Paul regarding the way each individual may be transformed into the image of God,

> All of us, with unveiled faces, seeing the glory of the Lord as though reflected in a mirror, are being transformed into the same image from one degree of glory to another; for this comes from the Lord, the Spirit. (2 Cor. 3:18, New Revised Standard Version as cited in, p. 19)

Jensen suggests that the artist must detach from and transcend their transformative experience to evaluate how well it tells the truth. He notes, "we need to wonder how we are changed or moved to change through the experience of art" (p. 19). This is also true in professional practice. The right relationship with self means that when looking in the mirror, the individual is in a good relationship with their reflection.

Kolb (1975) developed a reflective model to describe the way information gained from experiential learning is transformed into knowledge. He required nurse practitioners to reflect on their experiences after any kind of significant event or situation. The result was a rich description of the event and insights that led to the application of new knowledge, by the practitioner. Kolb's (1975) suggested that self-reflective practice enabled the individual to gain new knowledge by building on prior experiences.

Psychotherapy can provide a means of self-reflection. Duncan, Miller, Wampold, and Hubble (2010) explain the essence of psychotherapeutic change, suggesting that common factors operate in different forms of psychotherapy and noting that theory and technique are less important than the person who applies them. They contend that the specific details and procedures of particular therapies are relatively insignificant and suggest that four elements: extratherapeutic variables; common factors; hope, expectancy and placebo; and model or technique (p. 33) work together in therapy, as effective catalysts for change. Duncan et al. (2010) contend that, regardless of theoretical orientation, therapies that include ongoing evaluation of progress and provide feedback to the client, achieve superior results. These factors are also relevant to self-reflective practice, and it may be suggested that including ongoing evaluation of progress and feedback to the individual could result in sufficient insight for change.

Johns (1995), who examines the role of self-reflection in practice, finds that it helps practitioners to, "Access, understand and learn through, his or her lived experiences and as a consequence, to take congruent action towards developing increasing effectiveness within the context of what is understood as desirable practice" (p. 226). Integration of the lived-experience into practice is an important element of self-reflection. Duncan et al. (2010) suggest that, during therapy, the client decides what they require and continuously evaluates therapeutic developments, while actively working to arrange events to suit their purpose. This could also be true for the art therapist in their self-reflective process.

Johns also explores the benefits of sharing perceptions with a colleague, to determine whether sharing is beneficial. He suggests that becoming an effective practitioner involves processes of personal deconstruction and recognition to acknowledge who they are and making the necessary changes to move toward who they want to be. Johns describes the practitioner looking within and looking out at the situation they experience and outlines three categories of knowing for the practitioner. First, he defines the individual's personal way of knowing as "knowing of self" (p. 229). Second, the author addresses the ethical aspects of knowing in professional practice, noting the importance of paying attention to the conflict of values within self. The third way of knowing is called inter-relatedness or the aesthetic response of interpreting knowledge to fit a specific situation. Having different ways of knowing, when thinking and learning about experiences, increases the likelihood of the individual integrating knowledge into practice. Johns (1995) observes that while empirical knowledge is obtained from science, self-understanding is gained from personal knowledge. This self-understanding informs empathy and the understanding of others. This is exemplified by the practitioner's ability to imagine self in the client's position. While ethical awareness involves understanding moral questions and choices, aesthetic awareness includes: being in the present moment; acknowledging the uniqueness of the client; and being aware of the larger environmental scenario.

Johns (1995) concludes that engaging in structured reflection "is a valid way to help the practitioner frame his or her learning through practice", and adds, "recognizing the value of aesthetics and the dimensions of the personal and ethical ways of knowing enables nurses to see, value, embrace and know human caring in deeply personal ways" (p. 233). This is also true in the wider range of professional practice. In her research on nursing, critical thinking and reflective practice, Price (2004) outlines several arguments in favour of health professionals engaging in reflective practice. She notes that it promotes better understanding of values, motives, feelings, and perceptions as well as suggesting useful changes in the practice setting. Price (2004) states, "Without an inquiring and insightful workforce, health improvements will not be achieved" (p. 46). Jasper (2013) concurs, observing that reflective practice is associated with improved quality of care, as well as the stimulation of personal and professional growth.

Schön (1983) interviewed therapists from five different professions, finding that each had improvised a creative "reflection-in-action" repertoire that he described in his analysis of therapist/supervisor dialogues. Schön (1983) observes, "Once a story has been told, it can be held as a datum, considered at leisure for its meanings and its relationships with other stories" (p. 160). He suggests that, in inquiry, "thoughts and feelings can be seen as sources of discovery" (p. 161), adding that the therapist's ability to maintain inquiry, as a source of discovery rather than as a trigger for action, is based on the therapist's ability to self-reflect on their own experience and detect counter-transference.

Bruce L. Moon (1997) suggests that self-reflection with the use of art results in the emergence of a new vision that reveals the individual's sacred passion, stating that they can experience "authentic, vital and creative interactions between self and the world" (p. 27). With the use of materials in art making, Janson (1986) states,

> The hand tries to carry out the commands of the imagination and hopefully puts down a brush stroke, but the result might not be quite what had been expected, partly because all matter resists the human will, partly because the image in the artist's mind is constantly shifting and changing, so that the commands of the imagination cannot be very precise. (p. 11)

In the artistic method, the subconscious has a voice.

Janson (1986) suggests that for the image to come into focus, the first line drawn becomes the only fixed part of the image; a starting point. The image itself has yet to be born and requires a new leap of imagination for the second line to be placed on the page. This initiate creating the "ever-growing mental image" (p. 11), until the last line is drawn which gives the image form. The resulting image provides the fodder for contemplation.

To engage in self-reflection and become more aware of self, the individual must be able to connect with multiple aspects of the self, the inner, outer, past, future, true and false selves. Janson (1986) states "All art involves self-expression" (p. 16) and all art involves contemplation or mindfulness.

Mindfulness is about being in the moment. Bruce L. Moon (1997) describes the process whereby artistic expression leads to mindfulness, stating, "My art comforts me when I am in distress and afflicts me when I am too comfortable" (p. 32). He contends that the artist's creative expression is the result of their mindfulness, which uncovers the creative anxiety that leads to action. Possibilities for increasing self-awareness and self-healing occur when the self remains in the present moment.

Bruce L. Moon (1997) also suggests that self-healing results when the artist engages in deepening mindfulness and creative expression. It is believed that taking time to sit in a quiet place, to self-reflect and/or to engage in the creative process allows the individual to pay attention to aspects of reality that they would not otherwise perceive. This awakening of awareness enables them to connect with the self as their past, present and/or future concerns, hopes and dreams are revealed. Moon (1997) describes this phenomenon, stating "Terrors of the past, traumas of the present and worries of the future are transformed into the symbols of the work" (p. 50). In this regard, B. L. Moon (1997) comments that the more the art therapist attends to the internal artistically, the less those disturbing internal images are manifested in behaviour.

The foregoing discussion substantiates the value of art therapists or other professionals engaging with the self through introspection or self-reflection (Baumeister & Bushman, 2001; Johns, 1995; Kolb, 1975; B. L. Moon, 1997). Self-reflection is a spiritual ritual which can enable healing and transformation (Jensen, 2004; B. L. Moon, 1997). Further, the four elements (i.e., extratherapeutic variables; common factors; hope, expectancy and placebo; and model or technique which work together in psychotherapy (p. 33) are also catalysts for change in self-reflective practice (Duncan et al., 2010). Therefore, there is value in self-reflective practice to incorporate ongoing evaluation of progress and feedback (Duncan et al., 2010). The next section examines the personal and professional experience of the art therapist.

Art as therapy

An important objective of self-reflection is to obtain access to the unconscious. It is understood that certain aspects of everyone are known to them, while an indeterminate number of other elements are unknown. As Erikson (1980), Freud (2010), and Kohut (1971) suggest, unknown elements of an individual's personality significantly influence behaviour. Here, I explore the important role of art within the self-reflective practice, as a means for seeing into the unconscious to surface awareness.

Reflecting on his work, McNiff (2004) observes, "As an artist committed to healing, I cannot begin to be of use to others until I am attentive to the transformations of the healing and creative process within myself" (p. 52). He notes that, traditionally, healers have focused on restoring the soul and "reunification of body and spirit" (p. 231), observing that, to the contemporary artist, "the soul is imagined as locked inside a self that does not realize its potential for expression" (p. 232). When the rhythm of life is disrupted, the individual's self-expression shuts down (p. 232).

Allen (2001) defines art-making as a spiritual practice because, by exploring life's dualities, it promotes the emergence of personal wisdom. She describes the soul as confined within the everyday, indicating that when the soul connects with beauty, a door to the soul opens, flooding the experience with a sense of awe and reverence. Allen (2001) states, "we create our spiritual connection by attending to soul" (p. 75). He observes that the soul gives life to the body and states, "images reveal our relation to soul and spirit" (p. 75).

Ulman (2001) observes that, as spontaneous art-making creates a connection between the artist and their subconscious, they become aware of their inner core of conflicting drives. Given that releasing the unconscious is a necessary element of increasing self-awareness, LeClerc (2006) examines the therapist's role in aiding the client to make sense of the unconscious material manifested through art therapy. She asks an interesting question about the somewhat paradoxical nature of the unconscious, "how do art therapists know that something pertaining to the realm of the unconscious is manifesting itself in session?" (p. 130). The same question applies to the art therapist who is engaging in self-portraiture, as a self-reflective practice.

Freud (2010) theorized that the unconscious manifests itself in dreams, slips of the tongue, and/or symptoms and observes that a symbol represents, illustrates or embodies some aspect of whatever it symbolizes. LeClerc (2006) suggests that, in a similar fashion, the image in art therapy is an indicator of, or a witness to, the emergence of unconscious material, contending that the image reveals the presence of something that is partly hidden and/or not fully exposed. For instance, despite training, a therapist might be blinded to elements in the client's artwork that the therapist does not want to acknowledge. Janson (1986) notes, "The fruits of our investigation must, however agree with our observations" (p. 20) to grasp the meaning behind the self-portrait.

Ten years after an interview with Tony Merry (1997), Rogers discussed her use of art therapy in private practice with Sommers-Flanagan (2007). She described her continued use of art-making as a means of self-healing. Rogers found that using her own art-making allowed her to express self through a different language. She indicated that she trained as an art therapist because clients reported that they found the use of art helpful. As art provides a means for Rogers to self-reflect, it also offers the same potential for other art therapists.

Ulman (2001) describes the creative act as a means of "bringing order out of chaos – chaotic feelings and impulses within, and bewildering mass of impressions from without" (p. 26). He adds that, in the creative process of art therapy, "inner and outer realities are fused into a new entity" (p. 26). Keeling and Bermudez (2006) examined art as a means for externalizing problems (i.e., conflict between an individual's inner and outer realities). Working with 17 participants who used sculpture and journaling for four weeks, they found that "The intervention helped participants express emotions, increased their awareness of personal resources and agency, helped separate problems from self, decreased symptoms and problem behaviors, and fostered a sense of empowerment" (p. 405).

American author, artist and art therapist, Shaun McNiff (2007) associates illness with diminished contact with the individual's soul. He suggests that the experience of being in the art studio and working with creative expression, allows the artist to identify those characteristics that are neither helpful nor authentic. This is an important consideration for the art therapist who must nourish self to maintain balance and fulfillment in their work. When experiencing waning vitality, they need the means to increase self-awareness.

McNiff (2007) found that when clients took the risk of revealing the shadows, in their inner lives, they expressed authenticity. He indicates that art therapy enables clients to: expose personal pain; reveal things that the client did not like about him/herself; reveal what the client had not accepted about self; and identify problematic behaviours and other issues that compromise relationships. Participation in the art therapy revealed previously shadowed material, enabling the client to accept and understand self, and become more authentic. McNiff (2007) notes that during the clients' self-exploration new insights were revealed, smoothing the way for them to experience beauty and self-love.

De Botton and Armstrong (2014) suggest that art can provide a means of channelling empathy into an individual's own psyche while facilitating better understanding of their emotions. An increase in self-awareness can provide the vantage point from which an individual engages with the self to provide insight and expose inauthentic elements. This may or may not lead to self-acceptance. De Botton and Armstrong (2014) suggest that the desire to be authentic indicates that the individual desires to be true to their sense of self, despite external pressures to be different.

Therapists have a professional responsibility to be aware of and work through their own issues. Creative expression which fosters authenticity allows the art therapist to explore their self-identity, while exposing and expressing problematic issues (McNiff, 2007; B. L. Moon, 1997). Bruce L. Moon (1997) suggests that the primary purpose of engagement in psychotherapy is to heighten self-awareness. He observes that the artist accomplishes this by giving form to their essential story and themes, in order to "concretize the essence of human experience" (p. 30), and "the nature of conflict as a symbol of life in process" (p. 49).

Bruce L. Moon (1997) concludes that giving form to both story and conflict makes self-understanding possible. Documentation is a means of making the individual's experiential story and themes real on paper. As a result, whatever the stories reveal and represent can no longer be avoided. Noting that to be alive is to be in conflict with our needs, wants, and aspirations, and with those of others with whom we have a relationship, Moon observes that the active work of art-making with images and imagination, deepens the artist's experience which leads to authentic relationships, satisfying work and enhanced personal meaning. He adds that creative work enables the art therapist to be truly responsible for self by attending to their own soul. Bruce L. Moon contends that each therapist must be their own therapist, adding that if they unable to attend to self, a therapeutic relationship is required.

Bruce L. Moon (1997) describes creative endeavour as the act of evoking compassion by expressing pathos, a quality evoking sadness, sympathy and/or compassion (p. 3). He suggests that when art is used for self-reflection, it elicits the artist's compassion for self, in the same way that it would evoke a therapist's compassion for the client. Moon (1997) suggests that imagery serves two purposes; first, as the expression of unconscious conflict material, and second, as a means of diagnosis.

Bruce L. Moon (1997) describes the image as a "friendly messenger" (p. 4), mirroring its creator and revealing hidden mysteries. "The image never comes to hurt you" (McNiff as cited in B. L. Moon, 1997, p.3). Moon contends that when conflictual material is revealed no interpretation is necessary, adding that analysis is not useful at this time. He emphasizes that the meanings and interpretations of symbols are particular to each creator because analysis does not provide a generalized interpretation of symbols. In self-reflection, when the art therapist reflects on their created image, they are paying attention to the symbols of self, expressed therein. Their reflection reveals and expresses unconscious conflict material. What was hidden is revealed and can be articulated. In this way, the artist is enabled to contact the self and know self more fully.

Allen (1995) posits that art is a way and a means to know self, stating, "Art is a way of knowing what we actually believe. Knowing what we believe requires confronting ourselves, our fears and our resistance to change," (p. 3) and adds that when we "know what our real beliefs are we can allow them to evolve and change if they do not serve us" (p. 3). Permitting our beliefs to change, allows transformation to take place.

In *Art as Therapy,* philosophers Alain de Botton and John Armstrong (2014) support B. L. Moon's (1997) and McNiff's (2004) observations that art is a therapeutic medium. They suggest that art's purpose is to guide the viewer, to compensate for their psychological frailties and thus enable them to transcend self. In phenomenology, the term 'transcendent' refers to that which transcends, or rises above, the individual's consciousness. Bruce L. Moon (1997) observes that, through the act of creation, art transcends death; bringing the created image to life. He adds that art gives meaning to existence; deepening and enriching daily life, while promoting awareness and acceptance of the everyday.

De Botton and Armstrong (2014) link seven human frailties (i.e., forgetting, pessimism, despair, disintegration, habits, comforts and taking things for granted) with seven ways in which art functions: remembering, hope, sorrow, rebalancing, self-understanding, growth, and appreciation (pp. 64-65). These concepts harmonize with B. L. Moon's (1997) description of pathos depicted in inner portraits, noting that they explore triumphs, tragedies, hopes, fears, pleasures and pain, while bringing, "order amongst chaos" (p. 15). By liberating emotional expression, art-making promotes greater self-understanding and "rebalancing". It enables order to be created when deep unconscious content and/or human frailties are exposed. By using art as a self-reflective practice, the therapist can enhance self-revelation to facilitate personal growth, self-acceptance and self-compassion (de Botton & Armstrong, 2014; McNiff, 2004; B. L. Moon, 1997).

Chilton, Gerber, Bechtel, Councill, Dreyer, and Yingling (2015) observe that positive emotions are mirrored in responsive art, because of emotional experience. They suggest that engaging in the process of "emotional resonance" or the emphatic response to emotionally-charged, lived-experiences involves clients in a new way of knowing themselves. Further, the authors list essential skills and abilities for the therapist, including, "emotion simulation/regulation, imagining the perspective of another, performance of verbal and non-verbal expressions of empathy, and ability to perceive emphatic resonance are essential components of their ability to establish therapeutic alliances" (p. 21). This suggests that when the art therapist engages in self-reflection through art-making, they can expect both negative and positive emotions to emerge, and that by experiencing an empathic response to each, can grow and change (de Botton & Armstrong, 2014; Duncan et al., 2010; Hanes, 2007; Hocoy, 2007; McNiff, 2004; B. L. Moon, 1997).

Art as therapy is important because it serves as a vehicle for self-expression, self-exploration, and can lead to self-acceptance (Nouwen, 1979). Whatever the artwork reflects elicits communication with the self, exposing hidden realities and fostering insights that can lead to healing (McNiff, 2007). Art-making, as a spiritual practice, (Allen, 2001) can be a way to externalize problems that brings order out of chaos (B. L. Moon, 1997; Ulman, 2001), while documenting experiences of frailties, functions and pathos (de Botton & Armstrong, 2014; B. L. Moon, 1997).

Art and lived-experience

The lived-experience is filled with actions and re-actions, and functions and frailties (de Botton & Armstrong, 2014), all which surface through the process of self-reflection. The ability to perceive empathic resonance is an essential component of establishing and maintaining the therapeutic alliance. The lived-experience of empathic response to negative and positive emotions that surface through the process of self-reflection is an essential element for the maintenance of self-care. This section explores the different components for balancing care of self through art and the lived-experience, including: becoming one's true self (Van Katwyk, 2003); the need for understanding one's self-concept (Emery, Walsh & Slotter, 2015); and the identification of emotion (de Botton & Armstrong, 2014; Lum, 2002).

Van Katwyk (2003) contends that becoming one's true self can be described as the process of balancing care for the self and the surrounding world. He observes that moving to self-integration involves processes of continuous growth and change, within which self-creation occurs. The author describes the stories of an individual's life- experiences as meaning-making. He adds that the nature and identity of the self are articulated in a story within which the individual's life experiences are organized. It may be inferred that if an artist's life story does not meet their needs, there is an opportunity to change the story.

Researchers, Emery, Walsh and Slotter (2015), contend that "peoples' understanding of their self-concepts determines willingness to engage in self-growth or self-exploration" (p. 264). They observe that an individual must have a clear sense of self before they can engage in self-exploration. The authors state that, "If people lack a clear sense of who they are, they avoid adding more attributes to the self-concept" (p. 264). They theorize that an individual might be less interested in adding to their self-concept because they fear that "doing so would only increase their confusion about the self" (p. 264), observing that, "sometimes a previously clear sense of self becomes murky after experiencing self-change" (p. 265).

De Botton and Armstrong (2014) identify emotion as an important element of individual experience such as sorrow, loss and frustrated hopes (p. 26). The authors define hope, as the holding of idealized conceptions regarding some parts of life, noting that retaining an idealized, hopeful vision is precious because life seldom satisfies human desires (p. 20). Discussing sorrow, the authors observe that art provides a vantage point from which to survey one's disappointment, sorrow, sense of loss and frustrated hopes, and grief (p. 30). They contend that a great deal of artistic achievement is the result of the artist having sublimated sorrow, and effectively communicated this transcendence to their audience. As a self-reflective practice, creative art enables the therapist to release sublimated sorrow. When the therapist becomes aware of this release, they recognize that transformation can occur. De Botton and Armstrong state,

> The term sublimation derives from chemistry. It names the process by which a solid substance is directly transformed into a gas, without first becoming liquid. In art, sublimation refers to the psychological process of transformation, in which base and unimpressive experiences are converted into something noble and fine – exactly what may happen when sorrow meets art. (p. 26)

Therapists engage with sorrow every day. They bear their own sorrow, as well as the sorrow imparted and released to them by clients. Lum (2002) notes that every therapist accumulates sorrow and suggests that compassion fatigue results when sorrow accumulates beyond a certain limit. De Botton and Armstrong (2014) contend that each individual carry baggage comprising their personal history, relationships, life experience and work responsibilities that leaves them off-balance. Being off-balance occurs when their emotions incline too far in one direction or another. The therapist must be aware of their internal emotional experience to recognize when this occurs. It is equally important for the therapist to maintain and sustain balance in their life.

With regard to the therapists' personal life, de Botton and Armstrong (2014) suggest that art can connect them with what is missing in their life and/or experience and help them to find balance. They observe that individuals are not always transparent to themselves and emphasize the need for self-understanding, adding that a viewer can discern personal feelings and/or meanings in objects. For example, the viewer may feel a sense of kinship with a work of art when they experience the values it expresses more poignantly and clearly than they consciously realize. Recognizing that this has occurred increases the viewer's self-knowledge (de Botton & Armstrong, 2014; Duncan et al., 2010; Hanes, 2007; Hocoy, 2007; McNiff, 2004; B. L. Moon, 1997).

De Botton and Armstrong (2014) contend that viewing art serves to communicate internal emotional experience. The communication expresses: emotion that may not consciously be known to the individual; something that words might not be able to articulate, which might have been thought but not expressed; and to others know who we are and what we believe, "and is an excellent way of communicating" (p. 47). The authors observe that words can be clumsy, and art can capture aspects of an individual that cannot be verbally conveyed. They illustrate this by suggesting that an individual could point to an image and say, "That's what I am like sometimes; and I wish I were like that more often" (p. 48). This conveys a complex emotional truth about self, without needing further explanation in words. Art is a reminder of familiar truths about ourselves, who we long to be, and helps us recognize the need to rebalance (de Botton & Armstrong, 2014). Therefore, art reminds the artist of their need for self-care.

De Botton and Armstrong (2014) suggest that engagement with art promotes the personal growth of the individual, observing that art presents them with previously unknown, provocative material. This induces the viewer to make efforts to understand and deal strategically with a topic or issue that they had not previously perceived. The authors assert that an individual who does not engage in viewing art may never awaken critically important parts of their inner and outer worlds. It is important to consider this in relation to the lived experience of the therapist. They require self-engagement to: awaken insights and issues which might be unknown; connect with the beliefs and values which are important; and grow. The authors concur with Jensen (2004) and Lum (2002) who suggest that the viewer remains unchanged until externalized events motivate them to shed light on personal issues (de Botton & Armstrong, 2014). They contend that the viewer experiences growth when they acknowledge and understand their connection with such previously-unrecognized issues.

De Botton and Armstrong (2014), eloquently describe art as a guide to the extension of experience that leads to appreciation. They contend that art is a re-sensitization tool, providing a means to experience appreciation and discover a new way of viewing those phenomena that individuals tend to overlook and/or disregard. When an artist uses self-portraiture for self-reflection, the question is, will the art therapist experience the process of re-sensitizing to their core?

This section explored the work of de Botton and Armstrong (2014) and how art and lived-experience interconnect. As individuals we are complicated beings, with many layers to who it is we are. Art can surface those various layers. A part of the process of both art and lived experience is that of dialogue. Dialogue and the creation of art is a back and forth movement in the engagement of lived-experience. Art is another means of dialogue, conveying what often is difficult to put into words. A discussion follows that amplifies the dialogue that occurs between the artist and the image.

Dialoguing with images

This research assumed that as the artist reflects on their self-portrait, dialogue occurs with the image. The image looks back at its creator, who converses with it as an object separate from self.

McNiff (2004) describes the process of dialoguing with images. He observes that this conversation takes the individual into a deeper, intimate and creative exchange which allows them to move beyond explanation and one-way speech. Here, the image becomes an independent partner. He defines the image as an "other" and encourages the individual viewer to speak as self, thinking of the image as another person, and allowing that person to speak. He states, "Because images do spring from our inner lives, personifying enables us to dialogue with feelings and concerns that are not easily accessible to conventional thought" (p. 91). The personified image can then convey its observations to its audience. McNiff (2004) contends that simply describing what the viewer sees in the image causes them to feel emotion within. By evoking the feelings contained within the image, the viewer can experience those feelings

McNiff (2004) directs his students to become the voice of the image; to ask the image what it needs; what it wants the viewer to know; and how it feels when viewed as the 'other'. Using this strategy enables the art therapist to have a conversation with self about self. The 'other' is a reflection of self that communicates at a specific moment in time what the artist needs to know. Artwork is a tangible means to explore the artist's feelings at a particular time.

De Botton and Armstrong (2014) and Nunez (2009) suggest that artists need to produce art to: express their emotions, define their identities, make important statements, and to feel better. Nunez (2009) contends that by channelling and transforming pain, art-making raises the artist's self-esteem. When an artist dialogues with their created image, they express self, releasing whatever concerns they have been holding onto and/or holding in.

The creation of art enables the artist to release, and transform their pain, and bring identity issues to the surface. Art enables the artist and the art therapist to experience a sense of increased competency in the process of creation (de Botton & Armstrong, 2014; Erikson, 1997; Lowenfeld & Brittain, 1975; B. L. Moon, 1995; Rogers, 1959). De Botton and Armstrong (2014) contend that good artwork expresses a core significance for the viewer, whereas bad art merely reminds the viewer of an undefined something, with the essence of the event slipping away from memory and meaning so that they cannot connect with the important experience that should be recalled. Whether reflecting on good or bad art, the therapist is directed to pay attention to the symbolism of the self, inherent within the art.

One of the most valuable results of engaging in artistic practice is the participant's ability to release previously hidden issues onto the page, as an essential part of his/her desired transformation and transcendence (Jensen, 2004; Kenworthy, 1995; LeClerk, 2006; B. L. Moon, 1995; Smith, 2008). Nunez (2009) observes that an artist must engage with art, and make art, in order to self-explore by sustaining on-going, self-revealing dialogue between self and their artwork. Janson (1986) also contends that "Art has been called a visual dialogue, for it expresses its creator's imagination just as surely if he were speaking to us, though the object itself is mute" (p. 18). Learning how to respond to the art is important, requiring our active participation (Janson, 1986). Finding the right answers requires asking the right questions, and Janson (1986) suggests taking into account all the evidence to form our personal interpretation.

One question that surfaces from this discussion concerns the difference between the processes of journaling and art-making. It seems clear that practical differences exist. Both activities provide opportunities for self-reflection, but the artistic process allows the art therapist to make points of connection with their inner artist (Cameron, 2007). They are able to relate to significant aspects of the artwork, thereby further exploring the personal reality of their contextual environment (Gilroy, 2004; Lowenfeld & Brittain, 1975; B. L. Moon, 1997). The next section of this discussion explores this question further by examining the use of visual journals and responsive writing in self-reflective practice.

Visual journals and responsive writing

In this research, self-portraits were created weekly over four weeks as a visual journal. The participants were also required to do weekly written reflections immediately following their art-making. Visual journals provide artistic documentation of the artist's life over a period, while responsive writing records the artist's dialogue with their visual images (Cameron, 2007; Merry, 1997; Welkener & Magolda, 2014). Stuckey and Nobel (2010) found in their exploration of art and healing that expressive writing and journaling is another way to access the unconscious self (p. 260), and has positive consequences, such as improvement over pain and mood (p. 261). The processes are synergistic in surfacing previously hidden, subconscious truths.

Douglas Coupland (2015), an artist and writer in a discussion about his travelling show, *Everywhere is Anywhere is Anything* with Ann Webb, indicated that art takes place largely in space, while writing takes place largely in time. There must be sufficient space to accomplish the work; a safe space to self-engage; adequate space on the page; and enough space to allow the viewer to step back and see their series of artworks. By contrast, writing is a documentation of time, requiring very little space. Self-reflective practice involving journaling and art-making require participants to make both time and space commitments. Coupland (2015) notes that writing and art-making use different pathways in the brain. While both allow the individual to express ideas and be creative and analytical, art enables them to try new techniques, engage with new media and explore creatively in a more tactile, "repeatable brain sensation" (p. 24).

Deaver and McAuliffe (2009) examined the internship experience of eight students using three methods: visual journaling, written self-reflection of the visual journals; and interviews with the researchers concerning their reflections. Participants reported that they found the combination of art making and responsive writing to be a particularly effective reflection of their internship experience. For example, they found that participants gained insight or discernment about the underlying meaning of a situation, emotion or behavior, and that art-making revealed meanings to them while promoting stress reduction (p. 615).

Ganim and Fox (1999) agree with the work of Deaver and McAuliffe (2009) who indicate that focused art-making and reflective journaling are premised on two points: that imagery reveals inner feelings; and the use of words can help to make cognitive sense of the writer's created images. The two methods of reflection, visual and written journaling, provide different means of dialoguing with the self (Coupland, 2015). Both methods work synergistically providing multiple means of linking data.

Deaver and McAuliffe (2009) also described how participants struggled to find time to carry out their weekly reflection practice, with many reporting that they had to force themselves to engage in the process. Despite the struggle, participants reported they experienced a positive result using both processes. They believed the methods formed a connection between the physical act of art-making and the cognitive act of eliciting meaning and insight from the created image (Deaver & McAuliffe, 2009, p. 616). Participants found that the inclusion of responsive writing served an integrative function, maximizing the reflective potential of their art-making (Deaver & McAuliffe, 2009, p. 626).

Sutton, Townsend and Wright (2007) agree that learning journals provide opportunities for: catharsis; individuals to connect with and express their thoughts and feelings; and facilitating reflective learning. The authors emphasize the importance of reflection for therapists, as the therapist could compromise their therapeutic approach and decision-making by unknowingly involving their personal beliefs within the therapeutic process with a client. They concur with the observations of Ghave and Lillyman (1997), J. A. Moon (1999), and Walker (1985), who claim that participants who re-read their journals reported learning more about themselves and reflecting more profoundly on the personal and professional changes they experienced over time.

Bruce L. Moon (1997) observes that created images are metaphors, holding symbolic meanings from the artist's conscious and subconscious, adding that the images' purpose is to "articulate, teach, free and define their creator" (p. 82). The images can be interpreted in multiple ways, while paradoxically and simultaneously existing as "authentic portraits of selfhood" (p. 81). When the artist acknowledges this paradox and the multiple roles played by their created images, they can experience self-transformation. The artistic process "is an allegory for life" (p. 85). The creative act serves to allow the individual to express what is inside them, including issues and concerns they may not be aware of as "an externalized presentation" (p.29).

Bruce L. Moon (1997) asserts that with the creation of a visual image the artist recognizes and clearly "sees" these reflected issues and concerns within the artwork, as they surface in consciousness. The author suggests that the pleasure derived from art encourages self-transcendence and self-restoration. He adds that art-making cannot take place unless the artist is deeply involved psychologically, indicating that "soul work happens when the artist's own creative forces give rise to change by transforming conflict and ennobling painful struggle" (p. 84).

Self-care is a best practice for art therapists, suggesting that the therapist engage with their own artistic practice to: explore emotions (Chilton et al., 2015; de Botton & Armstrong, 2014; Keeling & Bermudez, 2006; B. L. Moon, 1995; Nunez, 2009); unearth hidden issues and concerns (Jensen, 2004; Kenworthy, 1995; Le Clerk, 2006; McNiff, 2007; B. L. Moon, 1995; Nunez, 1995; Smith, 2008; Sommers-Flanagan, 2007); enhance self-knowledge (de Botton & Armstrong, 2014; Duncan et al., 2010; Hanes, 2007; Hocoy, 2007; McNiff, 2004; B. L. Moon, 1997); understand their strengths, (Allen, 1992; B. L. Moon, 1995) wishes and needs (de Botton & Armstrong, 2014; McNiff, 2014; B. L. Moon, 1997); and achieve self-acceptance and self-appreciation (Alter-Muri, 2007; de Botton & Armstrong, 2014; Malchiodi, 2007; McNiff, 1998, 2007; B. L. Moon, 1997; Nouwan, 1979;) . The next section discusses three established arts-based assessment techniques, in which a portrait of a person is used for assessment purposes.

Arts-Based Assessments in Art Therapy

The major projective drawing and subjective assessment techniques are explored to surface the ways in which art therapists have used a drawing of a person to elicit assessment in therapy. Those techniques include: D-A-P, House-Tree-Person and the objective approach. Art therapists use these techniques, as a strategy to increase their insight about the client. These techniques provide a means to unearth a lot of information quickly and simply. The purpose of exploring these techniques is to acknowledge they may be known to the participants and may be intuitively used by them while reflecting on their self-portraits. However, within the context of this research, I am specifically not using these techniques; instead I am facilitating art therapists to surface their own meaning.

Draw A Person (D-A-P)

The D-A-P is a projective test developed by Karen Machover (1949) that requires an individual to draw human figures. Williams, Fall, Eaves, and Woods-Groves (2006) indicate that these human figure drawings are employed to gather information on cognitive ability and are useful with populations that are difficult to assess (i.e., children). Handelzalts and Ben-Artzy-Cohen (2014) believe that this test results in a symbolic, or indirect, drawing, and that individuals draw themselves either as they see themselves to be or wish to be. The same authors also indicate that same-sex drawings have been found to be related to inner body perception. Machover (1949) contends that features of the drawn figures reflect underlying attitudes, concerns and personality traits, enabling the researcher or therapist to make an overall assessment of the individual's personality.

For example, when engaging a child in the D-A-P test, they are asked to draw a man, woman, child and then a self-portrait. The child is not given any time limits to complete the assignment. Each drawing is subsequently evaluated and given a score based on whether: all body segments are depicted; the body segments are attached properly; discriminating factors such as hair, eyes, nose, details of fingers are incorporated; and the proportions are accurate.

Kinetic-House-Tree-Person (K-H-T-P)

Burns (2009) describes the K-H-T-P as a projective test that requires the individual to make separate drawings of a house, a tree and a person. According to Burns (2009), the drawing of the tree reflects the individual's process of transformation, the drawing of the house is believed to reflect their physical aspects, and the drawing of the person reflects the ego function. Burns (2009) also indicates that a larger and more complex metaphor is revealed when the individual is requested to draw a person in conjunction with the tree and/or draw the person doing something.

Oster and Crone (2004) examine the K-H-T-P technique, noting that it is an established standard method of directed drawing used in psychological testing, and is one of the most commonly employed methods of gathering data about personality integration, cognitive maturity, and interpersonal connectedness. The authors elaborate on the inferences drawn from the drawings, noting that the drawing of the tree refers to the client's role in life and feelings toward self, and the reinforcement they receive from their environment. The house drawing is thought to convey the client's connectedness with their home life and family, and the drawing of the person provides the client's perception of self in terms of who they wish to be and not who they may be.

Oster and Crone (2004) note that, as an assessment or an intervention, "the drawing of a person apparently stimulates conscious awareness of bodily image and self-concept, both physically and psychologically" (p. 108). This assessment tool provides a multi-layered perspective on an individual, including: what is happening on the surface; what they are experiencing at deeper inner levels; and what is occurring in their contextual environment. The authors observe that adding drawing directives allows clients to view themselves more objectively, within a safe framework, and may elicit problematic issues that would not have been recognized/assessed by conventional psychological testing. They suggest that adding drawing to therapeutic sessions provides a unique means of releasing blocked intrapsychic distress, while providing a vehicle for reflection and insight. Clients can express their concerns and conflict in a contained environment, confront themselves, and learn new strategies for problem solving.

The objective approach

In their work, *Drawing Out the Self: The Objective Approach in Art Therapy*, Dewdney and Nicholas (2011) ask clients to draw recognizable figures and note that this requirement often causes discomfort for clients who worry about lacking artistic skills. Drawing a figure that is recognizable as opposed to drawing a figure that is abstract is very different. Abstraction, which is usually based in the use of colour and shapes, is defined as "to draw away from or to separate" (Jansen, 1986, p. 681). Despite this, Dewdney and Nicholas (2011) contend, "it is easier to hide behind color and shapes; however, drawing recognizable images with a pencil is very revealing" (p. 73). The authors found that drawing the self as a projective drawing provides a simple means of gathering a significant amount of information about an individual. The projective drawings and the act of drawing within the therapeutic process surface information about the client as well as revealing what lies beneath.

Dewdney and Nicholas (2011) also describe their use of images and verbal expression in personality assessment. The client is sent a series of specific assignments, directing them to see self the way others see them. Each drawing activity takes at least 15 minutes and continues for as long as necessary. The client is then requested to describe their artwork as objectively as possible, "as though they had not done the work themselves" (p. 145). The therapist asks a series of questions about the artwork (e.g., age, gender, size, groups of figures, what is missing, etc.). Dewdney and Nicholas (2011) also ask the client to use the pencil and eraser to identify differences between their intention and the artistic outcome. The authors believe that the need to erase reveals areas of conflict and difficulty. This approach combines the individual's drawing, the therapist's questions, and the client's comments on the same page. The authors contend that, as a result, there is a "double remembering" for the client and therapist.

LeClerc (2006) succinctly observes that "projective identification involves a subject making another person experience an affect or an emotion, on a non-verbal level, particularly when the subject is not able to represent this emotion to him or herself" (p. 133). She suggests that the visual image in art therapy acts as a locus, not only for projections, but also for both transmission and reception of verbal and representational forms of communication which, when experienced and translated into knowledge, participate together in the mutual construction of meaning. LeClerc (2006) also observes that, for transmission to be effective, an individual must be in a state of attentiveness or stillness. It follows that the art therapist is: the subject and the object of knowledge; the object of subconscious communication; the subject of deep intersubjective experiences; and subjectively responsible for making intelligent order out of what is being presented. There is no need to establish this intelligent order within the context of problem solving. Rather, it is a form of self-transcendence, much like meditation, creativity and the use of the imagination (C. H. Moon, 2002).

Further, Hanson and Poston (2010) examine various therapeutic models of art assessment, concluding that assessments have clinically meaningful benefits when combined with personalized, collaborative and highly-involved client feedback. They observe that the feedback can take the form of a mini-treatment or intervention and note the need for more research regarding associated change mechanisms. This suggests that the same result could be achieved when the therapist reflects on their self-portrait, and subsequently engages in reflective dialogue with me.

This section examined the use of art in the therapeutic assessment process and underscored that drawing specific figures can provide structure and safety when an individual is engaged in self exploration (Burns, 2009; Dewdney & Nicholas, 2011; Gilroy et al., 2012; Handelzalts & Ben-Artzy-Cohen, 2014; Hanson & Poston, 2010; LeClerc, 2006; Levick, 2012; Miller, 2014; Oster & Crone, 2014; Weisz et al., 2011; Williams et al., 2006). As a self-reflective tool, the projective drawing process unearths and reveals greater understanding of the self for client and therapist. With reference to the research, I chose not to include projective drawing tests, as they blur the boundary between an artistic self-reflective process and formal assessment. The purpose of including these processes is to acknowledge that there are established tools that use the drawing of a person for assessment purposes in therapy.

The next section explores how symbols represent the self and are related to identity. The interpretation of the symbols within the drawing moves the artist beyond the aesthetic surface of the picture to a deeper dialogue with the unconscious.

Symbols of the self

The literature emphasizes that artistic images lend themselves well to self-reflection and self-review (Betts, 2006; Burns, 2009; Dewdney & Nicholas, 2011; Oster & Crone, 2004). This means that inherent within the artwork are symbols that express the artist's relationships, context, environment and psychology (McNiff, 2012). This section discusses the method of interpretation of art and the use of symbols as a means for self-discovery.

Gross and Stone (1964) define identity as "the substantive dimension of the self" (p. 357), adding that identity describes the placement, or situation, in which others place an individual as a social object in social relationships. The authors note that everyone maintains symbols related to their identity, such as "the shaping of the hair, painting of the face, clothing, cards of identity" (p. 358), and roles and activities. All identity-related symbols, roles and activities afford the therapist an opportunity to explore with the client their perception of identity.

Ulman (2001) indicates that the goal of art therapy is to elicit the client's interpretation of their work including, the meaning behind their symbolism. She adds that the therapist should not serve as an interpreter. She contends that art therapy encourages the spontaneous creativity that provides the raw materials from which art emerges. According to Ulman's (2001) interpretation, when a therapist observes and studies their self-portrait, they can interpret the signs and symbols because the spontaneity of the creative process has released unconscious material.

B. L. Moon (1997) also suggests that art-making is a symbolic expression of hope, noting that hope is an essential part of psychotherapy and of healing. He adds, "Hope requires faith" (p. 53) to permit us to look beyond crisis to new life and new opportunities. To be hopeful is to have faith that there will be a new day when we will be born again, and that whatever happens has meaning and purpose. Furth (1988) suggests that symbols are manifestations of the unconscious and states that, "Through such drawings we come closer to the use of symbols as a healing agent" (p. 1).

Gross and Stone (1964) note that identity symbols are important to self-representation and list five categories: spaces, props, equipment, clothing, and the body identity-symbol (p. 357). Furth (1988) discusses the process of interpretation as: noting one's initial emotional experience; identifying what art materials are used and size of the artwork; looking at colour, shape, direction, focal points and movement; determining the relationship of size of the image and paper placement; and assembling this information into a whole description (p. 33).

De Botton and Armstrong (2014) discuss the rendering of images, observing in this context that, "the apparent opposite to idealization – caricature – has a lot to teach us about how ideal images can be important to us" (p. 22). The authors note that simplification and exaggeration define caricature, adding that, when the essence of matters and experiences is revealed, valuable insights that might have been lost or overlooked in ordinary experience, emerge.

McNiff (2004) suggests that "literal-minded psychological interpretations often amount to the form of image abuse that obscures the deeper meanings of art expressions and blocks their healing powers" (p. 70). He suggests that we need to give artistic expressions their autonomy, as there are many different interpretations which provide the opportunity to explore the world of experience shifting the process of interpretation from "explanation to empathy" (p. 70).

Glaister (1996) indicates that symbols of self-concept issues are reflected in the size, colour, detail, pressure, line quality, symmetry, and placement of the self-portrait. He contends that low self-esteem is expressed by: small size; lack of colour variation and sparse detail; missing body parts reflecting feelings of inadequacy, and powerlessness; and incomplete, broken, or faint lines corresponding to lack of self-confidence (p. 313). She also observes that off-centre drawings and placement near the edge of the paper indicate feelings of insecurity or inadequacy. Furth (1988) and Glaister (1996) observe that, as an individual experience an increase in self-esteem and security, their self-portraits became firmer, clearer, stronger, centred, and symmetrical. Table 2 outlines the different symbols and "focal points that draw the therapist's and client's attention" (Furth, 1988, p. 33) that can be interpreted within a drawing. This research used this method to interpret the symbols within participant self-portraits.

Table 2

Approach to Picture Interpretation and Symbols of Self

Focal Point	Response	Symbols of Meaning - Conscious or Unconscious
What does the picture convey?	Initial Impression	Feeling
Anything out of the ordinary	Odd representations	Specific problem area, may or may not be aware.
Barriers	Blockages in communication	Difficulties between individuals
Missing elements	Absent or left out	Could be what is absent from life
Central	Core of significance	What is most important or the problem.
Size	Proportion of objects to people	Emphasize or devalue
Shape distortion	Something needed to return distortion to normality	Problem areas where more understanding is needed.
Repeated objects	Number of objects	Representing units of time or events of importance, in past, present, future.
Perspective	Consistent or not	Inconsistencies with life
Enter into picture	Feel, hear, see how elements behave	Better understand relationship to individual elements to whole of picture
Shading	More time and energy invested	May represent fixation on, or anxiety about what shaded object or shape represents
Edging	Edge of picture	Being involved partially, not fully committed.
Compare to surrounding world	Context differences	Country, culture, race, religion, season of year
Out of season	Significant holidays out of the actual time for the holiday	Something that might have happened or needs to be repeated

Focal Point	Response	Symbols of Meaning - Conscious or Unconscious
Encapsulation	Enclosure	Boundaries around the self – fear of or need to have
Extensions	Tools drawn in the hand	Exertion of greater control over environment, having or needing to have
Underlining	Grounding	Underlining is indicative of being grounded
Abstract	What does it look like to you or remind you of	Represents something hard to understand, difficult, or concealed. An avoidance.
Filled in vs. Empty	Representing an individual's life – empty or full	Overcompensating, ill, lack of energy
Trees and age	Balanced, healthy leaves able to breath rootedness	Life symbol
Colour in place or out of place	Psychological or physical factors	Feelings, moods, tone of relationship. Balance or imbalance.
Erasures	Redrawn or improved	Conflict material in life or deteriorated in life
Words	Words add definition to statement so not misinterpreted.	Feared point not clearly conveyed. Has or is something been misinterpreted not trusting the non-verbal communication.
Lines	"Something" psychologically overhead	Burden being carried
Transparency	Seeing into a taboo area	Seeing through a barrier or something within
Movement and flow of colour or design	Follow trajectory of movement	Overflow or moving toward

Note. Adapted from *The Secret World of Drawings: Healing Through Art*, by G. Furth, 1988, pp. 32-100. Copyright 1988 by Sigo Press.

Oster and Crone (2004) observe that, when drawing is added to therapy sessions, the expression of visual symbols can become a means of self-expression enabling the individual to share personal conflicts and frustration, and talk about previously hidden, painful issues. This permits the individual to experience emotional satisfaction, renews and enhances their sense of identity, and allows them to more easily accept self as competent. Cederboum (2009) discusses the use of words incorporated in the self-portrait. For Cederboum (2009), words used within art represents the tension between what is conscious to the artist and expressed, and what is not expressed which may be either conscious or not conscious to the artist. He states, "Assuming that the printed text represent speech, its appearance or disappearance describes the tension between hiding and exposure, between silence and speech" (p. 136).

Art therapists can provide clients with a wide variety of media in their therapeutic practice. For example, some art therapists prefer soft materials like paints, while others prefer harder materials like markers. The choice of art materials in art therapy facilitates the expression of emotion. For example, Furth (1988) suggests avoiding the use of markers, as their use makes it difficult to shade images.

For this research, the participants were directed to use the hard material or markers with the intention that their use would yield realistic self-portraits. However, Janson (1986) asserts that "The advantage of realism at face value is that it seems easier to understand" (p. 11) while the disadvantage is that representational art is "always bound to literal meaning and appearance of the everyday world" (p. 11). Janson (1986) suggested that truth is relative because in the appreciation of the artistic result, it is not only what our eyes reveal to us but also what is revealed through "the concepts to which our perceptions are filtered" (p. 11). Janson (1986) suggests that to understand meaning we also need to understand visual symbols and responses specific to everyone's specific culture and outlook of the artist to understand it properly. Colour can symbolize feelings, moods and tone, amplifying the objects and action within a picture. Colour can be difficult to interpret accurately as many theories abound about the use of colour (Furth, 1988).

The way in which different cultures describe the meaning of colour varies around the world and it can be beneficial to culturally contextualize the meanings of colors. Furth (1988) provided a compilation of the common interpretations of colour based upon the psychology and associations of Western culture (p. 97). The work of Christina Wang (2015) broadens the interpretation of the symbolism of colour by looking across the globe for interpretations of colour in different cultural contexts and outlines how different countries attribute different meanings to color. However, according to Adams and Osgood (1973) in their analysis of eighty-nine previous studies of colour, they found that there are cross-cultural similarities which indicate strong universal trends of affective meanings in the colour domain. As a result, this research used the common interpretation of colour symbolism explored by Furth (1988). Table 3 outlines the different interpretations of the symbolism of colour.

Table 3

Meanings of Colour

Colour	Psychologically	Physically
Red	Problem/surging emotion/danger	Illness/infection/fever
Pink	Resolution of a problem or illness just past	Colouring flesh or cheeks to show a healthy look
Purple	Need to possess or control need to have others control or support burden	Seizures/controlling, gripping situation
Orange	Suspenseful situation/ life or death struggle	Decreasing energy rescue from a threatening situation
Golden Yellow	Emphasis on spiritual or intuitive nature	Life-giving energy
Pale Yellow	Precarious life situation	
Bright Blue	Health	Energy
Pale Blue	Distance/contemplation	Fading away/ withdrawing
Dark Green	Healthy ego	Healthy body growth/ newness of life
Pale Yellow Green	Weakness	Fading out or coming back into life
Dark Brown	Nourishment	Healthy/in touch with nature
Pale Brown	Struggle to overcome destruction forces to become healthy	Rot or decay
Black	Symbolize the unknown	Negative dark thoughts
White	Repressed feelings	Life completion
Royal Purple	Sovereignty/spirituality/ supreme power	

Note. Adapted from *The Secret World of Drawings: Healing Through Art*, by G. Furth, 1988. Copyright 1988 by Sigo Press. Adapted from *Symbolism of Colors and Color Meanings Around the World*, by C. Wang, 2015.

Betts (2006) indicates that research on the use of projective tests in therapy needs to account for symbolic, conscious, or behavioural variables. She states, "self-concept was also identified as a quality that should be evaluated, since it has impact on the individual's decision-making process and behavior" (p. 429), noting the importance of examining "symbolic or private personality traits, since people are often motivated by their unconscious drives" (p. 429). She notes the necessity of a strong framework within which to identify the individual's self-concept and recommends using theories, such as developmental theory to facilitate greater understanding.

Lowenfeld and Brittain (1975) discuss how constructing through the creative act is a constant process of assimilation and projection. The creative art experience consists of the relationship between artist and environment, self-identification with the experience expressed, and the art materials by which it is expressed. The completed project is the true expression of the self, which "is as true at a very young age as it is for the adult artist" (Lowenfeld & Brittain, 1975). Lowenfeld and Brittain (1975) suggest that learning takes place through art and the interaction between a person and their environment. The authors (1975) suggest that at about age 12, self-identification becomes key and that individuals have the opportunity through art expression to develop their own individual voice and explore their individual identity. They suggest that, at this stage, two different types of expression in drawings can be identified. The authors observe that a visual-minded person is aware of the realities of what is seen, such as the wrinkles in clothing, stating that their art focuses on recreating a concrete, objective mirror of the actual world. By contrast, the haptic person is concerned with subjective, bodily experience and uses distortion, lack of depth and flat colour for emotional effect in their artwork (p. 283). The authors contend that the objective of art-making is not the artwork itself but developing greater awareness of self.

Lowenfeld and Brittain (1975) identify six stages of development: 1) the scribbling stage; 2) the pre-schematic stage; 3) the schematic stage; 4) the gang age; 5) the pseudo-naturalistic stage; and 6) the period of decision which are described in Table 4. These stages of development were used to interpret the drawings.

Table 4

Six Stages of Development

Stage and Main Markers	Description
1) Scribbling Stage. 2-4 years of age. • The first visual image created. • The beginnings of self-expression. • The child begins with disordered scribbles. • The child then advances to controlled scribbles. • The child then advances to named scribbles around the age of 3.5 years of age. • Media choice needs to reflect ease for grasping and scribbling.	Scribbling starts with lines chosen without direction and moves to controlled scribbles. There is a developing connection between motion and marks on the paper. Control over the scribble is also reflected in control over parts of the environment. Trying different colours and filling the page leads to discovering a relationship between drawing and the environment. Art expression changes from kinesthetic thinking to imaginative thinking, playing with colour, drawing with intent and no preconceived notions as to what the finished scribbling will look like. The marks evolve into clearly recognizable pictures of subject matter with colour choice to match objects depicted.
2) Pre-Schematic Stage Ages 4-7 years • In this stage the first representational attempts are made. • Copied symbols are visually repeated in a stiff and inflexible fashion. • Media choice needs to reflect ease in drawing, and as such markers are suitable for this developmental level.	Colors are selected based on mood and colour is used for its own sake. The egocentric view of the world is a view of self with controlled marks related to environment, developing a sensitivity to body parts and the first representation of a person is head to foot and is not a copy of a person. Space is conceived as primarily related to self and body. The emotionally sensitive child will exaggerate things or parts where emotion is involved.

Stage and Main Markers	Description
3) Schematic Stage. 7-9 years of age. • In this stage the achievement of a form concept occurs. • Developed is an awareness of how to represent three-dimensional quality of space usually represented by two dimensions. • A base line is used to indicate motion, on which things stand, and represents the surface of the landscape. • A skyline is drawn at the top of the page with the space between sky and land identified as being air. • Folding over is a process of creating space concept by drawing an object that appears to be drawn upside down. • The more active the artist is the more likely they are to give the drawn figure movement and action. • If the artist becomes bound up with one part of a drawing by losing all ties with the rest of it and if forms that are created are separated from the whole of the artwork they will lose meaning and the emotional response of the artist is no longer emotionally normal (maladjusted).	The drawing is the symbol of the mental image of the object which is an indication of the way information is interpreted and comprehension of experience. The drawing of a human figure is a readily recognizable symbol and will change from day to day and includes symbols such as hands, fingers, clothing, feet and the can be created in profile. There is a definite order in space relationship, with everything placed on a base line. Important symbols are exaggerated in size, with a change of symbols used for significant parts and neglect or omission of unimportant parts, or suppressed parts. Emotions are visibly expressed by exaggerations of size of body and facial expressions. Different time sequences and separate activities experienced can be represented within one drawing. The environment is drawn increasingly more objectively, and toward the end of this stage the drawings are increasingly influenced by the visual perception of the environment. Relationship to colour is based on the individual.

Stage and Main Markers	Description
4) Gang Age. 9-12 years of age. - The dawning of realism stage. - There is a stiffness in drawings with a movement from rigid color object relationship to a characterization of color. - There is an expression of sex differences with the subject matter being the subjective relationship of man to the environment. - Self-expression is no longer flowing freely. - Media best suited in this stage needs to reflect the artists concern with drawing detail.	The artist moves from egocentric thinking to thinking socially, and looking from the outside in, representing experience had with an object. There is a greater visual awareness, and a greater awareness of self and environment. A free use of exaggeration and distortion for emotional effect that represents more attention payed to parts that have emotional significance. There is an importance of identifying with oneself at a moment, and as the artist changes so does the artworks expression. Two different creative types evolve: visually minded and haptic.
5) Pseudo-Naturalistic Stage. 12-14 years of age. - The age of reasoning. - There is more interest in human figure drawings from females and more interest in satirical depictions from males. - The most difficult drawings at this stage are identified as drawing the self as it required coming to terms with one's own identity and a reflection of one's ability to face the self. - Between the ages of 12-15 the self is looked at negatively and described in derogative terms.	The developing self-awareness is expressed through a self-conscious approach to the environment. Sexual development is not included in drawings which might suggest fear of these changes, and there is an increased awareness of own physical development and curiosity about opposite sex. Expression of emotional relationships are expressed directly or symbolically. The use of colour is determined based on impact of past experiences.

Stage and Main Markers	Description
6) Period of Decision. 14-17 years of age. • Very little opportunity for self-identification is experienced in this stage which in a lot of cases ends the pursuit of drawing as students no longer have to take art classes in school.	In this stage the artist feels responsible for what is being done and is self-critical, introspective and idealistic. There is a growing concern about the relationship with environment, the expression of feelings and emotions and the need to master a portion of one's life.

Note. Adapted from *Creative and Mental Growth*, by V. Lowenfeld and W. L, Brittain, 1975. (6th Ed). Copyright 1975 by Macmillan Publishing Co., Inc.

Karen Hamblen (1984) reviewed the major theories of child art and the assumptions of stage theory to develop an explanation of artistic expression that allows and accounts for relationships between children's drawings and adult art. She found that there are cross-cultural similarities and differences that suggest there are universal factors shared by both children and adults that are still operative, although socially relative and developmental factors predominate (p. 2). She suggests that describing and analysing child and adult art with a socio-psychological framework provides a more adequate assessment of the graphic expressions of child and adult art at various chronological ages and developmental stages (p. 4). She suggests that a major assumption of stage theory is that a child's level of graphic expression is indicative of achievement in other cognitive domains, however stages can be skipped, reverted to or combined and there has been found to be developmental differences across domains. Cultural value differences have been found to be a factor as well, which suggests that classical interpretations of stage theory need to be modified (p. 7).

Hamblen (1984) suggests that "In an almost mirror-like fashion at the other end of the developmental and chronological continuum, innate factors have often been denied to have an influence on art" (p. 10). She suggests that spontaneous configurations in children's drawings reappear in adult art and as such adult art is a recollection of childhood expression that is "remembered, enhanced and repeated" (p. 18). Art therefore is not necessarily an improvement over time, "but is rather a barometer of socio-psychological orientations toward variable options" (p. 22-23), of recognizable patterns within individual psychology and cultural values. Therefore, Hamblen (1984) concludes that artistic expression consists of a non-linear path which is "circumscribed by the imperatives of time, place, and level of skill acquisition" (p. 2). As a result, the interpretation of adult art will be viewed through the lens of the stage theory as explored through the work of Lowenfeld and Brittain (1975).

For a therapist engaging in self-exploration, the foregoing observations suggest important ways to maximize their understanding of insights revealed through symbols, and to achieve closer contact with self. The interpretation of art using symbols is vital to art therapy and arts-based research. It enables the viewer(s) to identify the different elements of the self (Betts, 2006; Furth, 1988; Janson; 1986, McNiff, 2004; Oster & Crone, 2004).

Research Implications

This literature review had many implications for the research design and analysis. First, the literature revealed that, while there have been several studies concerning the exploration of the self-portrait; none have occurred with art therapists using their respective self-portraits. This research seeks to do just that. Second, the exploration of the "self" enabled me to be better prepared to observe, query and comment on the self-portraits. Third, the literature emphasized the importance of self-care, as a professional responsibility, reinforcing what I believe and practice. For example, Allen (1992) and Brown (2008) illuminate the need for art therapists to continue their own art work and engage in self-reflection, while carrying on their therapy practice. This is important to preventing burn-out, compassion fatigue, and clinification. Fourth, the literature informed the use of self-portraiture and reflection over a specified period with further reflection through verbal discussion with me at the end of that timeframe. Here, the literature affirmed the use projective self-portraiture as a self-reflective process for providing each participant with an objective view of self. This simple and quick projective drawing could allow the participant to reflect on their current perceptions of self and who they would like to be. As well, the discussion with me provided a witness to their lived-experience. Fifth, the literature affirmed the use of Furth's (1988) symbols and Lowenfeld and Brittain's (1975) stages of development to view self-portraits. Their method was used for this research.

CHAPTER TWO

METHOD

As previously mentioned, the research question for this study was: what is the art therapist's lived-experience of drawing a full-bodied self-portrait each week for four weeks? The goal of this study was to contribute to a better understanding of self-portraiture as a process of self-reflection, and as a strategy, whereby art therapists can increase self-understanding and address the self-care responsibility mandated by their profession. Three research objectives were developed to inform this goal:

1. To describe self-portraiture as self-reflective practice from the lived-experience perspective of art therapists;
2. To examine art therapists' subjective, personal experience of self-portraiture as a weekly reflective practice; and
3. To examine the reported perspectives of art therapists regarding personal changes and/or insights about the need for personal change that occurred during their engagement in this practice.

This research question directly influenced the selection of the research design and its implementation. This chapter: offers an overview of qualitative research and the research paradigm or the set of underlying beliefs and assumptions that guided this research; identifies the methodology and methods used to answer the research question, including participant selection, informed consent, data collection and analysis, credibility, dependability and trustworthiness, and reflexivity; and reviews the ethical considerations and procedures followed throughout this research. The discussion begins with an overview of qualitative research.

Cresswell (2014) notes that qualitative design based on open-ended questions and verbal communication can facilitate deeper understanding of the lived-experience of a phenomenon. He also observes that constructivist research seeks to understand the meaning of the phenomenon being studied, from the perspective of those who participate in that phenomenon. Cresswell (2014) suggests that qualitative research is conducted in an inductive manner, enabling the researcher to focus on the meaning which each participant derives from the experienced phenomenon. Chenail (2005) describes qualitative research as "attempting to make sense of the world" (p. 191), noting that it is a useful means of making a systematic evaluation of an experience that happens during a particular period. Creswell (2014) contends that it is an approach seeking to explore and understand the meaning that individuals ascribe to a complex situation.

The basis of this research project is in the artistic practice of creating art. Arts-based research provides a process for the exploration of non-linguistic knowing (Blumenfeld-Jones, 2016). Blumenfeld-Jones (2016) describes his process regarding his arts-based research as not a verbal process, but as "a motional awareness process" (p. 325). The process outlines the aesthetics of the moment paying attention to tone, imagination, feeling, body awareness, and emotion. He describes the reliance on the aesthetic moment as "a concatenation of all these dimensions of my being over and against the material reality that I am encountering. I am available to these dimensions of my response to the reality" (p. 325).

Since the process of the creation of the self-portrait is not a tool so much as it is a way of awareness, phenomenology provides a basis for conducting this qualitative, arts-based research. Prior to discussing the methodology for this research, it is useful to understand the set of beliefs that guided this research.

Research Paradigm

The research paradigm or set of underlying beliefs that guided this research was a constructivist/interpretive paradigm. Topolovčan (2016) suggests that the constructivist paradigm "points to the social (co-)construction of our understanding of reality" (p. 1143), while visual art and creativity is a language and a way of knowing that goes beyond language. The qualitative methodologies of constructivist learning point to the connection between the individual, their culture, language and communication and the creation of understanding and meaning of ones' own learning process (p. 1146), which can be researched by means of arts-based research. In arts-based research, introspection or the internal processing of "thinking, doubts, conflicts, redefinitions and ideas occurring in the creator when making a particular work of art or learning" (p. 1150) is an important component. At the same time, phenomenology focuses on researching the same phenomenon by different people through introspection, interpretation, and description of their experience of the phenomenon (p. 1151). As such, Topolovčan (2016) concludes that, from an ontological and epistemological view, arts-based research belongs to qualitative research with an emphasis on phenomenology, and a compatibility with constructivism, that is based on the co-construction of knowledge as a creative process.

The social construction of reality is a theory of knowledge that examines the way knowledge is socially constructed and maintained through social interaction (Berger & Luckmann, 1966). Social construction theory examines the structure of experience and the individual's conscious awareness of what is happening, both outside and within the individual (Riley, 1994). The theory's comprehensive perspective is based upon the notion that perceptions of reality are inter-related and contribute to a common knowledge of reality (Riley, 1994). For this reason, the social construction of reality incorporates signs, symbols and patterns of behavior that are all elements of an objective reality that can be negotiated, and communicated by individuals, as common knowledge (Berger & Luckmann, 1966).

Riley (1994) observes that social constructionism provides a lens through which the researcher can observe, learn about, and understand art therapy processes and interventions. She examined the effectiveness of social constructionism, as an integrative approach to family art therapy, noting that a pertinent message is embedded in the art work itself. When further examined, the message revealed significant information regarding the way the author has invented/created his/her personal reality (Riley, 1994). Riley (1994) cites the work of Duncan, Parks, and Rush (1990), who suggest that individuals can describe their lives in a cohesive fashion because they construct meanings which shape and organize their experiences and perceptions into patterns. Riley concurs with Watzlawick (1984) who notes that individuals invent the world in which they live by the way they use language, and in their interpretations of past and present events, noting that they connect these reality-shaping discourses and interpretations sequentially.

Berger and Luckmann (1966) state, "Only a small part of the totality of human experience(s) is retained in consciousness" (p. 67). The authors suggest that experiences become memorable entities, noting that, unless this "intersubjective sedimentation" (p. 67) happens; individuals cannot make sense of their personal biographies of knowledge. They add that 'common knowledge' results when those with common biographies share and incorporate experiences. Berger and Luckmann (1966) note that such experiences can be transmitted from one generation to the next by means of a linguistic sign system. The sign system can also be transmitted by utilizing physical objects and actions. These serve as the means to objectify new experiences and incorporate them into the existing knowledge base.

Berger and Luckmann (1966) contend that the intersubjective world is shared with others and differentiates every-day life from other conscious realities. The individual takes everyday life for granted, as reality. In order to challenge his/her reality, the individual must "engage in a deliberate, by no means easy effort" (p. 24). When the continuity of every-day life is interrupted, "the reality of every-day life seeks to integrate the problematic sector into what is already unproblematic" (p. 24). The authors observe that theatre, or other art forms, serve as transitional realities embodying their own meanings and order, which are different from those of every-day life. They contend that these "finite provinces of meaning" (p. 25) enable the individual to turn his/her attention away from the reality of his/her every-day life. After engaging in a transitional experience such as theatre, a radical change takes place in consciousness. The individual returns to every-day reality and begins to translate the coexistence of the other reality into every-day experience.

Riley (1994) suggests that motivation to change arises when "a world view, an understanding, a conclusion, a truth, the perception of how events are sequenced has proven false or unsatisfactory" (p. 33). For an individual to rebalance their life, they must change the way in which he/she perceives the problematic situation before resolution can occur. Riley (1994) contends that, from a social constructionist viewpoint, a large social context, such as a family system, can contain a wide and varied range of individual beliefs because everyone's reality is shaped by their interpretation of their beliefs.

In a similar context, Riley (1994) notes that it is essential for a therapist to bracket his/her own invented realities, to keep personal bias from intruding into a therapeutic relationship. It is pertinent to note Keeling and Bermudez's (2006) observation that social constructionism concurs with phenomenology's imperative that the researcher must endeavour to set aside their preconceived notions. The essential themes derived from research data can only emerge when the researcher maintains sharp focus on participant's lived-experience, as described in self-reports about their engagement in the artistic process, and reflections on their aesthetic creations (Keeling & Bermudez, 2006).

An individual's reality is determined through social interaction and conversation (Berger & Luckmann, 1966). The intrinsic life and meaning of words have an additional impact on the individual, leading him/her to explore multiple possible variations of meaning in any verbal communication (Berger & Luckmann, 1966). Riley (1994) notes that story-telling is the first level of communication allowing the therapist to enter into the client's world. Riley (1994) concurs with Hoffman's observation (1990) that the second level of communication comprises an ability to reflect that there are many possible versions of interpretation. Riley (1994) adds that this ability enables the therapist: to become a participant-observer; to offer interpretations; to reframe meanings; and, to speak the client's meaning-related language. She indicates, that it is through the process of art therapy the family is provided the opportunity to illustrate the family story and, "that the families descriptions and stories can be refocused through art expressions" (p. 66). The social constructionist view suggests that the therapeutic art task becomes integrated into the family's concept of reality, so that each member completes the task with the creative response that he/she needs to express (Riley, 1994). About such tasks, Riley (1994) observes that the client's stories and artwork provides a fresh lens with "depth and dimension which introduces new constructs into the client's recursive, symptom-bound tale" (p. 60).

Riley (1994) concurs with Anderson and Goolishan's (1990) observation that the researcher offers the client a creative task as an alternative mode of communication. It serves as a process of speaking what has not been spoken; opening the client's narrative and moving the therapeutic dialogue forward (Riley, 1994). Riley (1994) notes that artwork created by clients during the therapeutic process becomes an additional observer to both client and therapist offering another way to look at a situation, while also serving as another means of looking at the self.

Berger and Luckmann (1966) explain that both art, a system dealing with symbols, and language, which constructs symbolic representations of everyday realities, allow individual detachment from everyday experience. The authors describe the body of knowledge of everyday life, as including "knowledge of [one's] situation and limits" (p. 41) and suggest that when it is presented to an individual, as an integrated whole, it can serve as "the means to integrate discrete elements of my own knowledge" (p. 43). They add that the individual takes it for granted that their knowledge of everyday life is valid until they become aware that their knowledge is failing to work in a satisfactory manner (Berger & Luckmann, 1966, p 43).

The constructivist/interpretive paradigm was considered best suited for this research given my research question. Social constructionism provided the lens through which art interventions were examined. This decision allowed me to enter the world of the participant to learn something about how the participant makes sense of their world through their social interaction and their conversation.

Methodology

As previously mentioned, the methodology best suited for this qualitative research was descriptive phenomenological, arts-based research. The assembly of methods used for this research is grouped under the broad headings of qualitative enquiry, phenomenological research, with the theoretical orientation of arts-based research and constructivism. This section provides an overview of phenomenology and arts-based research, and describes the methods selected to implement the inquiry.

Phenomenology.

Phenomenology was founded by Edmond Husserl who was interested in the pure description of lived-experience and integrated both psychology and logic into a theory of intentionality (Dahl & Boss, 2005). Husserl contends that everyone perceives reality through their lens, which shows them a world, based upon how they conceive it to be (Oteros-Pailos, 2010). This implies that intention is fundamental to the operation of everyone's consciousness as he/she makes meaning out of lived-experience by assigning meaning (Berger & Luckman, 1966). The individual's awareness of their lived experience is the object of study for phenomenology. Husserl's phenomenological research method investigates experience from a transcendental perspective, which takes as a given, that the way phenomena constitute elements of an individual's experience depends upon how those phenomena appear to that individual. Amedeo Giorgi (1997) describes the three steps comprising Husserl's research method as follows:

1. the researcher adopts the transcendental phenomenological attitude;
2. the phenomenon to be explored is brought to consciousness, using intuition; and
3. the description of the essence of the experience that has been discovered is then carefully described (p. 240).

Giorgi developed his phenomenological method as an alternative epistemology for human science research, while closely following Husserl's descriptive, phenomenological method (Giorgi, 1997). His approach is distinguished from Husserl's by its attention to both descriptive and interpretive elements; using empathic immersion to obtain the deepest possible understanding of the participant's actual, lived experience of the phenomenon under investigation (Dahl & Boss, 2005). Giorgi's modified-Husserlian research method specifies four steps (Dahl & Boss, 2005). They are:

1. the researcher must read and re-read the entire description of an observation or experience many times, in order to gain a general sense of the whole;
2. having obtained a general sense of the whole description, the researcher must read through the text once more, with the objective of discerning meaning units;
3. the researcher transforms the meaning units by expressing the psychological insights they contain more directly, in order to articulate their lived-meanings; and
4. the researcher synthesizes all the transformed meaning units into a consistent statement regarding the participant's experience. (p. 74)

The phenomenological method relies upon participants' self-reporting of their individual experiences. Willis (2001) notes that the phenomenological process requires the researcher to analyze each participants' self-report, while searching for the patterns and themes held therein. Giorgi (1985b) suggests that interview data can be collected by recording and transcribing the verbal information. Once recorded and transcribed, the researcher reads and re-reads the text several times before beginning to analyze the data. The researcher then selects certain passages within the text, sections, which Giorgi (1985a) calls meaning units. The researcher recognizes a meaning unit when he/she reads a passage indicating, that within the participant's consciousness, a shift in meaning has taken place (Giorgi, 1997). A meaning unit is identified based upon the different words and sentences that are used by participants to convey different themes (Giorgi, 2012). The researcher then appropriately clusters the meaning units into themes that are relevant to the topic under investigation. Giorgi (2012) observes that the resulting descriptive analysis transforms the naturally diffuse nature of the participant's description into phenomenologically significant discourse.

Giorgi (2012) contends that phenomenology requires the researcher to assume a phenomenologically reductionist attitude. Reduction allows the phenomenologist to return specifically to an individual's experience, and to focus on the essential nature of the phenomenon. Giorgi (2012) defines eidetic reduction as the bracketing of contingent and accidental considerations in order to determine the essential nature of objects and acts of consciousness. According to Giorgi (2012), the researcher achieves eidetic reduction by engaging in the process of imaginative variation. Free variation comprises subjecting the phenomenon of a participant's conscious experience to a series of variations, systematically paring the phenomenon down to its essence (Giorgi, 1985b). It is pertinent to share Giorgi's (2012) suggestion that phenomenological reduction heightens the individual's conscious awareness of their experience, adding that this results in suspending extraneous beliefs about the experience.

The researcher carries out a second eidetic reduction, using imaginative variation whereby they imagine each emergent theme to be anything other than it is, while evaluating the phenomenon under investigation, to determine its relation to any other phenomenon. The researcher enlarges the realm of possible meanings derived from each participant's data by imaginatively varying and/or abstracting emergent themes (Giorgi, 2012). Moustakas (1994) explains that imaginative variation provides the researcher with opportunities to search for underlying themes, vary possible structural meanings and consider structural properties, such as time, space, material and causality. He adds that imaginative variation also enables the researcher to search for examples which validate the themes which emerge during the researcher's attempts to uncover hidden frames of reference.

It is important for the researcher to bracket his/her experiences, biases and preconceptions when determining the essence of a phenomenon or theme and/or when examining the organization and expression of raw data (Giorgi, 1997). Giorgi (2012) notes that, by identifying and bracketing biases and prejudices, the researcher can be more aware of, and attentive to the phenomenon under examination.

The researcher describes the essential structure of the participant's lived-experience from the perspective of the psychological discipline they are utilizing and analyzes the participant's concrete experiences to determine their eidetic meanings (Moustakas, 1994). Reduction has the advantage of allowing the phenomenologist to return specifically to the participant's actual experience and, thereby, to focus on the essential nature of the phenomenon (Giorgi, 1997).

Giorgi (1997) elaborates on the interpretation of data as follows, "Phenomenon within phenomenology means that whatever is given or presents itself is understood precisely as it presents itself to the consciousness of the person entering the awareness" (p. 238). When interpreting research results, the phenomenological process helps the investigator to discover and focus on newly-revealed elements and themes emerging from the data (Giorgi, 1997). The participants' reflections, once transcribed and compared with other participants' interview transcripts, reveals repetitions of experience providing opportunities for coding (Giorgi, 1997).

Giorgi based his work within the parameters of phenomenological philosophy, science and psychology, contending that phenomenological theory would provide more information than the, historically-established, research focus on empirical data (Dahl & Boss, 2005). His descriptive phenomenological method provides a methodological process that can be applied to social science research (Dahl & Boss, 2005). For example, when using Giorgi's method to conduct psychological research regarding consciousness, the researcher uncovers psychological themes distributed within the data and clarifies the meaning of the phenomenon/experience under investigation (Giorgi, 1997).

Arts-based research.

Qualitative researchers and arts-based researchers integrate both artistic activity and research. McNiff (1998) indicates that artistic activity is a form of research, as art has its own language. As previously discussed, McNiff (1998) dialogues with works of art to find out what it is that the artwork is saying, using this interpretation to determine the message that the artwork is trying to convey. The resulting artwork provides the findings and the dialogue that the creator and researcher conduct with them is the interpretation (Blumenfeld-Jones, 2016).

Van Lith (2008) relates the belief that art therapy and art expression assist individuals "who are trying to find themselves in the world through visually expressive self-projections and looking inward to create new meaning" (p. 25). Both Giorgi (1997) and Willis (2001) add the important clarification that, although phenomenological studies investigate the meaning of objects and/or how objects are perceived, the meaning of the experience is not inherent within the object itself. In reality, the meaning of an experience is located within the lived-experience of the participant/viewer (Willis, 2001). The above considerations indicate the importance of focusing on the meaning of each self-portrait in relation to the lived-experience of its creator.

As Janson (1986) states, "We must remember that any image is a separate and self-contained reality which has its own ends and responds to its own imperative, for the artist is bound only to his creativity" (p. 11), and therefore the viewer has to ask why the image is made this way as opposed to any other way. The artists, through their work, are trying to make conscious elements of self and context that are hidden, and as such are trying to attain conscious awareness of what is happening, based on past, current, and future experiences of self, their social construction of reality.

Finlay (1994) discusses the importance of arts-based research as a means of inquiry with multiple ways of seeing and multiple ways in which experience can be constructed. Blumenfeld-Jones (2016) suggests that investigating the self is a multilayered interpretive process. Arts-based research is grounded by feeling and states, "Phenomenologically, I must account for 'feeling' as what is common among all actions I take" (p. 326). The author describes that all the feeling ways of awareness point to an open and ongoing process, revealing new dimensions of the phenomenon and the participant's relationship to it (Blumenfeld-Jones, 2016). The process is interactive and non-linear.

Witnessing, as discussed by Blumenfeld-Jones (2016), is looking at the scene of the creative activity to see what is there, including; bodily positioning, the media used, the full-body of the participant, and if parts are missing. The researcher must be present to the creative act and no matter what the researchers' interpretation is of the of the creative act, attain what it is that the participants see in regard to the symbols within their artwork and how these symbols speak to them. Blumenfeld-Jones (2016) asserts that there are "feeling ways of awareness", a transpersonal process, which he terms "determining, immersing, objectively observing, bodily remembering, and assessing rightness through feeling" (p. 326).

Three types of determining provide a means for witnessing what is present in the scene. Blumenfeld-Jones (2016) offers some questions to consider when viewing the artistic scene: what is of importance; what is central; and what is the artistic nature of form, motion, colour and space. He describes the need to release from the scene in order to allow understandings and connections to be made. Immersing himself determines the essence, cultivating a focused attention to feelings, while the bodily sense leads to insights in which the artwork speaks to the researcher, and he states, "Look at what you are drawing, not the drawing itself" (p. 329). While bodily remembering is the remembering of the moment, to be able to recall the feeling, motion, emotion, and thoughts that were unfolding in the process and determine if what adds up resonates "with my aesthetic sensibilities and understanding" (p. 330).

Shaun McNiff (1998) discusses the necessity of personal participation in creative arts therapy research and contends it is consistent with the conditions of practice. It is the participation of the artist-researcher in the experimental activity that distinguishes arts-based research from any other. McNiff contends that personal involvement is a direct extension of the practice of the creative arts therapy (p. 36). The goal in creative arts therapies is to find out how the process of creation "affects us and what works in different therapeutic situations" (p. 36). As such, the examples of arts-based research illustrate the process of inquiry that can further the effectiveness of professional practice, "which grows from the trust in the intelligence of the creative process and a desire for relationships with images that emerge from it" (p. 37).

McNiff (1998) believes that the key to keeping the art as the primary mode of psychological inquiry is based in experiments with media "just as the chemist works with physical substances" (p. 26) in the controlled laboratory experiments of the physical sciences. It is the task of making the artwork that offers a clear structure and reliable method that provides "the structure for a sustained therapeutic experience." (p. 26). He also suggests that no matter how systematic the enquiries of arts-based research are, the arts-based research will "always produce results that simply 'happen' as a result of the unique conditions of the particular process of investigation" (p. 43).

A qualitative, descriptive phenomenological, arts-based research methodology offered the closest alignment with this research. For example, feeling is the basis for the arts-based phenomenological account and undergirds all the ways of awareness (Blumenfeld-Jones, 2016; Finlay, 1994). Determining the inside feeling of the phenomenon in question, considering the participants symbols as interpretation, surfacing the participants lived-experience and awareness are all elements of witnessing in arts-based research (Blumenfeld-Jones, 2016; McNiff, 1998). The conversation with the research participants allowed for retrospection as an outside feeling as "the art is but a response to the phenomenon" (Blumenfeld-Jones, 2016, p. 332).

Methods

Fifteen art therapists were selected from approximately 30 therapists who conveyed interest in the research. Each agreed to set aside one hour at the end of each week for four weeks to spend five minutes doing a full-bodied self-portraiture followed by 55 minutes of reflective journaling. Therapists self-selected the location for completing this self-reflective exercise. Following the four-week period, each art therapist agreed to participate in a one-hour telephone and/or Skype interview to reflect on their four self-portraitures, as a serial, with me.

This section describes: the recruitment and selection process for the participating 15 art therapists; the data collection procedures; the approach to data analysis; reflexivity of the researcher; and the means for ensuring credibility, dependability and trustworthiness.

Participants.

Purposive and convenience sampling were used to recruit participants. Participants were recruited from an exclusive population of art therapists or art psychotherapists who were either Registered or Professional by designation with the Canadian Art Therapy Association or the Ontario Art Therapy Association. For example, registered art therapists have undergone additional supervised practice with another registered art therapist and meet criteria set out by the Canadian Art Therapy Association, in addition to being professional members. Further, there are relatively few art therapists within the greater population of psychotherapists. As a Registered Art Therapist, I had personal access to the art therapy community through my educational and vocational ties.

An electronic invitation (Appendix A) was sent to the Canadian Art Therapy Association, the Ontario Art Therapy Association, the Vancouver Art Therapy Institute and the Toronto Art Therapy Institute with a request to post or email the invitation to their membership. The organizations indicated they either posted the invitation on their website and/or emailed their respective members. Both Institutes are educational bodies with membership in the Canadian Art Therapy Association. Thirty art therapists responded to the invitation. The researcher subsequently electronically mailed information about the study and an informed consent form to each of the 30 art therapists. The information letter introduced me, as the researcher, stated the purpose of the study, described the criteria to be met by participants, explained the selection process and discussed the expected duration of the project, its risks and benefits, issues of confidentiality, compensation, contact and consent, feedback and plans regarding publication. The information about the study included a description of the participant's weekly reflection process and questions that participants would be required to answer. Participants were not selected until information had been sent to all those who responded to the invitation.

Respondents, who were interested in participating, were directed to provide the required information and electronically mail this, along with their signed consent documents, to me. I responded by telephone or electronic mail to questions from potential participants, making sure that each participant was fully informed and understood what participation required, before signing the informed consent.

Although 30 art therapists responded to the invitation, only 15 met the criteria required for participation. Participants were purposively selected based on their Professional, or Registered designation as Art Therapists, and their current use of art therapy in a practice setting. The selected participants signed the informed consent before the research process began. Table 5 provides a description of the participants selected for this project. Of the 15 participants, only one identified as male, and the remainder identified as female. The dominance of the female voice in this study is not surprising, given that, at this time, most of art therapists and therapists in general, are female. The participants have practiced art therapy for an average of five years, and a range between one and 23 years. Three participants were previously known to the researcher as peers, having studied with her in the Art Therapy Diploma program of the Vancouver Art Therapy Institute.

Table 5

Descriptive List of Participants by Category and Number

Category	Type	Number of Participants
Education	BA and Diploma	9
	Masters and Diploma	5
	MSW and Diploma	1
Self-Care Method	Journaling	5
	Art	6
	Physical Activity	4
	Supervision	2
	None	3
Age Range	30's	2
	40's	7
	50's	5
	60's	1
Spiritual/Religious	Spiritual	5
	Muslim	2
	None	8
Employer	Agency	3
	Private Practice	12
	Full Time	7
	Part Time	8
Memberships	Registered CATA	5
	Professional CATA	10
Location	Ontario	7
	Alberta	1
	British Columbia	2
	New Brunswick	1
	Saskatchewan	2
	Yukon	1
	Outside of Canada	1
Gender	Male	1
	Female	14

Due to the limited number of art therapists, and the fact that most are female, the researcher anticipated that most participants would be female. Given that the purpose of the study was to explore the lived-experience of art therapists, the fact that equal numbers of suitable male and female research subjects could not be found, was not considered a major barrier to obtaining meaningful results. The sample selected for this project comprised 14 females and one male art therapists, and for this reason, the resulting data cannot provide data reflecting gender-based factors.

The data collection procedure.

Each participant received verbal instructions whilch summarized the instructions provided them by electronic mail (Appendix B). Each participant was asked to set aside one hour at the end of the work week each week for a total of four weeks. A specific location for this reflective practice was not specified enabling personal preference. The participants were instructed to make sure that they had coloured markers, photocopy paper measuring 8.5" x11" and a journal. Each participant was asked to take five minutes to draw a full-bodied self-portrait and to use the remainder of the hour for journaling reflections about the past week, and the just-completed self-portrait, including what he/she saw within, or missing from the self-portrait. The participants supplied their resulting self-portraits and journal to the researcher at the conclusion of the four-week period. The resulting journal entries were not coded; instead participants used their journal entries as a helpful tool to reflect on their experience of creating each self-portrait.

Primary data collection comprised conducting an in-depth interview with each participant following his/her completion of four weekly self-portraits and written self-reflections. The goal of the interview process was to unearth evidence, from each participant's self-assessment, regarding whether their engagement in the self-portraiture had affected their lived-experience. The intent was for participants to tell the story of what they could see within their resulting artworks, and also what was hidden within their artworks as well. Appendix C provides the interview guide used in conducting the semi-structured, in-depth interviews. Participants were asked 13 questions, which facilitated conversations about their lived-experience of the self-portraiture and reflection exercise. The question sequence was followed loosely, permitting each participant to guide the interview process in a manner that allowed him/her to express whatever he/she felt was most essential to his/her lived-experience.

Each interview was conducted at a time and place that best suited the participant's schedule, via his/her choice of Skype or the telephone. The one-on-one interviews ranged in length from approximately 40 to 100 minutes. Each interview was audio recorded, and subsequently transcribed at the rate of 50 percent of the speed at which it had been recorded. During transcription, the interviews were anonymized, removing all personal information and possible identifiers from the resulting records.

As outlined by the work of Furth (1988) before the interview process, I took the opportunity to reflect on the four artworks provided by the participant. I noted a general comment on each artwork. In the interview process, I asked each participant if they would like to tell me anything about each self-portrait. As I had already viewed the self-portrait and knew something of the scene, I had to navigate how best to witness the participants' descriptions of their lived-experience. This required me to bracket what I thought I knew about the art therapist "socio-political-cultural position" (Blumenfeld-Jones, 2016, p. 324) and what I thought the therapist knew about the situation to be able to see through the eyes of the participant (Blumenfeld-Jones, 2016). The goal for me, as witness, was to feel "the bodily 'attitudes' on display" (p. 327), by recording positioning of each figure, connections, form, motion, colour, space and what stands out as important within each artwork, not only through intellectual response but also through sensory response (Blumenfeld-Jones, 2016).

The conversation with each participant was meant to enable each of them to reimage their artworks as a series, rather than as separate artworks. Each participant had the opportunity to reflect on his/her written journal, in order to notice, make sense and remember what he/she was doing and perhaps seeking to know, understand or to be (Blumenfeld-Jones, 2016).

I listened very carefully to the comments in the discussion as well as the tape-recorded interviews later after the interview was over. If I did not recognize an object or design, I asked about it, and encouraged the participant to "Tell me more" with open ended questions. My interest was to explore self-symbols, as well as, the interpretations by the participants of what was presented in the self-portraits. As in social constructivism theory, I anticipated that participants would choose symbols to represent their context, in order to "share intimate information of their personal selves" (Furth, 1988, p. 31). In summary, the picture interpretation process was based on three steps (Furth, 1988):

1. I gained an initial impression of the resulting self-portraits, not interpreting each picture, but instead identifying an initial feeling. I bracketed the initial feeling and any personal associations identified, so that participants could speak to their own reflections on their work.
2. Questions were asked to gain insight into the unconscious voice from each self-portrait so that each self-portrait could be analyzed objectively by the participant. A chart was created from the work of Furth (1988), to attain information about colour used, shapes drawn, direction of movement within each self-portrait, placement of images, repeated objects, and/or missing items.
3. The third step was to synthesize the information gained about the different components of the self-portraits and assemble all the information garnered into a whole. The different information garnered about the focal points of each artwork pointed to a story and a theme for each participant.

These steps were to gain knowledge in the "ways of awareness" in order to make meaning (Blumenfeld-Jones, 2016). Both the resulting artworks and the process of creating them held the knowledge that occurred through action and reflection of that action (Schaverien, 1995). The language of art, in the use of symbols, creates an object of knowledge which is open to interpretation, and holds the meaning that the artist engaged in self-portraiture is seeking to reveal. Both the artist and I engaged together as observers, reflectors, and interpreters of both what could be seen on the surface of each work, but also what was hidden, and underlying being revealed through the subconscious through the interpretive process (Blumenfeld-Jones, 2016; Furth, 1988).

It may be pertinent to note that the research methodology did not include a measurement tool based upon the researcher's evaluation of the artwork itself. This contrasts with the work of Machover (1949) who developed the D-A-P test, a qualitative approach to be used, also without time constraints. It is important to note however, that the D-A-P test relies on the interpretation by an outside, clinified observer, whereas this research project is truly qualitative, being focused in every respect on eliciting the participant's experience.

Data analysis.

Once the interviews were transcribed and read, I began a manual coding process which comprised the consolidation and elimination of redundant codes, categorizing the codes, and comparing meaning structures interpreted from the data. I identified within the different transcripts similar phrases about the participant's lived-experiences which provided the basis for a code to be categorized. A descriptive code was used when it appeared to be accurate and appropriate to the data. Different colours were used to identify the coding. When an existing, consolidated code failed to capture the nuances of meaning in a quotation, a new code was established. I subsequently compared the meaning structures of the participants' transcripts and created a chart visually depicting the comparison of data, which in turn provided the themes to be identified.

The steps taken in the process to attain descriptive and interpretive elements were based on the description by Dahl and Boss (2005). My approach was to use empathic immersion to obtain the deepest possible understanding of the participant's actual lived experience of the phenomenon under investigation. The approach was to identify similarities as well as differences in the lived-experience of the participants.

In addition to the phenomenological approach to data interpretation, the social constructionism approach was utilized. The resulting artworks and interview questions were further examined to determine underlying messages that could reveal significant information regarding the way the author had invented/created their personal reality (Riley, 1994). I maintained the perspective that everyone created his/her personal reality in his/her own mind, based upon his/her own experience.

As well as personal lived-experience, the social construction of reality incorporates signs, symbols and patterns of behavior that are all elements of an objective reality that can be negotiated, and communicated by individuals, as common knowledge. The goal in both the arts-based method as well as social constructionism was to attain the broader context of the lived-experience of the art therapist and the integration of the experience into the life of the art therapist. Participants had the opportunity to explore in conversation with me, upon reflection of the four resulting artworks, their larger social context, problem areas, as well as individual beliefs. In order for individuals to rebalance their life, they must change the way in which they perceive the problematic situation before resolution can occur (Riley, 1994), and as such, the interview allowed the participants to explore their lived-experience and how they integrated the information they achieved from their own self-reflection into their life and work.

The essential themes derived from the research data emerged because I maintained sharp focus on participants' lived-experience, as described in their respective self-reports about their engagement in the artistic process and their reflections upon their aesthetic creations (Keeling & Bermudez, 2006). The primary focus was upon identifying and understanding each participant's meaning from within the data. I elicited complex personal experiences, drawing out rich descriptions and deep meaning from participants' descriptions of their weekly self-portraiture and journaling experiences.

Reflexivity.

The research design of this study incorporated the collection of data on the lived-experiences of art therapists engaged in self-reflective, self-portraiture. It was necessary to capture everyone's perceptions of his/her experiences in order to obtain and understand the range of meanings, including differences and commonalities in the participants' lived-experiences.

Given Finlay's (1994) contention that reflexivity can be understood on the basis of the investigator's research paradigm, it seems pertinent to note here that the researcher's epistemological and ontological views correspond to the constructivist paradigm. Riley (1994) observes that the theoretical framework of social constructivism can serve as a suitable vantage point from which to view, learn about, and understand art therapy interventions/ explorations, noting that, within constructivism, the operation of reflexivity helps to explain how meanings, recognized as reality, are experienced in the moment for the participants by the researcher.

Groenewald (2004) comments that the most important element in research for Giorgi, is the description, stating that the aim of the researcher is to "describe as accurately as possible the phenomenon" (p. 5), and that this is accomplished by suspending as much as possible "any pre-given" (p. 5) information or experience, while remaining as true to the facts as possible. Reflexivity contributes to an understanding of the phenomenon being studied because the experiences and meanings derived by others are taken as valid and true (Groenewald, 2004).

Finlay (1994) observes that researchers must examine personal motives implicated in their research topic, to uncover bias that might affect their research. My motivation and interests in this project arise from my lived-experience with self-portraiture and interest in self-reflective practice as an art therapist. I am interested in providing art therapists with an opportunity to share, using their own words and images, their experience of incorporating a self-reflective practice into their everyday lives.

I acknowledge that, while my own experiences have provided profound motivation, this may result in bias regarding others with similar experiences. It is also pertinent to note that my preconceived notions have shaped the literature review, methodology and interview questions. Further, through previous experience, three of the participants were known to me. As a result, influence of prior knowledge could bias the results. Finally, my decrease in use of art therapy in practice as well as my decrease in self-reflective practice, led me to this research question.

My role as researcher was to maintain a reflexive praxis throughout the research process. This meant a conscious and constant reflexivity to assess my own preconceptions and allow for the emergence of clarity that moved beyond accepting data at face value.

Credibility, dependability and trustworthiness.

A phenomenological approach in qualitative research assumes that participants' views and reports provide the only credible, justifiable and valid results. In such types of research, the term credibility refers to the degree to which the results of the data analysis meet with participant agreement (Cederboum, 2009; Dahl & Boss, 2005). According to Cederboum (2009), credibility has to do with "the number of variations that will emerge from the continuous occupation with the subject" (p. 80); the resulting self-portraits. In order to ascertain credibility in this project, I electronically mailed each participant's quoted comments to him/her, inviting him/her to review them for clarity and accuracy and to add further insight and information as needed. Sprenkle and Piercy (2005) concur with Allen and Piercy (2005), who observed that constructionist research in the social sciences yields rich information but note that both therapists and researchers must be scrupulous about the credibility of their findings. All participants reviewed their reflections and indicated approval or approval with clarification.

In arts-based research, dependability refers to the degree to which results are consistent with the data obtained in the execution of the process of the creation of the self-portraits (Cerderboum, 2009). To increase dependability, it was important for me to consider, the context within which the research took place. For example, participants could select the location for their reflective session. Nine or 60 percent of the 15 participants created their self-portraits and engaged in journal writing at work, while the remaining (six or 40 percent) did so at home. Further, participants were also given the opportunity to select the way interviews were conducted. Thirteen interviews with participants were conducted by Skype, and two were conducted by telephone. In both instances, the freedom to select the location for reflection and the way the interview was conducted were intended to enhance rather than restrict engagement.

Keeling and Bermudez (2006) observe that to obtain trustworthy research findings is to: "preserve the immediacy of lived-experience, to represent the experience as participants intended, and to convey the account adequately to support its conclusions" (p. 411). Stiles (1993) contends that interpretations of qualitative data can be validated on the basis of the degree to which the interpretation is internally consistent, applicable to, and an accurate reflection of the information obtained. To promote the trustworthiness of obtained data, I listened to participants' interviews multiple times at various stages of the analytic process and bracketed my preconceptions regarding the phenomena. Groenewald (2004) contends that bracketing of the researcher's preconceptions of the phenomena helps to ensure trustworthiness of his/her results because it keeps the description of the lived-experience as close to the description of the phenomena as possible.

Validity within qualitative research is to gain in understanding and interpretation of predictions of behaviour (Cederboum, 2009). According to Lincoln and Guba (1985) validity is achievable in the identification of patterns that the researcher has exposed. The more that the descriptions, unearthed by the researcher and provided by the participants are rich in description and deep in interpretation, the more the findings are valid and transferable (Cederboum, 2009).

To attain the highest possible degree of validity in this study, I maintained my connection with the participants' experiences by viewing each series of artworks and journal reflections along with each participant as he/she reflected on his/her experiences of the weekly process and his/her experience of viewing his/her series of works. During the Skype or telephone interviews, each participant maintained his/her connection with his/her created images and journal entries by having the portraits and journal pages literally spread out before him/her as he/she related his/her reflections to me. Further, I linked the present study with previous research with regard to scholarship on the self, self-portraiture, self-reflection, art therapy, arts-based assessments and art therapists.

These research processes and strategies were systematically implemented to ensure the credibility, dependability and trustworthiness of the research findings. Prior to closing this chapter, it is important to discuss the ethical considerations and procedures that were addressed throughout the research process.

Ethical Considerations

Permission to proceed with this study was reviewed and approved by the Wilfrid Laurier University Research Ethics Board. The purpose of the research and the anticipated benefits and emotional risks were addressed with participants in the informed consent form. Risks to participants were minimized by allowing them to choose whether or not to disclose personal information and by permitting them to withdraw at any point in the study, at which time their data would be destroyed. The information letter and informed consent also discussed the potential for emotional risk incurred by participants, as they created their self-portraits and reflected on their drawings, adding that I would address any discomfort that participants experienced. I elaborated on this commitment, noting that if necessary, participants would be referred to their own/usual resources to work through problematic issues and stating that, if these resources were inadequate, participants would be given information about therapists and/or counselling agencies in their local vicinity. All participants received a copy of the signed consent form.

Confidentiality and anonymity of participants was ensured, as all data collected by the researcher was coded to maintain confidentiality and anonymity of participant's identities. The image data did not include participant's names. Participant names were replaced by pseudonyms and other identifying information was removed or substituted. These measures were taken during the transcription phase, so that only each participant and I knew participants' real identities and other personal/private details. All collected data were stored and managed in a locked filing cabinet in the researcher's home office. Audio recordings and their transcripts were saved on a secure, password-protected computer and backed-up on a secure, external hard drive kept in the researcher's locked office. Only the researcher had access to the data.

During the interview process, I asked each participant for his/her permission to include his/her artwork in the research presentation. All participants gave their permission for the artwork to be included and shown. The researcher volunteered to remove any identifiers of the artists from their artworks before presenting them, but no participant felt that this would be necessary. Finally, I intend to send each participating art therapist a copy of the approved dissertation.

CHAPTER THREE

RESULTS

This chapter presents the self-portraitures and reflections of 15 art therapists, insights that surface through their respective interviews and the resulting analysis. The chapter begins with an exploration of the essential themes identified from the analytic process. The themes are subsequently explored with at least one participant exemplar followed by the voices from other individual participants. While I offer some initial impressions of the serial portraits, the primary data surfaces from the therapists. Important is that I have purposefully avoided providing any detail regarding the backgrounds of the art therapists, in order to insure anonymity. All participants' names have been replaced with pseudonyms. Prior to beginning the discussion, additional information is offered concerning the process for analyzing the data.

Analysis of Data

The interviews provided the most salient and personally significant aspect of the participant's experience, as the interviews focussed on their stories. Following the interviews, I adhered to Giorgi's (2012) methodological outline which included: reviewing the detailed descriptions provided by the participants; identifying and organizing the meaning units; and surfacing the essence of each participant experience through phenomenological psychological analysis (Dahl & Boss, 2005).

To obtain the essential meaning of each participant's experience, themes were identified and abstracted from the interview data (see Table 6). Entering this information in a table made it easier to visualize the data and facilitated the process of making comparisons regarding different structures of meaning. It also helped me organize the meaning units to derive the essential themes contained in the raw data, by noting the number of passages where specific units/structures and themes were identified and calculating the number of cases where they occurred.

Table 6

Frequencies and Percentages of Essential Themes

Essential Themes	Number	
	Passages	Cases
Self-awareness through symbolism of environment	113	15
Symbolism expressed through use of media	72	15
Self-awareness through emotional, spiritual and bodily awareness	129	15
Construction of self through word in art	65	6
Self-awareness through engagement with inner-child	88	10
Self-awareness through transformation	112	15
Self-awareness of professional self	122	15
Self-awareness through self-care	185	15
Self-awareness of hope and appreciation	200	15
Total	1,086	

In summary, I studied each third person meaning unit to understand its psychologically-significant essence. My goal was to abstract themes that all participants would recognize and identify with. The last step required me to synthesize all the transformed meaning units related to each theme into a consistent statement regarding the participants' experience. After completing the transformational processes described above, I wrote statements expressing the psychologically-relevant essences of the fundamental themes that emerged from the data.

An interpretive process took place in response to each of the art works. The interpretation examined the significance of the signs and symbols that appeared in the artworks, as well as their context based upon the descriptions from the participants. The interpretive processes aim to present the wealth of information obtained from the contents of the self-portraits, and on the participant's immediate experiential reactions during the interviews. Each participant showcased a particular theme. As becomes apparent, there was overlap rather than discrete boundaries between the themes.

Thematic Analysis

This section presents each of the eight themes, including: self-awareness through symbolism of environment; symbolism expressed through use of media; self-awareness through emotional, spiritual and bodily awareness; construction of self through word in art; self-awareness through engagement with inner-child; self-awareness through transformation; self-awareness of professional self; self-awareness through self-care; and self-awareness of hope and appreciation. The first theme explores self-awareness through symbolism, particularly with reference to the use of the environment to create meaning.

Self-awareness though symbolism of environment.

The thematic exploration that follows, concerns the use of symbolism about the environment which consists of the surroundings and context of the participant. The self-portraits and reflections of Linda are presented followed by additional insights from Bessie.

Reflections of Linda.

Linda offers a rich artistic use of environmental symbolism in her self-portraits (see Figure 1). My initial impression of the artwork was that all the spaces were filled, and the entire page engaged, with the exception of the first self-portrait. I sensed the first portrait depicted a "looking within," as her eyes were closed. The hands were also held as if "centering self" was taking place.

Linda described her first portrait as gathering her resources. In her second artwork, she indicated that her initial impression of the artwork was that of the metaphor of "taking in the sheaths," gathering the wheat in the field. For the researcher, this is a metaphor for harvesting resources, and a symbol of religiosity for bringing souls to Christ before judgement. She noted,

> My idea for this image was gathering up the wheat or grasses, gathering up resources. But the picture of myself that I drew … I had a client that week, he was four years old, and he pretended to shoot me in session and I pretended to die. This is exactly my posture when I was dying. I found that was very interesting because when I looked at the image I thought that is a very odd body placement for what I had in mind. But, that is the way I looked when he pretended to shoot me and then I thought, maybe one of my resources is that I am ok with being shot and playing dead with a four-year-old. This is a good resource as an art therapist.

Figure 1. Self-Portraits by Linda

Linda discussed how she had placed herself at the centre of the portraits, which symbolically indicates an opportunity to reveal herself as centrally important (Furth, 1988). This could increase her sense of cohesiveness (Kohut, 1971). The incorporation of the weekly self-portraits provides a creative response to how her environment was not conducive to her sense of cohesion. Linda also reflected on the difference between her drawing and comments from clients, including the limitation of available coloured markers, or omission that occurred in the process. She observed,

> I wrote in my journal that I don't have a grey marker. Three clients this week commented that I had a grey streak in my hair. I don't know how to draw myself at my age. I am 51. I am trying to think how I would reflect my age. I didn't have a grey marker so maybe I avoided showing my age. So I couldn't do a grey streak in my hair.

Linda discussed her experience of reflecting on her artwork and how one item was constantly missing throughout the four images. Yet, she had no idea why and found that she could not connect to what this meant for her. She observed,

> I was surprised I never drew myself with shoes. It's so funny. Even in a drawing where I was standing and looking reflective and I wear clothes, I am not wearing shoes. You cannot see my feet in the nest, but I know I am not wearing shoes. I never go bare-foot; I wear shoes all the time. It is harder to draw feet then shoes. Shoes are consistently missing, and I don't even know what to make of that.

For me, as I reflect upon the work of Linda, my interpretation of the reason for the wearing of shoes, is that shoes serve to protect our feet from the environment. Without shoes, the feet have no protection. The metaphor for the lack of shoes suggests being childlike. To be childlike is to be innocent and free from the burden of real-life requirements.

Linda explained her experience of doing the self-portraits and being surprised by how much her environment needed to be re-organized to suit her work. She indicated that she found it very hard to incorporate the process in her work environment, and self-reflected that "This should not be so hard". As such, this created the need to change her environment in order for an increased sense of cohesiveness. She observed,

> Maybe what this process did was raise my awareness of my surroundings and how they are supporting me. When I noticed I was stressed out doing the self-portrait, I said to myself that I should be able to add this to my life. As a result, I am putting everything relating to my practice in my studio and separating home and work. My work has to go to the studio and my work has to stay there.

Furth (1988) discusses the need to reflect on the difference between the image and the actual world of the artist and to compare the two, which may be significant to the artist's psychology. It was interesting to observe that the third artwork depicted a bright golden yellow sun which, according to Furth (1988), indicates an emphasis on a spiritual or intuitive nature. In her final artwork, she depicted herself as a child with wings who was perched way up high in a tree. As noted by Furth (1988), the tree is a life symbol. The wings symbolise spirituality, flying or rising above, as she sits in the nest within the tree. The nest might represent Linda's home and/or work environment. While the colours chosen for each of her artworks; dark brown, bright blue, and dark green, emphasize health, growth, nourishment and being in touch with nature (Furth, 1988). Linda discussed how what she needed was reflected in her artwork. She said,

> It was reflected in my artwork towards the end because I looked so comfortable in my nest. Because my life is never going to be calm and predictable, I have to create an environment for myself that supports chaos... and so a nest, in my studio. I really like my studio so it is an easy move to make. I also integrated my experience by making art. Spending an hour at the end of each week, just making something, I think that is very important. I don't do a self-reflection process and this highlighted for me how important that is.

The analysis suggests the constructivist self-awareness of the different selves within the story and the existentialism expressed in freedom (Klugman, 1997). As Lowenfeld and Brittain (1975) indicate in their developmental mode for the "gang age", the subject matter represents the subjective experience of relationship between self to the environment, which is no longer bound up in the self from an egocentric view to looking from the outside in (p. 231). Further, Linda described recognizing transference when she was reflecting on her images. As previously mentioned, the second image depicted an experience during a session with a client. When she first drew the image, she believed it depicted harvesting resources. On later reflection, she realized that she had shown herself responding to a client by play-acting being shot. Other participants also reported experiencing awareness that they were more alert to their effects on clients and/or to clients' effects on them, adding that they were able to identify these effects within their artwork.

Participant Reflections.

One participant, Bessie, indicated that she experienced a revelation about her environment surfacing from her unconscious when she spoke about her images and reflections. While in conversation about her artwork, she realized that all four images contained symbolism related to birth, with the first image a womb. Bessie noted that initially she believed that she had drawn tears of blood to represent her feelings. Discussing her reflective experience surfaced Bessie's need to transform herself into what she considered socially acceptable for her age and stage. She had not previously recognized her pain concerning the continuing conflict she found herself in her work with her inability to manage herself in order to "fit". She was able to look at herself and the experience with new insight. Through the process of the self-portraiture she chose a date to retire.

As explored in this section, the realm of the subconscious is represented in art through the use of symbols as the participants reflected upon themselves within their particular context. By the participant exploring the meaning related to each symbol, the participant's relationship with their surroundings surfaced. The resulting exploration of symbols of the environment allowed insight and the opportunity for change to occur.

Symbolism expressed through use of media.

The following thematic exploration describes the association of the lived-experience and the theme of symbolism expressed through the use of media. For purposes of this research, the word media concerns the use of different materials to create the image. As previously mentioned, participants were directed to use markers. Markers or felts are a hard material, and somewhat difficult to use as they do enable shading and lines cannot be erased (Furth, 1988). Several participants chose to use different media such as pencils, chalk pastels, oil pastels, glitter, and pencil crayons. The self-portraits and reflections by Laura and Salina are discussed with additional insights from Bessie and Nike.

Reflections of Laura.

I found the portraits by Laura very energetic; with lots of movement (see Figure 2). They appeared to be fun and doll like. Alternatively, the colouring and hair appeared a bit frazzled, suggesting a feeling of stress.

Laura reported that she used her imagination to create each self-portrait which allowed her to experience a sense of freedom. Laura noted,

> I was surprised to find I actually enjoyed it. I have a complete aversion to drawing portraits of people. It is about being dedicated because I had to find space in my calendar for me to find time to do this, to actually do it.

Laura reported that she was able to connect with her child self, and that after initially worrying about creating the first self-portrait, she was able to relax and let herself go. Laura reflected upon the symbolism of the prominent feature of hair within each artwork. She used dark brown to depict both the trunk of the tree and the colour of her hair. According to Furth (1988), dark brown represents nourishment, health, and being in touch with nature. Laura indicated that this symbol of her hair allowed her to connect to a story from her past.

When I was a kid my mom used to cut my hair really, really short and I looked like a boy. It used to be short and now it's long and that's a big deal.

Figure 2. Self-Portraits by Laura

Laura discussed her experience of using the markers and how this led to the feel of a caricature in her artwork. She noted,

> I think that the fact I used the markers, because when you are a child you use markers, but there is something kind of free with that as well. Maybe that is what allowed me to just scribble away.

This connection with the inner child, as explored by Winnicott (1965), suggests that an accurate mirror of her experiences allows the individual to feel a sense of pleasure at being alive, inhabiting a reality that encourages continued true self growth.

Laura described the transition she felt happened within self, and was reflected in her artwork over the four weeks. In her initial artwork, she created herself within a mandala. Furth (1988) describes this as a barrier which he suggests is a conscious or subconscious blockage. There appears to be a number of barriers within her self-portraits. The first starts with the mandala in which Laura has placed herself safely inside a bubble. In this portrait Laura depicted herself in a red dress surrounded by golden yellow. According to Furth (1988), red symbolizes an identification of a problem, surging emotions and/or danger, while golden yellow places an emphasis on the spiritual or intuitive nature and life-giving energy surrounding her within the bubble. In the second portrait, Laura breaks free of the confines of the mandala to create movement. She appears to break free and is able to fly. It is noteworthy that the colour of her dress cascades from red at the top of her dress into golden yellow, as she breaks free of the bubble.

The next two portraits have an edging of trees on the right-hand side of the page which, according to Furth (1988), might be another element of being partially involved or not totally committed. The pale blue colour chosen for the background of the images might represent distance, or contemplation, or a fading away (Furth, 1988). The fifth portrait appeared to be contemplative, as though the artist was gazing into herself in order to create clarity. The color of her dress changes from red and golden yellow to bright blue representing health and energy, and subsequently, becomes a pale blue, representing contemplation (Furth, 1988). In the same portrait, Laura has depicted herself surrounded by an array of royal purple topped by red colouring, which might represent spirituality and/or power. As McNiff (2007) outlined, the image in the mirror is an imaginary self, hinting at the opportunity for wholeness, yet providing the distance needed from the separated self. McNiff (2007) states, "the soul is imagined as locked inside a self that does not realize its potential for expression" (p. 232). When the rhythm of life is disrupted, the individual's self-expression shuts down (McNiff, 2007).

As Santrock (2011) indicates, the particular characteristics of an individual's self are known as his/her identity. The identity is composed of internal mental images, or constructs, that create the individual's self-image (Santrock, 2011). As in this case, the artist seeks to establish personal identity. The differing elements that compose the self-image are what are exposed in the self-portrait. The symbolism expressed through media suggests the scribbling stage of development, in which her scribbling reflects control over parts of her environment (Lowenfeld & Brittain, 1975).

B. L. Moon (1995) suggests that the artist's goal is two-fold. First, the artist seeks to create an artwork that is an expression of the self and an expression of the soul. As Cederboum (2009) suggests, the artist creates and re-creates again and again searching in every artwork for identity, while trying to stave off, fear of loss of identity. Secondly, the artist wishes to acknowledge, experience, and observe their feelings; becoming more self-aware. Laura reflected on these thoughts as she gazed at her serial portraits. She observed,

> The first one is a mandala and I think a lot about what is really going on inside and all of my own personal issues, thinking about what people see on the outside. If I look at the drawing that's exactly how it would be. Like everybody on the outside of the scene are through people not knowing what is going on the inside. And if you are looking at the last one it is somehow liberating. And looking at that one is a little bit funny, because it sort of happens with the hawk. What that was about really, got me out of my safety, to do what I really felt I had to do, and it had such a profound impact on me, and it does feel like the drawing is something very real and very creative then.

The final artwork depicted an increase use of the colour golden yellow on the ground and is also the colour of the hawk, indicating an emphasis on the spiritual or intuitive nature and life-giving energy (Furth, 1988). The use of the light brown to depict her skin within all of the artworks could indicate a struggle with destructive forces to become healthy (Furth, 1988). Laura reflected on her symbolic scribbling use of media, and noted,

> It got me thinking, it got me to work on how to integrate it. It is like being more aware of how I was being in these self-portraits and then being in my work and how to order the mental state together. And I think that doing these portraits somehow freed me from sort of a part of myself.

Reflections of Salina.

My initial impression of the self-portraits by Salina (see Figure 3) was that of concern. The images appeared disfigured and empty. Anger appeared to be reflected in the second image. The third and fourth images, in particular, have a look of distortion that symbolically represented problem areas (Furth, 1988). Salina in her conversation with me expressed she gained self-awareness while reflecting on her images.

Salina described the importance of her hands and how their depiction in her self-portraits was important. She indicated the hands stored energy she did not know how to release. She associated this with feeling she was not exactly where she would like to be in her work, and the sense of not being able to do enough. Salina observed,

> But the hands, I mean they are still a work in progress, the hands, because for me it is a lot of stored energy, because there is so much. I mean I am looking at her and she has so much stored energy but she still needs a scale to really fit. So the hands are still a work in progress, that's like my career. I have got to where I am, I do a lot of teaching, supervision, training people, workshops, but I feel like there is so much more I want to do. I am not quite sure of how to release the energy, you know? Because my vision is that I have to grow the field here because I can't manage the requests for the services of art therapy assessment, I can't manage making referrals for all of them because everybody that I know is so busy.

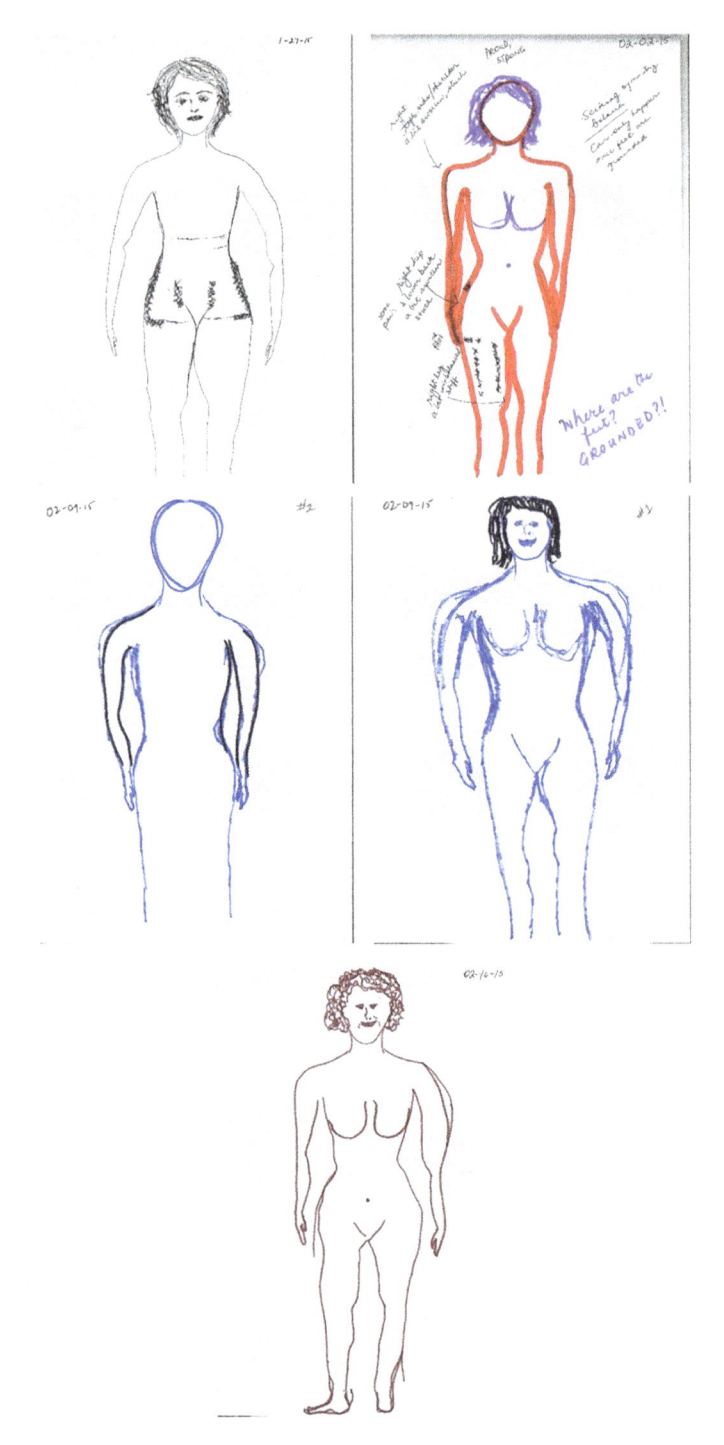

Figure 3. Self-Portraits by Salina

All four images were quite empty, void of being filled in, indicating perhaps a lack of physical energy (Furth, 1988). Salina discussed her surprise concerning how she physically depicted herself compared to how she actually felt. This supports the work of Orbach (2009) concerning the effects of embodiment upon the individual's sense of self, the impact of conflict within the mind and the body, and how both identity and the physical body are shaped and formed with reference to our visual world. The self and self-identification are reflected, in both whom we are on the inside as well as how we look on the outside, and how we are perceived by others. In essence, we are both the subject and object of our lived-experience (Orbach, 2009). Salina noted,

> In my self-reflection I began noticing how I represented myself, visually you know, and I was surprised. I was surprised by the steadiness and the symmetry of the lines of the image. There was a lot of strength. Whereas I am feeling extremely vulnerable also at the same time. It allowed me to see that there is a strength to the way I am standing, my shoulders are very strong, my hips are very strong, the legs are very strong, even though there is pain on the outside, there is a lot of strength.

All but one of the participants acknowledged an increase in bodily awareness by observing, as B. L. Moon (1997) predicts, that during the process they had recognized a need to change some aspect of their lives. The art therapists often described becoming self-aware of their own body-satisfaction, as they explored their images. Backos (1997) found similar results having identified positive growth and change, as she observed physical differences in the portraits and noted expressions of satisfaction in the self-images. She attributed these changes to increases in the artists' satisfaction with their own bodies. Salina discussed the important aspects that she needed to portray in her portrait. She explained that what she needed to commemorate was what was held within the body. She believed that this was important because it is her belief that the body holds memories and emotion, as well as experiences. The goal for her was to commemorate and externalize those aspects of self.

Two years ago I started studying qigong. So if you notice, there's a lot of focus on the actual physical alignment where I am holding tension in all of my drawings. Because that is my work. I'm very involved in body work practice. All of the pictures are naked, so very exposed.

Salina indicated that originally she could not identify with the red image. While reflecting on her self-portraiture experience, Salina described an experience during which she decided to draw a second image of herself in red. She observed that this duality confused her, and noted her ongoing struggle to discover the identity and significance of the second image. She observed,

> I'm definite this one does not make any sense. The one that does not make any sense to me is this one. Who is this? She looks young too. I can't really relate to her. This is very disturbing to me, this one.

In conversation with me, she was able to identify a particular self within the image. Salina indicated that she had drawn negative effects of early deficits from her past. Salina observed,

> This one is very disturbing for me this one. She is probably around the age of my trauma. She is at a very difficult state for me, faceless, gentle she is. She is how she is expected her to be. She is the most symmetrical, she has the best figure, she is standing the straightest. She has the least defined hands, like merging into her body and for me I just realized, it was my traumas around my gender and my sexuality, and it is her hair and her breasts that are purple, and it is separated from her entire self, it is split. I didn't see this one coming. Art is too powerful.

Throughout the process it was evident that the exploration of the self of the images indicated that the artist, as an adaptive mother, manipulated materials to repair the negative effects of early deficits in mirroring attunement. This observation supports Kohut (1984) and Winnicott (1953), whose work addresses the phenomenon of mirroring attunement, or resonance, as opposed to misattunement, or dissonance noted by Wright (2009). As Wright (2009) suggests, "adaptive mothering" occurs when the artist creates their own self-containing forms/images. The images developed by Salina are self-contained. It may be inferred that when a relationship develops between the artist and their artwork, within the safety of a trusting relationship, it can challenge/motivate the artist in the direction of further self-development. This suggests that as the artist develops the self, she can incorporate the changes she experiences into new or modified self-containing images/forms.

Salina discussed her increasing self-awareness when she was reflecting alone on her image compared to answering the question list and conversing about her experiences. Having a witness increased her sense of self-awareness and deepened her understanding of self when viewing and reflecting on her images. As LeClerc (2006) suggests, the image in art therapy is an indicator of, or a witness to, the emergence of unconscious material, contending that the image reveals the presence of something that is partly hidden and/or not fully exposed; it is unexplored and/or unresolved. The data indicate that, despite training, a therapist might be blinded to elements in the client's artwork that the therapist does not want to acknowledge. She observed, "Honestly when it is your own process you can notice things that colour our own lenses, you know even as art therapists we still have limited vision."

Salina, in reflecting on her images, indicated she created additional images because she thought she had made a mistake, only to realize that what was reflected in her artwork was her experience of releasing trauma through her broken body lines. Reflecting on the work of DiLeo (1983), Glaister (1996), Hammer (1967), and Kaufman and Wohl (1992), the portraits suggest low self-esteem, as expressed by small size, lack of colour variation and scarcity of detail, with missing body parts reflecting feelings of inadequacy, and powerlessness and incomplete, broken, or faint lines corresponding to lack of self-confidence. The use of black and white for the first and last image may symbolize the unknown and repressed feelings (Furth, 1988). The second image uses a significant amount of red to outline her body, which might symbolize an issue of vital significance (Furth, 1988). The third and fourth images are outlined in blue perhaps representing the vital flow of energy (Furth, 1988). It is noteworthy that, all images include the predominance of white (Furth, 1988). Also, data indicate that the therapist's counter-transference must be acknowledged and subsequently analyzed, as the art therapy process moves from a two-way relationship to a two-person relationship (Schaverien, 1995). Each self-portrait reflection allowed the participant to acknowledge counter-transference. They then had the opportunity to analyze the counter-transference. Salina also indicated a change that took place during the process which influenced her work. She observed,

> So I had gone for a trauma relief exercise workshop in which we were working on how the body holds trauma. These tremors you stimulate them and then your body involuntarily tremors. It brought up a lot of vulnerability. This is the picture of my vulnerability. Here I am it looks like I am a big hulk of a person and I can't be helped because I am so big. This did disturb me so much I made another one. There's movement, I did notice that, I just thought I messed up.

Salina also created an additional artwork during the third week (see Figure 3), reporting that she had identified a lot of physical tension being held in her body. She reported that she created the additional artwork because, "I thought I messed up." Upon reflection, however, she realized that the repeated outlines of her first figure depicted her physical sense of being. When reflecting on her first two self-portraits and her bodily experience at the time, she felt the need to keep changing. She had an intense feeling that she needed to go over her outline to have a sense of movement in her portraits.

Salina described her experience of how the images changed over time, particularly in regard to the missing elements of her body. For example, the first self-portrait made her aware of great vulnerability. Describing the image Salina said, "[it] doesn't feel strong, but hulky, and she can't be cared for, and so this did disturb me so much I had to make another one." This experience alerted Salina's to her the physical and emotional experience of vulnerable feelings. She affirmed, within her last self-portrait, that she was able to attain a grounded image on the page with all of the body elements intact. She said,

> You start with stance, you start with feet. So there would just never be any space for feet. And then the last one when I had to make feet, and it fits. I would want to make feet every time but it just wouldn't fit. The grounding was missing. It was a lot of focus up here, but the feet were missing, the grounding was missing. The last one is the brown one with the feet. Really, really, well grounded.

Salina described an enhanced awareness, as she explored her different ages and stages of life in past and present selves. She reflected that at the time she was creating her self-portraits she had no idea, even during the written reflection, that she had created different developmental images of herself. It is important to note Freud's (2010) contention that the greater part of what constitutes the self, and the manner in which its components function, are either preconscious or subconscious. Freud believed that preconscious and subconscious information are not consciously available to the individual in the present moment but have the potential to be called into consciousness. Perceptions and ideas which cannot become conscious and are therefore, not available to introspection, are termed unconscious in Freudian theory. The images reflect the pseudo-naturalistic stage in which the self is looked at negatively, and developing self-awareness is expressed through a self-conscious approach to the environment. The drawings reflect an increased awareness of her physical development. The choice of colour in this stage is affected by past experiences and the expression of intense feelings resulting from increased self-awareness (Lowenfeld & Brittain, 1975). Salina discussed the difference that she found developmentally in each of her artworks. She noted,

> There's a growing up, it was an age thing. This is the eldest for sure. It's almost like, teen, no not teen. That first one is when I was twelve. The first one is kind of flat-chested, there's no chest. Sixteen, fifteen, these must be my bad temper days. Twenty, getting out of my bad temper days, thirty, forty.

Reflections of participants.

Participants also commented that the experience of participating in the research project had: re-ignited their creative and imaginative flame; re-instilled the effectiveness of art therapy; reminded them about the importance of media; and made them realize how much their art-making had diminished over time. Two participants reported that they discarded their first artworks because their initial experience of producing an image caused them great discomfort. Two participants commented that they used a mirror to begin the process in order to calm their anxiety about creating the first image.

All participants noted that they initially experienced difficulty with not being able to change or erase lines due to the use of markers; however, all participants noted that they became increasingly comfortable with the process. With the increasing comfort over the period of time each participant used the media to reflect what they felt.

Describing her lived-experience of the self-portraiture process, Bessie noted her realization that her artwork had diminished over time. She stated,

> I see an inner emptiness [in my self-portraits] and that has made me realize that I need to get back to the work which is art therapy and incorporate that . . . I miss doing the art therapy.

Nike reported that journaling allowed her to experience her self-portraiture process and made her aware of an active need to respond to what she identified in each self-portrait. After her first self-portrait was created, Nike reported in her journal,

> I had completed the drawing and really saw and felt the need to allow any negative energies to fall away. I actually did the grounding cord meditation after this image and felt lighter, more clear-headed, more grounded. The image confirmed my feelings and provided an idea as to solving them through the use of the meditation.

Bruce L. Moon (1995) observes that self-understanding is attained through work with the image which enables the individual to reclaim his/her imagination. Participants repeatedly noted that their increased self-awareness enabled them to re-ignite their imaginative creative sparks and also recounted experiencing sorrow at having lost their engagement with art over time. Allen (1995) describes art as a way of knowing that provides spiritual fulfillment; suggesting that the created image paradoxically depicts what is and what could be. Bessie reflected, "I think the art is what helped me not to worry about time as much as it freed me up and connected me to my free spiritedness."

Participants reported feeling that they knew themselves more comprehensively as they became more self-aware. For example, the data suggest that using media associated with youth (i.e., markers) puts the artist in touch with the past, present and future themes and stories. Describing this experience, Laura stated,

> I think that the fact that I used the markers, because when you are a child you use markers, but there is something kind of free with that as well. Maybe that is what allowed me to just scribble away. What that was about really got me out of my safety to do what I really felt I had to do, and it had such a profound impact on me.

Nike explained her experience of creating art and doing reflective writing. She said,

> For me, writing certainly takes more time. Artwork brings things into concrete format. [Art] takes your emotions and your feelings and puts it down on to the page, but when you translate it into the written word it not only brings emotions out on the page, and once you name the feelings it makes them even more true. I feel like it makes it concrete in a certain way, when you draw it you go "ah ha" there's that emotion; there's the feeling that I am trying to tell you.

Self-awareness through emotional, spiritual and bodily-awareness.

The following thematic exploration describes the association of the lived-experience and the theme of emotional, spiritual and bodily awareness, with emphasis on the self-portraits by and reflections of Sade. Explored through the images of the participants is how the process of the weekly creation and reflection on the self-portrait facilitates the individual's self-awareness regarding their current functioning and sense of well-being through emotional, spiritual and bodily awareness. The self-portraits and reflections by Sade follow with some of my observations and highlights from participants.

Reflections of Sade.

Sade indicated her self-portraits depicted how her body internally felt at the end of each work week (see Figure 4). Initially, I experienced confusion in response to viewing these artworks. They were so different from any other self-portraits. I did not know what to think or how to respond to the portraits until I spoke with Sade.

Sade reflected that she followed a process that worked for her spiritually, as she reflected on her body image, and what was happening over the four weeks. Sade said,

> I wanted to experience the process of adding psychological symptoms in a drawing, so I chose to do an outline of a body image. I just wanted to do an outline of a body image without adding any other parts especially around the face. The reason behind that is we believe GOD is the creator of all things and we are just part of His creations. So, being a Muslim I had to think, how am I going to do this project that would be spiritually ok and at the same time allow it to have a productive process? So, creating an outline of a body image provided me with many options to design emotions and to structure where I could add them from personal experience.

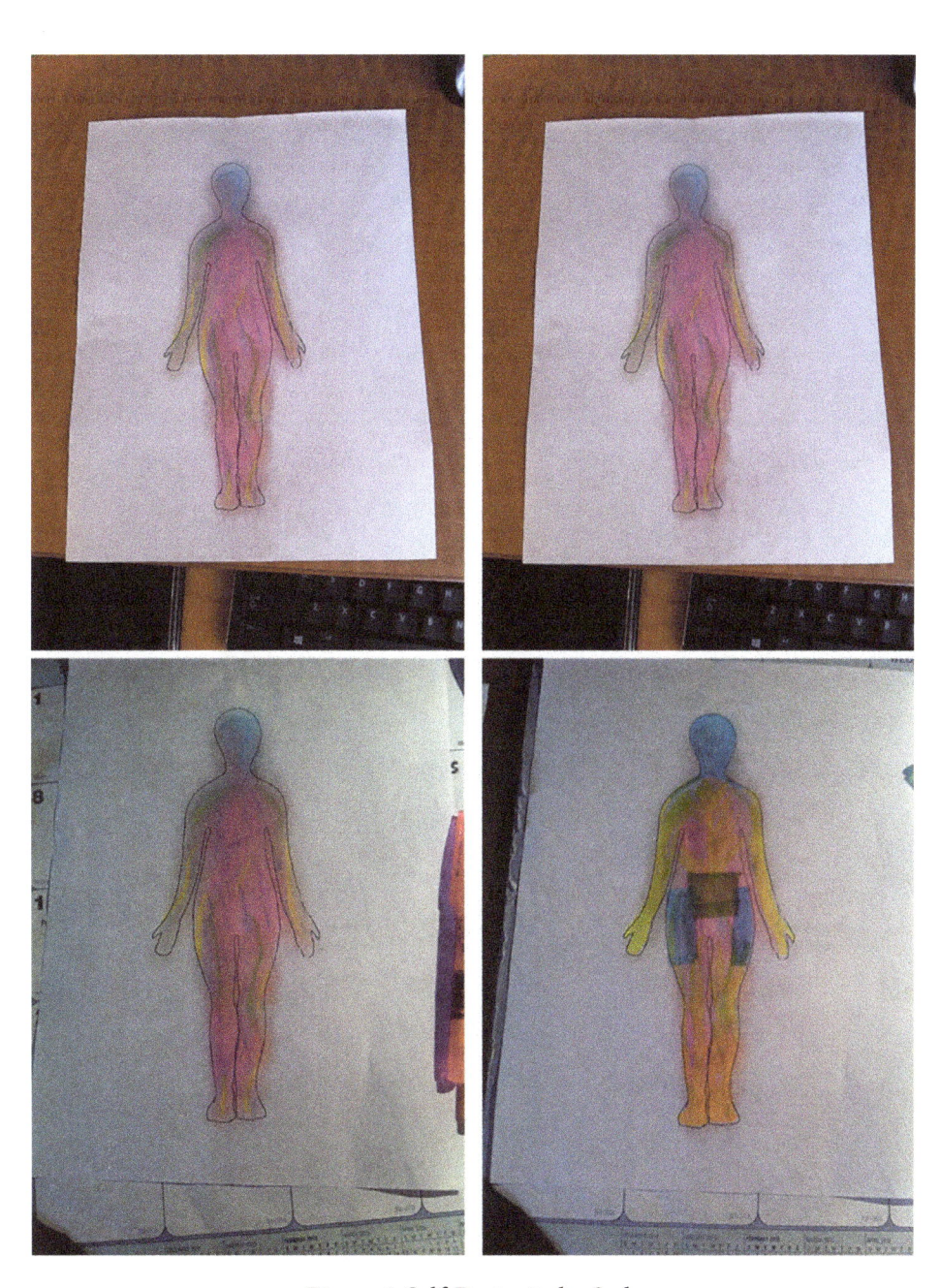

Figure 4. Self-Portraits by Sade

Orbach (2009) observes that Freud was captivated by the relationship between mind and body, examining physical symptoms for which there is no medical explanation and drawing links between mind and body experience, stating, "From there he drew links between what individuals had experienced, their construction and memory of what had happened and how they made sense of that experience in the light of their unconscious longings and conflicts" (p. 9). The data indicate the linking of mind and body experience in the construction of memory, as the images created reflected experience of unconscious longings and conflicts back to the artist.

Sade went on to explain her use of colour, saying,

> I decided to use colours that I believe reflected the energy that my body was producing. For example blue to show relaxed areas and pink to show tense areas etc. I also chose to show some of my organs by creating them in different shapes. For example the heart organ was in a heart shape and the kidneys in a rectangle shape. This process allowed me to be mindful of my organs and their purposes.

Riley (1994) acknowledges the work of Duncan, Parks and Rush (1990), who suggest that individuals are able to describe their lives in a cohesive fashion because they construct meanings which shape and organize their experiences and perceptions into patterns. Sade described how the colours she used for energy on her body image made her realize that her body was alerting her that she had become out of balance. Sade observed,

> Few "Ah ha" moments came up especially around body parts that I unconsciously coloured to represent tense areas like the shoulders, neck and jaw areas. I looked at the image and noticed that my body was telling me something indirectly. So, I thought to myself, "my goodness, when was the last time I had a body massage or did any activities that relaxed me?" As I was going back in time in my mind, I also noticed that in all four drawings I had indicated similar tense areas in all the four pictures. I questioned if this was what I presented, as myself, to the world as being very stable on the outside but internally

I can felt tense and anxious by the end of the day. So, I decided to partake those pictures as my client's work. What suggestions would I make or what questions can I explore?

According to Furth (1988), colour indicates psychological or physical factors, and the out of place colours may indicate getting in touch with spiritual aspects as well as letting go of suffering. Repeated images may indicate an importance of past, present, and future (Furth, 1988). For Sade, this is the period of decision which represents the need to master a portion of her life, be self-critical, introspective and idealistic (Lowenfeld &Brittain, 1975). This developmental stage is an expression of feelings and emotions that I characterized by a growing concern about her relationship with the environment, and feeling responsible for what she is doing (Lowenfeld & Brittain, 1975).

Sade indicated learning from the process itself. She reflected that, in regards to her emotional, spiritual and bodily awareness and her professional self,

> Another thing I learned from this project is it is important to assess oneself daily from head to toe by running your hands over head down to your feet. If you find any pain or tension one can massage or stretch it out then just ignoring till it gets worse or one can do it through art as I did. I think I will use this similar tool with my clients instead of using a questionnaire one.

Participants reported that journal writing helped to concretize their experiences and enhance their ability to make connections and explore the emotions depicted in their self-portraits. They noted that this resulted in further awareness of self. Sade noted that as she progressed through the weeks of creating self-portraits, she began to focus on identifiable personal changes occurring as a result of reflective practice and observed that the background colours in her portraits were becoming lighter (see Figure 4). The colour choices of each of the images were similar until the fourth image. The first three images included pale blue shading of the head, a touch of golden yellow throughout the body with pink shading. According to Furth (1988), the use of pale blue could indicate contemplation, distance or fading, while the use of the golden yellow could indicate life-giving energy and an emphasis on spiritual or intuitive nature. The use of pink could represent an indication of health, a resolution of a problem or an illness that has just passed. She said,

> So now I was focussing a lot on my anxiety. [By the third image] for me I was talking about the anxiety I had. When I completed the fourth drawing I noticed there was a pattern emerging from all of them. I realized I was tracking my anxiety.

Sade noted, "Creating an outline of a body image provided me with many options to add psychological symptoms in a drawing, design emotions and to structure where I could add them from personal experience." Freud (2010) theorized that the unconscious manifests itself in dreams, slips of the tongue, and/or symptoms and observes that a symbol represents, illustrates or embodies some aspect of whatever it symbolizes. LeClerc (2006) suggests that, in a similar fashion, the image in art therapy is an indicator of, or a witness to, the emergence of unconscious material, contending that the image reveals the presence of something that is partly hidden and/or not fully exposed; it is unexplored and/or unresolved. The final portrait included bright blue shading of the head and hips which could indicate health and energy (Furth, 1988), and included an increase in the use of golden yellow and pink throughout the body. Sade also included a pale green in her mid-section to reflect an unexplainable pain that had developed. According to Furth (1988), pale green could indicate weakness, a fading out or a coming back into life.

Reflections of participants.

All the therapists expressed emotional, spiritual and/or bodily awareness within their portraits and in reflective conversation with me. Some observations with highlights from those conversations follow.

All of the participants described feeling overwhelmed when reflecting on their respective four artworks. They observed that, when viewing their weekly self-portraits and especially when reflecting on their series of four images, these experiences unearthed unconscious to conscious knowing. They explained that, with increased emotional, spiritual and bodily awareness, they were able to recognize the necessity to make changes regarding constraints in their personal or work-related lives. Participants found that including the full-body, in their self-portraits, further augmented their experiences of unearthing identity issues and revealing their inner states, particularly with regard to their need for self-care. Sally discussed experiencing increased self-awareness about: feelings as she engaged with her self-symbols within the artworks; and how the self-reflective process allowed her to work through her bodily experiences. She said,

> So much is happening in your body and that is really true of the experience of pregnancy too. All of the energy is being sucked away from my brain. That's what it feels like. That is what came out in the images.

Penny also experienced and increased self-awareness of her self-concept as she reflected on her body positioning on the page. She stated, "I fill the page-I like myself. I am kind, I feel confident about my personality. The feet point out and forward, to me this reflects hope and solidity. I am firmly planted on the ground -I know who I am."

Regardless of the manner in which participants began the intervention process, they all noted that they found the inclusion of the whole body to be of great importance, remarking that this led to increased sense of self, as whole individuals. They added that including the entire body in their self-portraits enabled them to express a fuller picture of their lived-experience.

Participants described the experience of seeing their mirrored images reflecting their experiences back to them, noting that this was a source of important personal information that they were not conscious of at the time. They also reported being able to identify how they were truly feeling at the time depicted in the image. For example, Mary observed, "I have a feeling in the second and fourth image I was feeling a lot less well, that I was having a bad week. That it is not surprising that my body looks less open."

Schaverien (1995) describes how the created image deepens the viewer's connection and self-awareness with the self through the gaze, and emphasizes the importance of the witness. The data suggest that participants' comments during their reflection indicate that even drawing an outline without facial features to depict the self, allow the operation of various gazes.

Four participants identified themselves as either having a religious affiliation or indicated they are spiritual in nature. Reflecting on her identity, Tracey stated,

> In my journal I expressed how I have a strong spiritual life and how it grounds me, in not only my personal life but in my work life as well, and that it focuses in God and trusting the process, taking care of myself when it is that I feel overwhelmed.

Participants often discussed an increased sense of self with regard to physical experiences. They attributed their increased awareness to depictions of their bodies and described a variety of experiences. Karen noted as she reflected on her first portrait, "I look at, for instance, in the first portrait there is a sense of sadness in that one for sure." Bessie reported becoming able to externalize her anxiety, as well as to identify and track the anxiety she was experiencing from within.

Her willingness to engage in the work of self-exploration enables her to experience who she truly is, from the inside out (Nouwen, 1979). This supports the work of Nouwen (1979), as Bessie also began to identify personal issues and concerns which might otherwise not be recognized. By exposing previously hidden issues and releasing the emotions associated with them, the artist experiences an increased sense of self and is able to heal (B. L. Moon, 1995; Nunez, 2009).

All but one of the participants acknowledged an increase in bodily awareness by observing, as Moon (1997) predicts, that during the process they had recognized a need to change some aspect of their lives. The art therapists often described becoming self-aware of their own body-satisfaction, as they explored their images. Backos (1997) found similar results having identified positive growth and change, as she observed physical differences in the portraits and noted expressions of satisfaction in the self-images. She attributed these changes to increases in the artists' satisfaction with their own bodies. Salina discussed the important aspects that she needed to portray in her portrait. She explained that what she needed to commemorate was what was held within the body. She believed that this was important because it is her belief that the body holds memories and emotion, as well as experiences.

Participants discussed their experiences when asked to include their entire bodies in their self-portraits. All of the participants commented that they had not previously drawn full-body self-portraits. They described experiencing nervousness and anxiety when engaging in the first self-portraiture because of this directive but reflected by the end of the process they were much more relaxed and able to do so.

The data indicate that greater understanding of internal emotional, spiritual and physical experiences can: foster increased self-awareness; help the individual to identify the need to modify specific behaviors; develop skills; improve his/her reality orientation; reduce anxiety; and/or increase self-esteem (American Art Therapy Association, 2013). As well, the data show that the process encourages true self growth by identifying the pathological and graphic traits of the false body, so that a range of authentic body feelings can emerge. This encourages a conversation with the critical self, and movement between and among, the body-self, the intellectual-self, the emotional-self and the contextual environment of self (Machover, 1949). Participants also expressed how, when making an image, the self-reflection fosters self-knowing and spiritual fulfillment, as the artist first addresses their relationship with self (Allen, 2001; Cameron, 2007; Jensen, 2004; B. L. Moon, 1997)

Construction of self through word in art.

The following thematic exploration describes the association of the lived-experience and the theme of construction of self through word in art. There is a dynamic element that develops when the self-portrait is joined with words. A dialogue is created between the various appearances of written text on the created images. Six (40 percent) participants used words to either title their images or describe ideas or thoughts on their portrait. The self-portraits and reflections by Tracey and Alice follow.

Reflections of Tracey.

Figure 5 depicts the self-portraits of Tracey. My initial response was that these portraits did not include her entire body. For instance, only the first image contained the whole body, while the remaining three focused on her head. Tracey reported that with the creation of the first portrait she was reminded how much she loves to create art. In the second self-portrait, she reflected that she felt "a little divided", and the third portrait was a reflection of the features of herself that she uses as a therapist. The last self-portrait she decided to reflect different emotions. Tracey indicated that she used this last self-portrait to explore self. She indicated this was a project she often asked of clients. Tracey reported that with the last image she gained a greater connection with her clients. She was able to get in touch with the notion that "I don't give myself enough time, especially as an art therapist to take the time to do art and use the process to do my own self-care."

The first image is her yoga pose. The body is up in the air, transparent, and surrounded by movement. Tracey reported that the first image is about "the stress around me and me in my peaceful pose despite it." Tracey noted that she could identify, within her images, a fragmented self and added that her third self-portrait depicted "what features I use of mine that are most beneficial in the work that I do."

Figure 5. Self-Portraits by Tracey

Tracey could identify her different working selves, as noted by Farrar, Stopa and Turner (2015). She reported a positive self-image and affect indicating she was able to connect with her spiritual side, as that grounds her. In her first self-image, depicting herself in an elevated yoga pose, Tracey surrounded herself with scribbles of dark and light blue. This could indicate being surrounded by health and energy or it could symbolise distance, contemplation, fading away, or withdrawing (Furth (1988). Tracey also outlined herself in red which, according to Furth (1988), might indicate a problem, a surge in emotion, and/or danger or illness. In her second self-portrait, Tracey depicted herself using the colours bright blue, red, orange, and golden yellow. The use of orange could suggest a suspenseful situation or a life and death struggle, in which Tracey is experiencing a decrease in energy and the need for rescue from a threatening situation (Furth, 1988).

Tracey reported that the second portrait depicted the different components of herself she uses in counselling. Within this self-portrait, there are only two colours used; bright blue and pink with most of the rest of the face being white. The bright blue, particularly for the eyes, could indicate health and energy (Furth, 1988), and combined with the use of pink, may indicate a resolution of a problem or recent illness. The majority of the portrait which is white might indicate repressed feelings and completion (Furth, 1988).

The first portrait depicts words around the head in red and the fourth portrait depicts the use of words all over the heads. Although Furth (1988) contends the use of words mean that the artist does not trust the process, Tracey reported that her focus on God allows her to trust and "take care of myself when I am feeling overwhelmed." She labelled the two sides of self as "Happy" and "Anxious." Tracey depicted each emotion using a side view portrait of her head. She labelled each side view using a black marker. For Happy, she chose the colour with bright blue writing. The use of pink might indicate a health and/or the resolution of a problem, and the use of bright blue indicates health and energy (Furth, 1988). The second head labeled Anxious is a dark green with red wording. The choice of dark green could indicate a healthy ego and body growth healing, while the red lettering could indicate a problem, surging emotions and illness (Furth, 1988). This image is different having been created on coloured construction paper; cut and assembled with written text in marker. This points to a multi-layered, multi-dimensional construct that represents intertextuality that creates an interdisciplinary dialogue which is stronger and deeper and expands the range of interpretations (Cederboum, 2009). According to Klugman (1997), the emotions expressed represent the existentialist self, whereas the constructivist self represented in the weekly reflections point to the many different representations of the self. Tracey reported that her last self-portrait shows how she uses her two sides in a positive way.

The data support the work of Cederboum (2009), who states, "Assuming that the printed text represents speech, its appearance or disappearance describes the tension between hiding and exposure, between silence and speech" (p. 136). He describes the use of words on images as a visual metaphor of a "wish to utter words but the inability to do so" (p. 136). In the schematic stage the drawing of a person can change from one day to the next with the drawing being a symbol of the mental image of the object and an indication of the way in which she interprets and comprehends information of experience. Also, emotions are visibly expressed by exaggerations of size of body, important parts and facial expressions with neglect or omission of unimportant or suppressed parts (Lowenfeld & Brittain, 1975).

Tracey determined that she does not use a witness for added reflection on her artwork, stating, "I have not done that since school" and concluded that, "I suppose it is a worthwhile experience to do that. Maybe I might give it a try in my next supervision session." She continued to reflect that the process of focussing on the self was a "good experience and a good reminder that I need to take time out for myself and reflect upon myself and my work and my life."

Reflections of Alice.

Alice also used words within her artwork (see Figure 6). My initial response to this work was it appeared to be a puzzle, or a map, and that the message held within appeared to be complicated. As Cederboum (2009) suggests, text is a kind of speech with substance, it becomes an object as words have power and they need to be integrated with the image. The act of underlining or circling strengthens the speech indicating that this is a visual metaphor that shows that the story of the self is a story "of materials for the artist's own story" turning the text into the artists own words (Cederboum, 2009, p. 137).

Figure 6. Self-Portraits by Alice

Alice reflected on how she uses writing with her clients and how it facilitates their awareness and points they wish to remember. She observed,

> With clients that struggle with language based learning disabilities I have found that allowing them to speak about their art, their understanding of the process, emotions and memories evoked from engaging in their work has provided them with a rich therapeutic experience. Often they will want to remember something they said or have become aware of, so I have taken on the role of note taker recording their thoughts and reflections, in their voice, allowing them to capture the meaning in the moment.

Alice explained her transformation during this process, indicating she began to look at things differently in her life; moving from a negative perspective to seeing the positive. She depicted herself, in her first image, wearing bright blue and green and surrounded herself in the second image with the same colour. According to Furth (1988), bright blue indicates health and energy. In the second image, Alice also included herself wearing a purple top that might indicate a need for control or support a burden, and/or her connection spiritually. She noted,

> The environment can be very negative and at times overwhelming. Decisions are not always made in a time line that supports various deadlines for the program. I found that recording the many activities including the pending feedback allowed me to take a step back from the busyness and appreciate how much was being accomplished even though several questions remained unanswered.

The data concur with the work of Erikson (1997) who, in his description of developmental stages, emphasizes that changes can take place in adulthood and that environment plays a significant role in shaping personality. Further, it highlights the importance of self-reflection for health and well-being.

Alice described her experience of looking at her self-portrait in week three, stating that,

> In week three there were several paths to choose from; however, I felt like I was on the outside of the picture, not quite certain where to step first. In reflection it doesn't feel like a self-portrait, instead where do I want to fit into the picture.

The data show how the self and self-identification are reflected in both who we are on the inside as well as how we look on the outside, and how we are perceived by others. We are both the subject and object of lived-experience (Orbach, 2009). Lum (2002) suggests that self-portrait and weekly journaling are creative ways to externalize the internal processes of therapists seeking to "heal and to prepare themselves to be therapeutically congruent" by resolving problematic personal issues (p. 181). The author describes the therapists' goal of facilitating personal awareness as becoming, "aware of inner process, accepting of what is, knowing one's self, and to be able to reflect upon oneself in order to develop awareness" (p. 182). This was true for Alice. As Alice reflected on her artwork, she added a number of written insights directly on the portraits. She was able to build upon the connections made through journaling and art, as noted by Rogers (Merry, 1997). In her third portrait, Alice used light blue writing which could indicate contemplation and/or a fading away or withdrawing. Alice indicated that, as she plunged further into connecting with her guarded feelings and thoughts, one expressive art form stimulated and nurtured another and ultimately resulted in inner healing. She said,

> Writing down all the details connected to my thoughts and emotions, as well as expectations from self and others have allowed me to make sense of and appreciate all the accomplishments that occur over the course of the week. My head may look like a complicated map; however, journaling has provided a focus and an opportunity to be mindful of the things that I can change.

Alice described that looking back over the four weeks of artwork stimulated the experience of self-reflection. This suggests that conscious and unconscious connections were made by Alice (Shaverien, 1995). Schaverien (1995) notes that the therapist's counter-transference must be acknowledged and subsequently analyzed, as the art therapy process moves from a two-way relationship to a two-person relationship. She suggests that an unconscious thread lures the artist and the therapist into the picture, deepening the therapist's connection to the artist's self. This intensification of the interpersonal relationship leads to the therapeutic interaction. As Alice said, "Being able to reflect on the art and make connections to conscious and unconscious thoughts is a powerful and tangible way to explore the notion of self-care."

Alice examined her self-concept, as she constructed herself and her images from self-exploration to her last image where she identified balance. As Cederboum (2009) described, "The presence of handwriting in a painting is the artist's invitation to look into her own inner and personal world" (p. 141) which points to a process of release and exposure. The underlying theme within the data are that of self-investigation and construction of identity. My experience of the images was that they "feel" like construction. The first image has perspective in which lines that represent walls directs to the self of the image; the second image has structure, with the feeling of "climbing up"; the third image looks through windows to the future; and, the fourth image looks like a stone building structure. All images included a lot of white, especially the first, third, and fourth images, which could indicate repressed feelings and life completion (Furth, 1988).

Alice also reflected that she had made a commitment to participate and chose to do the work on Friday nights. Initially, she had no difficulty with the commitment. However, for the last portrait, she found herself doing the portrait on a Saturday morning drive. Alice was able to identify patterns, as part of her construction of self. In conversation she realized, "So my commitment to doing it compared to the first three weeks was different, interesting." Alice reflected that the fourth portrait "shows the therapeutic engagement inner process that's going to be kind of like my own self-care for an hour."

For Alice, week four was different than the rest of the weeks. Alice depicted herself with dark green eyes which could indicate a healthy ego and/or healthy body growth. She indicated, "exploring the emotions attached to all the busyness in my head," as for the first time she was able to have "any kind of emotional connection to the experience." Alice lamented that the first three weeks were about how she was on the brink of caregiver burnout, "Ya, that's about burn-out". Our conversation allowed her "to realize [the] patterns . . . to actually realize even more patterns. I think it's super insightful." This data suggest that the self-portrait for the therapist can provide the process needed to incorporate new knowledge (Berger & Luckmann, 1966).

As Berger and Luckmann (1966) explain, in order for new realities to augment realities that have already been internalized through primary socialization, the new realities need to be "brought home" (p. 143), in a vivid, relevant, and interesting way that connects them to the knowledge already internalized by primary socialization. The new knowledge must be interesting enough for the individual to move away from the primary internalizations and accept the new "artificial internalizations" (p. 143). When this occurs, the new realities become newly acquired knowledge, augmenting the individual's self-concept. This insight is important in regards to the construction of self, as the individual self-reflects. These connections can be made with an art object, such as a self-portrait. In the schematic stage the drawing of the human symbol is readily recognizable, with clothing, hands, fingers and feet as symbols with a definite order in space relationship with everything placed on a baseline with a developed awareness of how to represent the three-dimensional quality of space usually represented by two dimensions. The baseline is used to indicate motion with subjective space experiences represented as a mixture of plan and elevation (Lowenfeld & Brittain, 1975).

The data indicate, as discussed by de Botton and Armstrong (2014), that artistic communication expresses emotion that may not consciously be known to the individual, and conveys an added dimension of words in art, not just on the pages of the reflective journal (Deaver & McAuliffe, 2009). Words in art can help to make cognitive sense of the writer's created images. Words themselves are symbols, and as Oster and Crone (2004) observe, visual symbols can become a means of self-expression enabling the individual to share personal conflicts and frustration and to talk about previously hidden, painful issues. The data suggest that expression of words represent speech and permit the individual to experience emotional satisfaction, renew and enhance their sense of identity, and allow them to more easily accept self as competent (Cederboum, 2009).

Self-awareness through engagement with the inner-child.

The following thematic exploration describes in greater depth the association of the lived-experience and the theme of self-awareness through engagement with the inner-child. The whole of the self-portrait is treated as one visual text. The story and interpretation is an integral part, of the interpretation, whether evident in the artwork itself or hidden within it. The conversation between the participant and myself considers the deep and rich description of the lived-experience of the participant and the resulting artwork to unearth deeper, hidden meanings. Participants identified that the use of markers allowed them to get in touch with their youthfulness as they reflected that it was at the age of being a teenager that they last used markers. This aspect of engaging with their youthful selves supported them getting in touch with their inner child (Cameron, 2007). As well, it allowed the participants to re-experience the different stages of self-expression as explored by Lowenfeld & Brittain (1975). The self-portraits and reflections of Justin and Sandy follow.

Reflections of Justin.

Figure 7 includes the four self-portraits created by Justin. My initial response to the artwork was that it was mostly achromatic, using pencil, and focused mostly on the face or upper body instead of his full-body. The images appeared to become lighter, with less focus on interiority over time, giving a feeling of moving from dark to light.

Justin identified that at first he was extremely worried about how to begin the process of creating a portrait. As such, he created his first portrait using his computer in order to gain a clear depiction of himself to copy. He also used pencil to add to the self-portrait. As discussed by Furth (1988), shading alludes to the notion that more time and energy has been invested in the creation of the self-portrait which might reflect anxiety. Justin indicated that the first, third and fourth portraits used pencil, while only the second self-portrait was created with the use of markers. The three pencil drawings also concentrated on his upper body, as opposed to a full-bodied self-portrait. Justin described his approach as follows.

I broke a lot of the rules that came in the instructions like not doing a full-body sketch and also, not adding colour to most of them. It's funny because I started with some kind of intention but ran out of room on the page.

Figure 7. Self-Portraits by Justin

Justin later identified that "I'm really in my head a lot of the time, so that's why my head is taking up more space." As Furth (1988) suggests, what is missing might allude to conflict with the missing element. I felt a sense of insecurity or shyness being expressed when I engaged with the first and third portraits. The third and fourth portraits seemed to reflect a sense of turning towards the viewer, a sense of confronting the self. I concur with Allen (1995) who indicates that the image, like a mirror reflects distortions and the incomplete ego-self. The mirror image serves to cultivate access to the self; opening the way to show the subject his whole image, yet presents what is hidden as well.

As the fourth and final self-portrait seemed to look directly at the viewer, the portrait gave the impression that the artist was ready to engage with the self. The data support the work of Dalley, Rifkind, and Terry (1993) and Hammer (1967) who suggest that the creation of a full frontal portrait indicates that an individual is ready to contend with reality; to face truths that may alter their self-image. Also, the transparency of the last two portraits, as they appear to be lightly sketched and not filled in, could indicate that this was a taboo area (Furth, 1988). The taboo area might be the process of looking within self. Alternatively, based on the work of Furth (1988), Glaister (1996), and Hammer (1967), as an individual's self-esteem increases they experience a sense of security, and as a result the self-portraits became firmer, clearer, stronger, centred, and symmetrical. For Justin, the images became more centred, symmetrical and clearer, however, not firmer and stronger, which might allude to self-esteem decreasing not increasing during the progression of self-portraits.

Justin discussed an experience which altered the way he depicted himself, which added a sense of emptiness to the last two images. He said,

> I had gone to a show, where part of the performance on stage the artist creates animation. One of the things she does is she paint's like a child's face that is projected on a big screen, and as the salt turns the overlay over it is an aging process and that was a bit frustrating for me. So I thought that if you add lines you add age. So, I thought maybe I will just stop adding lines here.

He wrote in his journal that he could have added more to these images, however, when he tried to do so he found that he aged himself. He decided not to continue to add lines. As the images were mainly left white, it could indicate repressed feelings and/or representative of life's completion (Furth, 1988).

The data indicate the creation of self is a social enterprise. As Berger and Luckmann (1966) suggest, individuals create themselves, noting that this does not take place in solitude, but is a social enterprise. The existence, within the individual's consciousness, of the generalized other, enables the individual's acknowledged self-identity to attain stability and continuity. The authors state that self-identification occurs when a "symmetrical relationship is established between objective and subjective reality. What is real 'outside' corresponds to what is real 'within'" (p. 133). Interpretation of experience leads to authenticity.

Justin lamented over his aging, and how it is that he used to look at people that were his age, as old, however now, "he actually feels alright". Justin identified that "the third one is the youngest, the last one is pretty much like me now, they are all various ages." Upon reflection, he noted, "they are all younger than me. . . . yup, that's how I feel; younger than I am." He stated, "I've been training to be fit like a teenager, so I don't think when teenagers look at me and think I'm so old." This data support the work of Argyle (2009) who suggests that the individual's sense of self in social encounters affects his self-image, as a result of the feedback he obtains from the reactions of others. Alternatively, the sense of emptiness within the artworks may symbolically allude to a lack of energy (Furth, 1988).

Justin reflected on the difference between his images and the self that he was portraying, with the temperature changes occurring in the environment. He observed,

> I do have a dark side. Where the cartoony sketch was a goofy whimsical week, the first darkest sketch was like minus thirty deep-freeze or something like that. And the third one the deep freeze was over and I was finally getting out and getting physical so it was more of a bare body sketch. The fourth one was balanced out because it just kind of settled from that craziness.

This data suggest that the drawings provide good indications of growth by depicting the individual's gradual progression from an egocentric point of view to an awareness of self as part of a larger environment (Lowenfeld & Brittain, 1975).

Justin also had an experience in his second drawing where his five-year-old accidently coloured his portrait. Justin had been working on an idea of what he was choosing to commemorate, and as such, this image was a preparation sketch. Justin drew himself with a black marker which could symbolize the unknown and/or negative dark thoughts, threat, or fear (Furth, 1988). However, when this happened, and his child coloured on his sketch, he made the choice that this finished self-portrait was what he actually wanted to commemorate.

It was funny to have my five-year-old contribute to the second week by colouring my portrait, I didn't know she had done this and when I came back to my desk she had already coloured it all in. It was just a rough sketch on writing paper. I thought "this is kind of great because part of me is like a kid."

While the self-portrait was not totally produced by the artist, the data affirm the work of Weiser (2008), who studied personal snapshots and family albums, describing the snapshot as a type of self-portrait; "a kind of 'mirror with memory'" (p. 1). She suggests interesting observations regarding the relationship between the insights generated by viewing photos and meaning-making that even when not produced by the client are still "tangible symbolic self-constructs and metaphoric transitional objects, silently offering them inner 'insight' about things that are less consciously-evident or verbally accessible" (p. 2). The data support this conclusion, as Justin highly identified a part of his self with the help of his child. His inner child surfaced (Cameron, 2007).

Justin provided an example of how, as an afterthought, he added an additional title to his last self-portrait. The title opened up a memory and he described how this experience brought back a life theme for him. He thought it was about participating in the project, however upon reflection, he realized otherwise.

As a kind of afterthought I wrote the title "For the good" on the last sketch. I was thinking of the greater good in participating in the research, but then the real subject that I journaled about is one of my life themes has been "to be good". When I was four years old, my sister got leukemia. My family went to a treatment centre and I didn't go. I went to Newfoundland to live with my grandmother, but my task assigned to me was to be good. I guess now as an adult I reflected on that and I realize that I had interpreted being good as my contribution to my sister not dying. If I am good then she will live. It has been an interesting theme about how to be good. So there is a bit of ongoing rebellion against being good. I am also a bit of a perfectionist so I consciously try not to try to be good.

This reflection indicates how the artistic creation could remind and link past self to psychological insight with the current story. The artwork was able to pin down the core significance for Justin. The pinning down of core significance allowed him to foreground the elements that could be hard to hold on to and evoke memories of a past experience (de Botton & Armstrong, 2014). Further, his emphasis on specific body parts may be representative of the preschematic stage. In this stage the emotionally sensitive child will exaggerate things or parts with which he is emotionally involved (Lowenfeld & Brittain, 1975).

Justin explored his own sense of what "good" meant for him with his last portrait titled "For the Good." Jensen (2004), in speaking about the spiritual aspect of the soul, states, "Beauty is not the goal or highest reality; its' source the Good is" (p. 8).

This self-portrait serial alluded to the difference between the true and false selves. As Winnicott (1960) observes, the true self is based on the individual's sense of integrity as a connected, healthy, whole self, while a false self maintains relationships in order to adapt, following social codes and complying with external cues. The serial portraits and reflections indicate that this might also reflect Justin's superego, which as Freud (2010) describes contains the ego-ideal, an imagined vision of the individual's ideal-self-image of how he ought to look and behave when at his best.

This mirror encounter provided the opportunity for Justin to engage, as B. L. Moon (1995) contends with the canvas-mirror which reflects the past, present, and future and also what is hidden, feared, or longed for. The window permitted Justin to look from what is on the outside, to what is on the inside, and create a self-portrait that reflects "a growing sum of who I am" (p. 139); a reflection of who the artist is, was, or wishes to be (B. L. Moon, 1995).

De Botton and Armstrong (2014) describe self-esteem as an individual's subjective emotional evaluation of himself and his worth in the world and observe that by fostering self-compassion, by acknowledging what is good and strong, as well as what is weak in the individual, he is able to self-appreciate and recognize his positive features. Justin was aware that his choices were meaningful and symbolic, and he was able to draw connections between memory and body experience (Feud, 2010; Orbach, 2009). This look within revealed what was hidden, enabling the artist to pay attention to the paradoxes of life. Finally, the data suggest that Justin's self-images shifted and changed, showing his different selves, based upon his self-experience and context (Creswell, 2011).

Reflections of Sandy.

Whereas most of the other self-portraits were drawn by visually-minded persons, Sandy's self-portraits looked haptic (see Figure 8). Lowenfeld and Brittain (1975) explain these two different types of expression in drawings. They observe that a visual-minded person is aware of the particular realities of what is seen, such as the wrinkles in clothing, stating that his/her art focusses on recreating a concrete, objective mirror of the actual world. By contrast, the haptic person is concerned with subjective, bodily experience and uses distortion, lack of depth and flat colour for emotional effect in his/her artwork. The authors contend that the objective of art-making is not the artwork itself, but is rather the goal of developing greater awareness of the self.

Sandy reflected on the use of markers and agreed with other participants that, "I felt like I did really kid like drawings because I felt like that is what I think of felts." She also indicated that the style of her drawings reflected the medium that she was using. Sandy noted,

> It reminded me of how art is a big piece and how it says so much. It made me think about mediums again. That was a huge piece with what the different mediums we use makes the difference with what we create. I felt like I did really kid like drawings because I felt like that is what I think of felts. I felt like that was

something fun I would do. A lot of my teens love felts. I felt like that is the kind of work that teenagers would draw. It reinforced how much I believe in art therapy.

Sandy reflected on the need for space and said,

> Part of creating art is about space. I keep dreaming that I have this amazing art therapy space that I can do art with clients. I have bags of stuff that I want to take art to do with my clients. But when you meet clients in a coffee shop you can't do art and when you take them out to eat you can't do art. But when they come to my office I can do art. It is about safe space. I visit some clients that are homebound. If I am visiting them at their house, then I can do art because they have a space.

Figure 8. Self-Portraits by Sandy

Sandy described her experience of her response to her images, and how, in two of her artworks, she could see herself. She said,

> The first two images look different then the second two because the first two I tried to do freehand. So then for the next one, because I thought that these look like cartoons, I best see what I actually look like.
>
> I think that the first two are a better reflection of me because I can see myself in them. The smile is huge. People always say you are always smiling, smiling lights up my face more than not. It is not a conscious thing. I smile even when I am not happy. I wouldn't know that except what people tell me. I think the smile is huge. That kind of made me notice. The first two do look happy so if I do look like that then I get why people say that I look happy.

Sandy reflected upon her self-portrait and how her image suddenly changed. She felt that she had changed her drawing style because she wanted her image to transform from what she called cartoony to being more human, and yet, when she reflected on her story, she realized that there was more at play. She noted,

> The second two images, I don't think they look like me. I had my birthday just before I drew the third and fourth one that I look way older and I turned 51 and you know how you reflect on aging every time you have a birthday. It is interesting that after I had my birthday the drawings changed. I turned 51 and the drawings changed. I thought that the drawings changed because I was trying to do a more realistic picture. I never noticed that I look way older. It is true, more realistically, I look older.

Sandy indicated that her portraits reflected different ages in her life. She observed,

> The first one looks like a teenager, the second one could be like 20's maybe and the last on like Kiss trying to look young but old, the third one, thirties, forties. The last two look like they are trying to look young, but actually look old.

In the first image the artist is not completely on the page, with half of her legs missing, whereas in the last portrait her image is at the top half of the page with a lot of empty space. Furth (1988) describes the empty space and only partial fulfillment of the space as a lack of energy or illness.

Within the second artwork, there appeared to be a heavy element at the back, which Sandy indicated was her backpack. For me, this appeared to be a distortion. Furth (1988) identifies this as symbolically representing problem areas, perhaps that of a heavy burden. Sandy reported that she had body image issues as she looked at her artwork. She called her third artwork awkward, as she had drawn herself with very short and awkwardly placed arms. In this last portrait, she indicated wanting to focus more on her dog and less on her awkward body positioning. All of Sandy's portraits used the same colour; black for her outline and hair which might symbolize the unknown and/or negative dark thoughts, threat or fear (Furth, 1988). The second portrait includes pale blue which might indicate contemplation. The first and third portraits consist of the same colour choices; black, blue and purple which might indicate health and energy as well as the need for control or support and/or a burden. The mouth changes from just a small line smile to a larger depiction, all using red, which might indicate an identification of a problem and/or an increase in a surge of emotion (Furth, 1988). Her portraits could be indicative of the gang age, as there is a stiffness to the drawings with a free use of exaggeration and distortion for emotional effect (Lowenfeld & Brittain, 1975).

Reflections of participants.

Participants described experiencing that their projective artwork revealed various aspects of their many selves and provided them with meaningful developmental insights. They realized that their inner child is still with them. The journey of self-discovery was confusing at times as multiple selves were exposed (B. L. Moon, 1997).

Participants reported that they were able to resonate and make connections with themselves, their feelings and contexts, affirming the work of Jensen (2004). For example, Bessie explored her feelings and experiences of being younger and "free-spirited". Laura indicated that her last portrait showed a "happier looking face, than it was at the beginning," and she attributed the initial portraits to the environment she "put herself in." She expressed a sense of freedom in her reflection which she termed "the wild of the image." She indicated that the image was not that of a woman "it's not graceful, it's not like a woman's body, it's just a girl." She reflected,

> If anything, it is the self-reflecting perception that I have always had of myself. That I've been older inside than what I really am, that I have experienced all that.

The data indicate that projective drawings can illuminate aspects of the mature self and reveal developmental deficits and significant insights regarding the manner in which the artist represents their multiple selves (Baumeister & Bushman, 2010; Cresswell, 2011; Glaister, 1996; Hanes, 2007; Otero-Pailos, 2010; Rogers, 1959; Smith, 2008; Winnicott, 1965).

Self-awareness through transformation.

This thematic exploration describes the association of the lived-experience with self-awareness through transformation. The self-portrait is an image, like a mirror, which reflects distortions and the incomplete ego-self, and cultivates access to the self enabling self-awareness (Allen, 1995). The process of self-portraiture can promote the insight, or conscious knowing, that is a prelude to change and transformation. Permitting beliefs to change allows transformation to take place. This section begins with the works of art composed by Penny, as part of the story and inner meaning of the visual text. The self-portraits and reflections of Mary follow with added insights from participants.

Reflections of Penny.

Penny drew four self-portraits (see Figure 9), identifying a growing sense of self, as she went through the four-week process. Penny examined her transformation with me, as her images changed over time reflecting a dynamic evolution of selves. Her transformation became a mirror that showed something of her inner world.

My first impression of the artworks was that the artist appeared to be confronting and analyzing self, with each figure situated in the centre of the page. There seemed to be a movement from security to insecurity and back to security again.

The first portrait did not appear to be grounded. This indicated, based on the literature, a lack of grounding or having secure footing (Furth, 1988). In the second portrait, Penny reflected "a sense of working on being." The closed eyes indicated that this might be a form of withdrawing into self. As expressed by Winnicott (1965), the child develops a sense of false self, necessitating their development of a façade, hiding their internal emptiness behind a pretended real self on the outside. Oster and Crone (2004) observe that, when drawing is added to therapy sessions, the expression of visual symbols can become a means of self-expression enabling the individual to share personal conflicts and frustration and to talk about previously hidden, painful issues. The third portrait reflected a transparency as seeing through an internal barrier and perhaps, as she identified, trying to come to terms with change in regards to a relationship. Penny expressed that the first three portraits were created at a time when she was increasingly in relational distress and coming to terms with emotional conflict.

Figure 9. Self-Portraits by Penny

The second and third artworks appeared to me, as an inclining movement towards the top of the page, perhaps indicating a growing sense of self. As Furth (1988) describes, this movement within the art indicates a trajectory. He also suggests that the filling up of the page may indicate vitality in the interactions with life, as each of Penny's self-portraits seem to be not only centred but increasingly take up more space on the page representing an increased focus on self-development. As described by Lowenfeld & Brittain (1975), the pseudo-naturalistic stage represents developing self-awareness through a self-conscious approach to the environment, and in coming to terms with one's identity which is difficult when drawing the self.

The third portrait expresses extremely tired and frazzled looking eyes. This image used a lot of black and white which might symbolize the unknown and/or negative dark thoughts, threat or fear, as well as repressed feelings and life's completion (Furth, 1988). The eyes and the body show what lies within a person and reflects this revelation back to the person. This suggests the artwork is reflected back to the artist as windows to her soul (B. L. Moon, 1995).

Penny reflected upon her growing sense of self. She identified how within each portrait she was able to express her differing selves, and how she experienced a sense of authenticity when she reflected upon her last image. Penny noted that she gained a sense of accomplishment when looking at her portraits. She could see within them a progression over time, from past to present, and how this afforded her insight into her future sense of self. Penny noted,

> At this stage of my life, I have decided to go back to school. I am learning, like my kids are learning now, how to be independent and find my way in the world – to be in community and to support myself. I haven't done this before. All my adult life I was supported, I was married, so this is new. At the same time as I am discovering what it is like to be an art therapist, I am also trying to learn how to be more independent.

As discussed in the literature, the data suggest that the internal mental images depict who the individual is in the current moment, and also contain images of their past and future selves (Glaister, 1996; Hanes, 2007; Smith,

2008). These selves intertwine and coalesce into a belief system about self that make up each individual's self-concept – providing the answer to the question, "Who am I?" (Berger & Luckman, 1966). Penny observed,

> My self-concept is that I am fairly competent but I struggle a lot in this particular phase of life and what is going on. I can keep going I can keep trying hard. I think I am self-actualizing at this stage of life. At the same time as discovering what it was like to be an art therapist I am also trying to learn how to be more independent.

The data suggest the act of self-portraiture reflects one's ability to face self (Lowenfeld & Brittain, 1975). As Lowenfeld and Brittain (1975) indicate, this activity may reveal developmental delays, noting that identifying such delays can greatly facilitate therapeutic changes in self-concept. Penny indicated that her hands, including what they were doing, were an important theme within the artwork. Her hands had various meanings for her. For example, Penny felt that her hands reflected her "ability to be independent and functional" and feeling "helpless with a lot of things that were happening." She also identified using her hands and arms to "keep my balance," and that she feels that "I am not yet fully competent or fully functional." Perhaps the tiptoe dance in her third portrait indicates a feeling of being off balance.

The process of self-reflection and interpretation of the self-portraits provided a means for Penny to experience movement from the problem dominated self to a new way of seeing self. She began to express her self-concept in terms of being an agent of the self (Klugman, 1997). There was also growth in the experience of self as an existential self (Klugman, 1997). The initial portrait was depicted using purple and white, which may indicate a burden, or the need for control or support, repressed feelings, and/or life's completion (Furth, 1988). Within the second portrait, Penny depicted herself sitting on a sea of pale blue which might indicate contemplation while wearing both dark green and brown could indicate a healthy ego, and healthy body growth, nourishment, and/or being in touch with nature (Furth, 1988). Penny noted that her first two self-portraits were "very emotional and sad and reflective," while in the last artwork, she felt "so much happier." She observed,

> The middle two pictures are kind of solemn. It is like a sandwich. The first and the last a little more optimistic. Somehow when I was feeling intensely lonely and unhappy I showed it in the middle two pictures, the second and the third pictures. So maybe the first one was a bit of a warmup. Then I felt more comfortable to show more in the last two pictures.

As Kohut (1971) suggests a time of fragmentation develops into the stage of the cohesive self, in which the individual's increased physical and mental self-experience is cohesive in space and has continuity over time, or authenticity (McNiff, 2007; B. L. Moon, 1997; Winnicott, 1965). For instance, the middle portraits may reflect a fragmented place for Penny, which she termed a place of "confusion and insecurity". In the last image, she was able to move back to a place of being cohesive, in which she stated, "everything felt better." The last image is very similar to the first image, with Penny being in the same pose, although admittedly by Penny, perhaps the difference between the two might be that she became more comfortable with the process.

As Penny looked at the second image she identified that she was able to dialogue with the image as separate from herself, and that the image "evoked emotion" in herself and "evokes a feeling of compassion for myself". The last image Penny represented herself as being larger, more forward on the page and presenting the self as clearly grounded (Furth, 1988). The inclusion of orange in this image might indicate a suspenseful situation, a life or death struggle, decreasing energy, and/or a rescue from a threatening situation. Furth (1988), Glaister (1996) and Hammer (1967) indicate that as an individual's self-esteem increases so does a sense of security, and as such their self-portraits become firmer, clearer, stronger, centred, and symmetrical.

Reflections of Mary.

As I glanced over the self-portraits provided by Mary (see Figure 10), the use of colour seemed out of place. For the first image, Mary used purple to depict her hair, pink to outline her body, and black to depict a heavy black skirt and shoes. The purple could indicate a spiritual or regal in nature, or depict a need to have other's support, and/or depict a burden. The pink could indicate an illness or resolution of a problem and/or to show a healthy look, while the black could symbolize the unknown and/or negative dark thoughts, threat, or fear (Furth, 1988). Dark green was used to depict the hair and shirt in the second image and was used again in the last image to depict the skin. According to Furth, 1988, dark green depicts healthy ego as well as healthy body growth; however Mary used the colour to depict illness. The feeling of the art was that of illness, especially the last image. Mary described that "some aspects of her drawings looked kind of masculine to me, and I don't think of myself as looking masculine at all really." Mary reported that her self-concept within the images to her "looked quite stable, solid and upright."

Mary explained that her images were incongruent with how she saw herself. She reflected how she had to become comfortable with her depiction of self. She described this as a transformative experience. She said,

> So I didn't try to change anything, and I didn't feel overly frustrated that the images didn't really look like me. If I didn't like the size of the arm I drew, I didn't bother to change anything once it was done, even if I didn't think that is what I wanted the arm to look like, for example. I just left it the way it was. I felt okay with what came out, even if it wasn't a literal image of me.

Mary indicated the third image depicts herself feeling really good on a trip to Cuba. She drew her arms as brown indicating the feeling of warmth from the sun on the beach and how this experience transformed her pain.

Mary described that, in the second and fourth self-portrait, she was "feeling a lot less well," as she suffers from chronic pain. On reflection she reported that "her body looks less open." She reported she could see a "sense of openness and function, like a level of functioning even when I'm not feeling well. [Further,] even when feeling a lot of pain, I have a shred of hope that is very difficult not to feel." For example in the third portrait, Mary was vacationing in Cuba and the colour reflects her feeling warm with a lot less pain. In her fourth portrait, Mary reported that coloured herself yellow because she was not feeling well. She subsequently changed the colour to green which left a yellow halo around her. She stated that "it's possible it is a subconscious message of hope, you know?"

Figure 10. Self-Portraits by Mary

Reflections of participants.

Eleven participants described similar experiences of transformation. For example, Bessie was able to transform herself from a place of being confused and anxious to being at peace with retirement. Participants clearly identified their differing selves during the reflective interview suggesting a post-modern focus on awareness of their differing selves. Tracey identified that she witnessed within her work a sense of a fragmented self as well as her differing selves. Specifically, she said her second self-portrait reflected that she, "felt a little divided and fragmented with different roles" (see Figure 5). Participants noted and findings showed that this sense of fragmentation could be identified in their artworks, as they connected with the sense of self over the four week period, highlighting the important implication of work disturbances. The findings showed that seeing the self clearly enabled working through and thereby integrating experience (Erikson, 1980; Kohut, 1971), which led to transformation.

Findings supported the work of B. L. Moon (1997) who underscored the significance of authenticity and multiple selves, as the participants recounted experiencing themselves in new ways. Laura (see Figure 2) noted that at first she was surprised by how her depicted herself, and that she needed to allow her depiction of self to speak for itself. She stated, "Actually I think that the story that emerged for me was, there is something in the self-portrait of myself that is about being really very authentic." It is relevant to note that eight participants indicated they believed that this process revealed their authenticity.

Participants described the experience of gazing at their portraits and the portraits gazing back at them, and their experience of me gazing at their portraits. For instance, Laura stated, "I think the picture that was looking at you, it's almost like saying look at me; this is who I am. I had to get more comfortable with it." As B. L. Moon (1995) contends, the self-portrait reflects the artist's self-concept and identity. He adds, whatever inhabits the individual's soul comes out in their drawing, noting that, by expressing emotions, the artist brings order from chaos, and exposes an image of their inner life. The responses of participants in this project revealed that during the reflective self-portraiture process they felt increasingly self-aware, and that this experience enabled them to identify and engage with a personal sense of authenticity. This supports B. L. Moon's comment that, "Authentic life demands contemplation" (p. 58). Participants' reports also validate B. L. Moon's suggestion that, as an individual's self-awareness increases, they become better able to connect with their inner and outer contexts, feelings and thoughts.

The data suggest that, as Cardinal (2014) contends, an individual can have both a cohesive and a fragile sense of self made up of many elements. Participants recounted experiences confirming this observation when describing the manner in which they identified their differing true and false selves (Machover, 1949; Tuber, 2008; Winnicott, 1958). Salina reflected on her surprise when she recognized a previous fragile self, eliciting a sense of true and false self within the image (see Figure 3). Nike had this to say about her self-concept, as she reflected on her four portraits.

I think I am fairly intact. I think I am fairly self-aware. I am quite solid as who I am as a person within my values, and my sense and my ideas and beliefs myself are quite strong and healthy and good.

Mary's images appear to reflect the schematic stage as the drawing symbolizes the mental image of the object with everything placed on a baseline (Lowenfeld & Brittain, 1975). The main symbols are exaggerated in size with emotions visibly expressed given the relationship between colour and object (Lowenfeld and Brittain, 1975). This is most evident in the first and third portraits exaggerated arms and body. The data indicate that self-portrait and reflection enable the therapists to release sublimated sorrow, and through this release, recognize that transformation can occur, leading to self-transcendence (Jensen, 2004; Kenworthy, 1995; LeClerk, 2006; B. L. Moon, 1995, 1997; Smith, 2008).

Self-awareness of professional self-identity.

This theme describes the association of the lived-experience with professional self-identity. The self-portraits and reflections of Sally and Bessie are presented followed by reflections from a number of participants.

Reflections of Sally.

My initial experience was that each image had a distinct feeling of pregnancy and personal discomfort. The first image seemed to outline the feeling of centrality of blood flow where all of the energy seemed to be directed. The red and orange in the centre of the body could depict a problem, a surge in emotions, illness, a suspenseful situation, a life or death struggle, and/or decreasing energy (Furth, 1988). Later, in conversation, Sally revealed that this reflected her pregnancy. The pale blue surrounding the figure could represent contemplation and/or fading away, while the purple area could represent spirituality or represent a burden or need to have other's support. The use of black could symbolize the unknown and/or negative dark thoughts, threat or fear (Furth, 1988). All images seemed to obscure her head which felt disturbing for me. Sally, in reflecting on her four images (see Figure 11), indicated that each image reflected her experience of pregnancy, and the way she saw herself at work. She indicated that her head was not really in a good place, and that was a concern given her work with clients.

The first image seemed more abstract in nature, and as Furth (1988) indicates, either something is hard to understand or there is avoidance. Sally created this image with pastels which allowed her to do some shading. The head of the figure appeared to be distorted which may indicate a problem area (Furth, 1988). Sally said,

> I have had some insomnia and stuff and so my head is not really in a great space. That is where I was at. Even so it did help me to look at some of that and reflect on some of that and see how I can fit that in with the stuff I had to do and kind of work through it.

Sally added that she was trying to "grapple with the struggle of trying to fight" with how she was feeling.

In the second portrait, Sally identified a duality, as she could see upon reflection that she had created an image that was bi-directional, an optical illusion that has more than one meaning. These images within one image depict the duality she felt within her self-image. One direction looks pregnant, while the other not. As indicated by Allen (2001), by exploring life's dualities it promoted the emergence of spiritual wisdom.

Sally also identified that she used paint, as she had just had her hair cut and found it depressing. She said, in the pregnant side depicted, it "looked so depressing, like a frumpy pregnant woman hunched over." As indicated by Furth (1988), colour can represent emotion. For example, the first image was very colourful in direct contrast to the black and white of the second image. According to Furth (1988), the use of black and white could symbolize the unknown or repressed feelings in the second and fourth portrait.

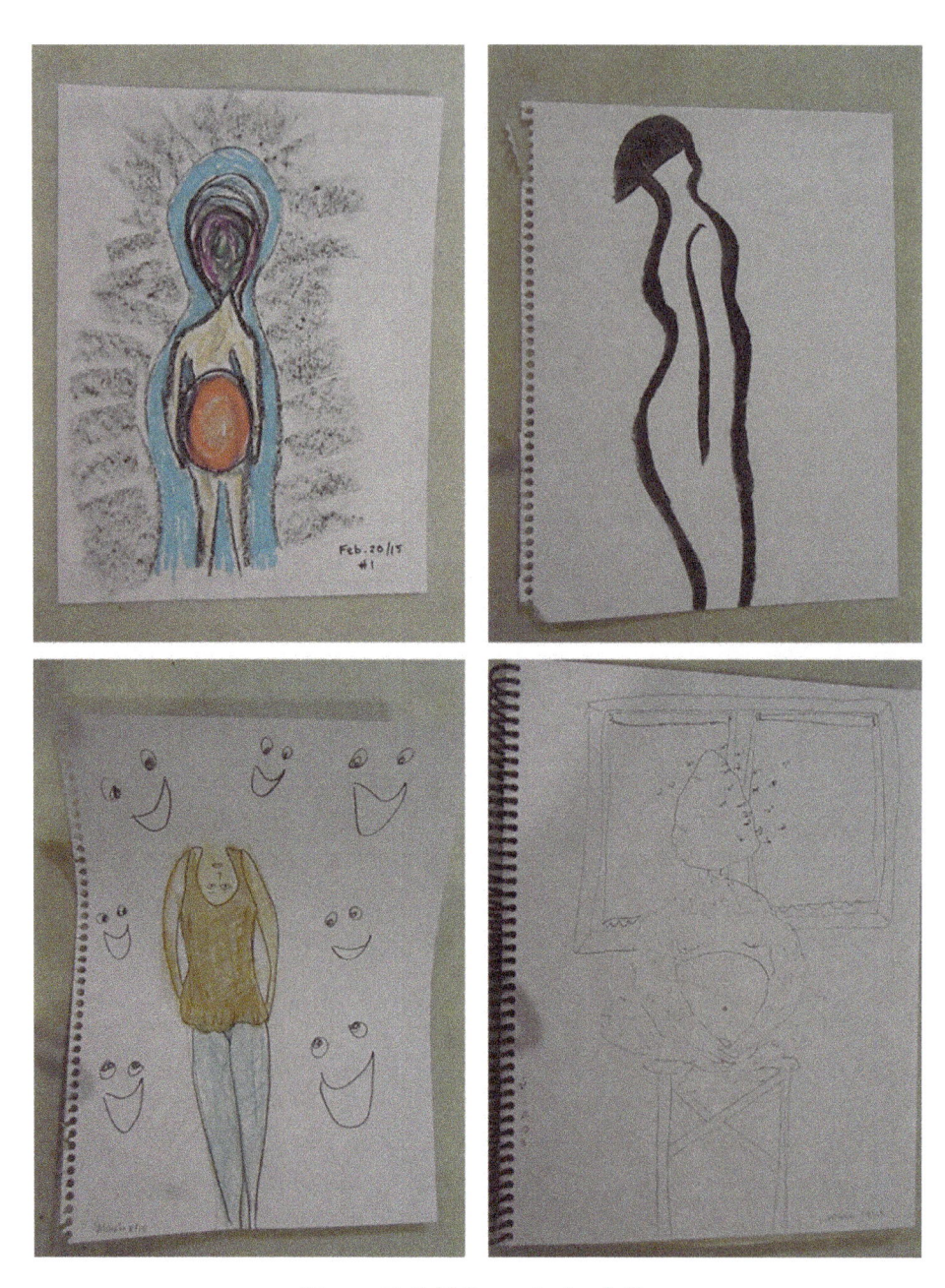

Figure 11. Self-Portraits by Sally

In the third image, the self of the artist is coloured in with markers indicating the central focus of the image is the self. The pale blue could symbolize contemplation and/or withdrawing, while the golden yellow could be an emphasis on the spiritual or intuitive nature and/or life-giving energy (Furth, 1988). The laughing faces that surround her image are out of proportion which may indicate they have power over the central figure (Furth, 1988). Sally observed,

> The third one is a common scenario that was sparked from a recent conversation. How I use my own defences in a way that don't always serve me, or how I try to protect myself that I think don't serve me well in the end. That day that I was really joking about it I had this sudden urge to cry, and I thought oh my goodness, what is that about?

This data concur with the definition by Gross and Stone (1964) of identity, as "the substantive dimension of the self" (p. 357), adding that identity describes the placement, or situation, in which others place an individual as a social object in social relationships. The individual is established as an identity in social terms within a social context. The authors note that each individual maintains symbols related to their identity, such as "the shaping of the hair, painting of the face, clothing, cards of identity" (p. 358), and roles and activities. All identity-related symbols, roles and activities afford others the opportunity to validate or invalidate the individual's perceived identity. In the pseudo-naturalistic stage, self-awareness develops, as expressed through a self-conscious approach to the environment and can be experienced using satirical drawings at this stage. This is the age of reasoning where an individual works on coming to terms with one's identity, looking at the self negatively, in derogative terms with emotional relationships expressed directly or symbolically with an increased awareness of one's own physical development (Lowenfeld & Brittain, 1975), expressed through both the work of Sally and Bessie.

Sally discussed her response to her final drawing in terms of feeling hopeful after reviewing the previous three, and how depressing and serious she found the previous images. Sally indicated artwork evoked a sense of professional imbalance with potential burn-out. She observed,

> I feel like the last one I did was really a lot more playful so it kind of reminds me, lighten up be playful in the moment, those kind of things, and don't be so serious. I think that the last one is playful but it does kind of feel like there is a little bit more hope, hope is not the right word, but I little bit more openness and possibilities and still recognizing that not all is pretty, and it is still kind of dark and it is still kind of tough but the space is still there.

For the fourth image, Sally used pencil. She said,

> I was thinking of what it would sound like to have a bee hive over your head; that it would literally drown everything else out, and be a bit irritating. And also like the posture of this gorilla, and sitting up crossed legged, seems really calming and the buzzing bees. It is like playing with those two sides, and it is hard to find the balance of moving between those.

Sally, in reflecting back over her work experience and this process said,

> In the moment you can't see a connection [to my professional self] but when you step back and look at the whole in that chunk of time there is something happening. That is why that is so lovely to be able to do that with clients. That process is another type of process in and of itself.

Reflections of Bessie.

The first two portraits by Bessie (see Figure 12) appeared disturbing; perhaps even painful. As Leonard (1994) points out, when something happens to the body, the individual develops insight. Bessie described her experience as follows.

The first one was actually quite disturbing. The burn out. I can't let it be seen because I can't let the team down. I can't believe I actually volunteered because my usual statement is that I don't have time, I am tired. But I did.

Bessie also described how she was experiencing herself, as she reflected upon her images.

I've been exhausted over the last couple of years. The never ending fatigue, burnout, my paperwork is atrocious, I can do the job but all of the energy goes there. I can do the work with my clients but there is no energy left to do much else after.

This data suggest that Bessie engaged with her agent self through her experience of her engagement with her self-portrait. As Kohut (1971) indicates, the cohesive self-experience incorporates all the different parts of self, resulting in the individual's increased awareness of personal well-being. In turn this manifests the agent self, which enables self-control for personal and professional healthy choices and living (Baumeister & Bushman, 2010). When cohesiveness is not achieved, dis-integration or loss of the central-self can occur.

Figure 12. Self-Portraits by Bessie.

The data suggest that the development of self begins with the individual's internal self-experiences and includes what is external to self. The first self-portrait depicted either tear drops or sperm with the use of red and black which could symbolize a problem, surging emotions, danger and/or illness or infection (Furth, 1988). Bessie noted,

> You know the first one actually looks like a womb in a way. I just noticed that. I am much younger in the portraits. I have been known to be free-spirited and I have lost that, or I had. I am slowly coming back. I am actually doing more, more that is important to me since I started this process.

Bessie believed the second portrait was a coincidence, as she had just worked with a client who was disfigured and thus drew herself with a large gash on her head. Within this portrait as well, the colours purple and black were dominant. While the gash on her head appears to be dark brown which would indicate nourishment (Furth, 1988), her story of the artwork suggests a better fit with the symbol of light brown which represents a struggle to overcome destructive forces, to become healthy. According to Schaverien (1995), the therapist's counter-transference must be acknowledged and subsequently analyzed, and suggests that an unconscious thread lures the artist and the therapist into the picture, deepening the therapist's connection to the artist's self. This intensification of the interpersonal relationship leads to the therapeutic interaction (Shaverien, 1995).

Bessie also described her sorrow of being overwhelmed and not being able to keep up with her workload. She observed,

> I have been through this before and I think that's the story. It's that I have put so much into my career and have throughout my life, and I keep on doing it and what I found in the story is that I stopped being me again. What I realize since I did those images, I had to make some decisions especially about my job.

This suggests that as Bessie accumulates sorrow, compassion fatigue could result (Lum 2002). As de Botton and Armstrong (2014) and Ulman (2001) indicate, each individual carries baggage comprising her personal history, relationships, life experience and work responsibilities that leave her off-balance, creating negative feelings of sorrow that within the self-portrait are sublimated into a transformative experience. This suggests that it is important for Bessie to recognize that she was off balance, as it can impact the therapeutic relationship with clients (de Botton & Armstrong, 2014).

The third portrait looked whimsical and the fourth artwork appeared quite peaceful. Within this portrait Bessie outlined herself with a pale yellow green which symbolizes weakness and/or a fading out or coming back into life (Furth, 1988). Bessie observed,

> I realize since I did those images that I had to make some decisions especially about my job. I have made a retirement date now. I have been avoiding. The experience of doing my self-portrait in January lessened my anxiety and gave me clarity. I can see more depth in the last one, I can see far, more hopeful.

The data indicate that self-interpretation is key to gaining insight in regards to illness. Leonard (1994) describes this phenomenon as follows, "one approaches illness as a rupture in the patient's ability to negotiate the world" (p. 53). She suggests that a practice to encourage self-interpretation, one that brings experiences that might otherwise be taken for granted into consciousness, enables the self to gain insight about the context of these experiences. As Bessie reflected on the experience of the portraiture process, she found the images offered her insights about her future needs.

Discussing her research findings, Brown (2008) asserts that it is imperative for art therapists to nurture their own creativity during professional practice, noting that failure to do so can lead to caregiver burnout. For Bessie, the self-portrait enabled her to surface her feelings in order to make changes.

I have done what I perceive as what other people wanted me to do. When I look at them [self-portraits], I also see strength. I see a lot of heaviness and some strength, and what I see with the sideways head [self-portrait] had some brightness because I had some clarity and I don't listen to myself.

Where the second artwork is heavy and weighted down, the third artwork appears to have a new growth popping from her ear, as she holds a chicken. Bessie remarked that she did not know why she had drawn herself holding a chicken, although she had just ordered chicken from a local farmer. Nunez (2009) asserts that self-portraiture is a powerful tool, capable of uniting both inner and outer images to discover the real self. The self-portrait unearths what might otherwise remain hidden, providing the artist with a significant opportunity to: know and accept self; perceive what the self is missing; what it might need; and what hidden desires should be expressed. Addressing these overlooked issues fosters an increase in self-awareness and promoting greater insight, meaning, congruence and self-acceptance (Nunez, 2009).

Bessie reported that this image of her holding a chicken with a new growth coming out of her ear made her laugh. She continued to express a new way of viewing what she disregarded. The prominent dark green leaf could symbolize a healthy ego and healthy body growth (Furth, 1988). She reported that, in her last image, she can see more of a future. In the last self-portrait, Bessie represented herself as a landscape and used a lighter colour palate. The colours used; pale blue, dark green, golden yellow and brown, could symbolize contemplation, healthy ego, an emphasis on the spiritual, life-giving energy and nourishment, and/or being in touch with nature (Furth, 1988). The colour choices seem to mirror the healing and transformation experience described by Bessie when she viewed her final artwork. The data concur with the work of Burns (2009) who claims, in terms of ego function, that drawing a tree can be understood to reflect the subject's individual process of transformation compared to the drawing of the person which reflects on the subject's self. Bessie observed,

> The last one I saw more open, and actually looking at this now I thought it was more of a beach scene, but now I am thinking it is more the mountains in the background where I live. I live in the mountains.

For Bessie, the self-portrait and reflection process enabled her to participate in inner healing and transformation. As McNiff (2007) observes, "As an artist committed to healing, I cannot begin to be of use to others until I am attentive to the transformations of the healing and creative process within myself" (p. 52). Bessie, in reflecting on her artwork, indicated the need to confront the fact that her current work was unfulfilling. She recalled experiences from her youth that were currently missing in her life. She observed,

> I realize since I did those images that I had to make some decisions especially about my job. I have made a retirement date now. I have been avoiding. The experience of doing my self-portrait in January lessened my anxiety and gave me clarity. I can see more depth in the last one; I can see far, more hopeful.

I think the art is what helped me not worry about time as much as it freed me up and connected me to my free spiritedness. The person that was growing up on one hand was free spirited and I did a lot of wondering at a very young age and very creative in a lot of ways. I was a very free spirited child that became more constrained as we all do as we grow up.

Her reflections concur with the work of de Botton and Armstrong (2014), who describe self-esteem as an individual's subjective emotional evaluation of self and their worth in the world. The authors contend that by fostering self-compassion and acknowledging what is good and strong and weak within the individual, they are able to self-appreciate and recognize their positive features. Further, Dewdney and Nicholas (2011) contend that adults develop qualities of the self from the time of being children and bring this child into the formation of their adult self.

The data support Van Katwyk's (2003) contention that becoming one's true self is the process of balancing care for the self and the surrounding world. The data support his observation that moving to self-integration involves processes of continuous growth and change, within which self-creation occurs. Bessie described her transformation when making the decision to retirement. Bessie noted,

> I am starting to let go not of my opinions but of my place, it isn't my place too anymore, for the future. It's like handing the torch over in a way. I have been thinking it is time for somebody younger to do my job. When I was new in the field I wished some of these people would retire. And now who is that person. What goes around comes around and it doesn't bother me. It is part of the way it needs to be. I made a decision. I have a retirement date now.

Bessie experienced the constructivist sense of self and existentialist sense of authenticity, moving from anxiety to self-awareness (Klugman, 1997). She was able to experience new insights and self-acceptance. When Bessie reflected on her future and how this process could be integrated, she said,

> It solidified the need for doing it myself in my own life to continue doing self-portraits. It also solidified that I need to continue using it with clients I am working with and groups or whomever, and it is something that I will continue to recommend because I have seen the benefit of doing self-portraits. I think it is so important for me personally, and I think it is important for all people that are willing to try it. It is an amazing insightful tool. It is so intimidating for people that don't understand it but it is so amazing.

Reflections of participants.

Participants noted their surprise when issues of self-care emerged on their journal pages. For example when Sally reflected on her images depicting how she portrayed herself at work (see Figure 11), she noted with surprise, how her own defenses at work do not always serve her and how her self-reflection allowed her to connect with how she can be off balance. Nike reflected on how off balanced she felt at work with an image that was black and white and quite empty. Furth (1988) indicates that black may symbolize the unknown. The emptiness on the page may also symbolize the artist having a lack of energy (Furth, 1988). Nike indicated she started to pay attention to her professional self and the build-up of negative feelings within her through this process. She said,

> The last day I don't know how it happened. I usually space people with similar disorders and the last day I had four people who were severely depressed in a row. I had one after the other just being more and more depressed in that space. By the end of the day in that picture, by the end of the day I said 'Holy Hanna" let's get rid of all that stuff.

In journaling and during interviews, participants reported that a variety of demands (e.g., travel for work, illness of self or family members, workplace conflict) overwhelm their daily schedule, preventing them from completing self-care routines and/or engaging in their own art-making. By decreasing engagement with art, the practicing art therapist can suffer from clinification and a lack of self-awareness (Brown, 2008; Gilroy, 2004). Alternatively, B. L. Moon (1997) contends that creative activity and the resulting artwork leads participants to experience heightened self-awareness. This was true for the therapists, as their reports reflected a focus on their own stories, aspirations and conflicting needs.

Nike noted that the process of reflection made her aware of an essential theme in her life and facilitated a "concretizing" of this perception, especially in regards to how she worked with clients. Nike reflected on the experience of exploring her artwork and sharing in the conversation. She observed,

> It is happening in the conversation that although the artwork brought out the emotion it wasn't necessarily in my consciousness until you spoke it. When I wrote the things it is like different levels of concrete setting, the artwork brings it out into the world, and then the writing sets it. It is almost like the two things bring a validation to the artwork. Normally when we have a conversation in the therapeutic space about the artwork the therapist and client verbalization about the artwork is what finalizes and validates that concrete setting, but when we are doing it a self-reflective setting it is necessary to bring it to the same place. I have learned from your ideas and reflections of the artwork because you are seeing different things in there then I am seeing or acknowledging. For personal growth even in a peer situation where you are reflecting with another therapist can be an extremely helpful tool.

This report reflects B. L. Moon's (1995) suggestion that the artist gives form to their essential story through their work, adding that this enables the artist to engage in a dramatic enactment of the essential theme in their life.

Participants noted the beneficial effects of reflection, describing it as a critical strategy to help them cope. There was simplicity to the intervention process, including the media directed for use and the manner in which each participant used it. While the use of markers limited shading, the lines drawn with markers became expressions. Karen reflected that in her professional experience she stays within her comfort zone. She indicated that this reflective experience moved her beyond her comfort zone.

Participants also reported experiencing awareness that they were more alert to their effects on clients and/or to clients' effects on them, adding that they were able to identify these effects within their artwork. Nike reported that she was able to "step into the shoes of her client's experience," when at first she felt uncertain about how to create her first portrait. Karen noted,

> I was able to put myself in the shoes of my art therapy clients who may be uncomfortable with what's in front of them, and uncomfortable with the process and uncomfortable with the materials, a perspective that I would not get otherwise. It was good to be in those shoes.

They also indicated their need for maintaining boundaries. Sade said, "I needed to start looking at [my inner self] in order to make sure I am present in the room for people and also to be present to myself as therapist and to maintain that balance of wellness."

Participants also reported that using the projective drawing task, as a weekly reflection tool, did not prevent them from accomplishing other tasks. They indicated that the directed projective drawing led to increased self-awareness of their professional identities and provided them with opportunities to experience insight in regards to their assessments with clients. Sade stated, "Another thing I learned from this project is it is important to assess oneself daily. I think I will use this similar tool, the self-portrait, with my clients instead of using a questionnaire one."

Participants also discussed having experienced increased self-awareness with reference to experiences with others and their contextual environments. They added that this self-awareness helped them acknowledge feelings of exhaustion and recognize their expectations of self. Participants reported that increased self-awareness motivated them to change, and make more effort to efficiently organize, prioritize, and manage their schedules. It also made them recognize that creating art was an essential aspect of self, and they needed to include it within their regular schedule.

While reflecting on the artistic self-reflection process, participants reported that, as a result of increased self-awareness concerning their professional self, they were able to more clearly address and define meaning in their lives, and to reflect on their personal and professional circumstances and relationships. They added that this also brought to the fore what their inner and outer selves were currently experiencing and where and what they wanted for the future. In the same vein, participants observed that the opportunity to reflect on the four images made them consciously aware of the difficulties they were currently experiencing and revealed insights regarding the changes they must make to become the individuals they longed to be. The increased focus on themselves enabled the therapists to engage in self-relevant, meaning-making and self-understanding in their respective lived-experiences.

Self-awareness through self-care.

Art therapists and other health care practitioners work within or with complex health systems, and must navigate the tensions between maintaining well-being with the demands of their practice. The challenge is protecting the time and means to care for the self. By doing so, the practitioners maintain their grounding to: be their own advocate; maintain a sense of agency; and assure effectiveness for self and other (Rogers, 1959, pp. 208-209). The following theme explores the experiences of Karen and Megan, as they reflected on self-care and its integration within their practices. Additional insights are offered by Sade.

Reflections of Karen.

My initial response to Karen's self-portraits (see Figure 13) was that they were very well drawn and looked really pretty; like a drawing of a modern doll. I learned in conversation that Karen was indeed a professional artist and had formal training in drawing. She had worked as an illustrator for many years. As an illustrator, Karen had a specific style that she did not want to use in her art therapy practice. She also specifically chose to set aside her artistic ability for this project, as she considered this project to be part of her art therapy practice. Karen describes,

> But when I do an art therapy piece I try very hard to set aside the skill and the technique just to be here in truth. It is difficult not to be worrying about what it looks like. I feel like that is good because I put aside the artist part of me.

The self-images reflect two components of self: the ego, as self-image, personal identity; and the unconscious, which have been exposed. As Freud (2010) indicates, the ego is the part of the psyche that mediates between the id and the demands of the individual's environment. The imagination, as explored by H.W. Janson, (1986), is the connector of the conscious and subconscious which holds together personality, intellect and spirituality.

Karen described her drawing style and reflected on the exaggerations indicating, "My head is awfully big. I make attempts not to read too much because I know that traditionally it is just a way of drawing but I also can't discount the undertones." This could suggest that simplification and exaggeration define caricature, and when the essence of what matters is revealed, valuable insights that might have been lost or overlooked in ordinary experience can emerge (de Botton & Armstrong, 2014). The drawing of an anatomical feature that is larger than what it actually is draws attention to that feature as important or significant and can symbolically represent emotion (Furth, 1988). The eyes are also exaggerated because the head is so big. They give the appearance of being able to see in both directions at the same time.

Figure 13. Self-Portraits by Karen

176

Karen reflected on what she saw as she looked at her artworks and noted,

> I look at for instance in the first portrait there is a sense of sadness in that one for sure that I can see right off the bat and just a look of insecurity that I noted in that one more than any other ones and I was truly feeling that way that week. Just feeling a little over my head with things and grieving from the anniversary of a loss and kind of feeling a little out of sorts and it shows. I really felt like it is a reflection of my self-care right now too, because it is kind of in the toilet. I just am not doing the self-care I normally would.

The data concur with the work of Freud (2010) concerning transference, as an element of unconscious behavior in which an individual redirects emotions from a past experience to another person. The drawing of the large head highlighted for Karen her feelings of being tired which she could link to her lack of self-care when she reflected on her serial portraits. Karen transferred her emotions from the past experience to the image on her portrait. These self-portraits reflect the schematic stage of development, in which the self-portrait is readily recognizable and includes clothing, hands, fingers and feet with the important symbols being exaggerated in size (Lowenfeld & Brittain, 1975). In this stage, everything depicted within an artwork is anchored by being placed on a baseline to indicate the place on which things stand (Lowenfeld & Brittain, 1975).

Karen discussed the constraints imposed by the process, and insights about the limitations she places on herself. She observed,

> As much as the constraints of time and the materials and having to draw my entire self were a little frustrating at the time, they were really good learning for me. I learned that it is ok for me to go outside my comfort zone, as I would not normally put those constraints on myself while doing that. I think that was a good thing to step outside of what is comfortable.

I feel like I got more loose, as I went along. I did not put in the same effort. I think I did not put the same amount of thought in it as I went along.

It is interesting to note that Karen started with her depiction of herself in her first image using black which could symbolize the unknown and/or dark thoughts, threat or fear, and in her last portrait used mostly white which could symbolize repressed feelings and life's completion. The centre two portraits had more colour, with the second portrait depicting a red section of her top which could indicate a problem or surge in emotion, while the third portrait had the most colour using dark blue which could indicate health and energy (Furth, 1988).

Karen, while journaling about her portraits, identified an increase in self-awareness. For example, she said,

> No fingers again. Now that I am thinking about it, is it a "hands-tied" indication? I do sometimes feel that my hands are a bit tied. I know that I work too much, but I know that I will not always have this schedule. [I realize] a lot that I am missing... relaxation, self-care that has always been a part of my life is starting to slip, and that's not a good feeling.

When she reflected on what she gained from the process, Karen said,

> It gave me the time to do that bit of self-reflection and gave me more balance and a few less things on my own mind going into session. It gave me a bit of renewal as an art therapist to do my own process, a bit of self-awareness, a little more self-awareness about where I really am at. The artwork can allow you to see something that you may not have been recognizing and help you understand where you're at.

Reflections of Megan.

My impression of Megan's self-portraits (see Figure 14) was varied. The first and second portraits felt like spiritual images, although the facial features of the second image felt strained rather than peaceful. The third portrait appeared to be an image of a tree and felt sexual, while the last portrait seemed to convey the peaceful pose that the second portrait lacked. Megan recounted her experience of wanting to go deeper and needing to stay on the surface to maintain a sense of control over what she shared with me, as she did not know me. Megan observed,

> I would have liked the whole hour doing the portrait. I found that I didn't go as deep as I would have if I had more time. However I was very nervous and worried starting because I didn't want to expose myself too much. I was afraid of getting deeper so the process allowed me to stay more on the surface and that provided some security for me. So, really the process was good as it was. I would say art is about the soul and essence whereas writing is about documenting and detailing.

As she reflected on her fourth image, Megan explained that she needed to come to terms with herself and the need to care for herself. Megan noted,

> I had to come to terms with my self-care and boundaries [in regards to my employer's expectations and workload] especially, and I think that is what the story is. The agency I work for increased my work load, I saw 26 face-to-face clients weekly, with a caseload of over 50 clients. I could not keep up with the pace, and I don't think that we can do good work being so overwhelmed like that. The last one says to me that I need to incorporate boundaries, and I need to work differently. Boundaries with administration, to advocate more for myself that I cannot see that many clients, and do advocacy, reports, session notes, meetings etc. . . . The stress was becoming overwhelming in addition to my personal family crisis. I had to actually remove myself from work; go on stress leave.

Megan reported that the first image was before she found out that anything was wrong within the family, and that she was just back from vacation. The first image reflected a large rendition of herself, which on reflection, meant she had gained weight and needed to lose it. She depicted herself as a sort of mother-nature, donned in a fish necklace of symbolic peace, wisdom and spiritual growth. The first image incorporates a green headband with a purple background, in which the green could symbolize a healthy ego and healthy body growth with the purple symbolizing spirituality and/or a burden (Furth, 1988). There is also a use of light brown to outline the body which could symbolize a struggle to overcome destructive forces to become healthy (Furth, 1988). Megan reported that "at this portrait, I feel at peace and wise." Megan titled this portrait "Repose".

In the second image, Megan said she "added the chakras with the red and sitting on red stress." She indicated that she is "much like a volcano, sitting on a magma and trying to keep cool . . . feeling powerless." Essentially, the second image reflects maintaining a sense of calm and continuing with all her normal activities, despite her husband being diagnosed as ill. The pale yellow green used in this portrait could indicate, according to Furth (1988), weakness, fading out, or coming back into life. The purple and yellow background could symbolize spirituality, a burden, and/or a need for support (Furth, 1988). Megan titled this portrait, "Frustration".

Figure 14. Self-Portraits by Megan

In the third image, she stated that "you can see I am trying to remain in my relaxed place, but you can also see that my branches are drooping." Megan titled this portrait "Giving" indicating, in her journal, that all she feels that she is doing is giving. She also recorded these words on the trunk of the tree.

The fourth artwork reflects her decision to go on stress leave. The black and white of this image could symbolize the unknown, negative dark thoughts, threat or fear, repressed feelings and life's completion (Furth, 1988). Megan indicated that "the fourth one says to me that I have to take time for me, that I have to give to myself as well." Megan titled this picture "Holding On" which depicts her sitting on a "colorless beach, praying, naked and vulnerable." She reported that symbolically she is sitting at a side view in order to shut others out, both with work and timeframes. In the schematic stage, emotions are visibly expressed through exaggerations of body size and facial expressions, and the subjective space experiences are a mixture of plan and elevation. Toward the end of this stage, the drawings are increasingly influenced by visual perceptions of the environment with the need to identify, feel responsible for, and have some control over one's actions (Lowenfeld & Brittain, 1975).

Megan also added that her self-portraits speak of her strength; "That I am centred and I am a very giving person. . . . I will survive but I have to take care of myself and I have to pay attention to my self-care and boundaries."

Reflections of participants.

The majority of art therapists described realizing that they had neglected self-care. Eleven of the therapists indicated the demands of their practice were overwhelming, and prevented them from having sufficient time to devote to their own art-making or self-reflection. They felt off-balance with regard to their work and home lives. All participants added that they had not previously engaged in self-reflection, and noted that this had proven to be "an extremely useful experience". A few therapists observed that through awareness they surfaced some difficult emotions and/or what was missing or needed in their lives. Participants reported that, by engaging in self-reflective practice, they became aware that taking time for the self was essential. Sade noted,

> Doing this art project has increased my awareness about being mindful about one's health care [as an art therapist practitioner] and one should practice what they preach. I like journaling my art experiences and expressing it non-verbally.

I enjoy the art process because it allowed me to drift away from present stress or to get away from distractive mind. But best of all I can problem solve situations better or even see things from better angles.

Their observations support de Botton and Armstrong (2014) and B. L. Moon (1997) who emphasize the importance of artistic self-reflection.

Self-awareness of hope and appreciation.

According to Palacios et al. (2015), the relationship between self-concept and satisfaction with life is reflected in the ways one sees self, physically, academically, professionally, socially and privately. The authors contend that satisfaction with life is an indicator of personal adjustment. They indicate that the way the individual sees self, impacts their self-image, self-concept and sense of identity (p. 56). The whole self is able to: connect with soul and spirit; be inspired in artistic connection with the inner-child; and maintain a sense of hope and self-appreciation (p. 53).

Reflections of Nike.

This theme explores the awareness of hope and appreciation through the self-portraits and reflections of Nike, followed by insights from Alice, Penny, Bessie, and Salina.

The self-portraits by Nike (see Figure 15) gave me a sense of hope. There was a sense of getting in touch with important aspects of the therapist's self and appreciating those aspects while moving towards hope. All of her images evoked a motherly self within me. Her images (i.e., sitting by the fire, being grounded, and surrounded by images that seemed to depict a womb) indicated a distinct feeling of feminine growth, self-expression and joy, and seemed to lead to her mimicking a tree. The tree looks dormant, without leaves, yet her arms seemed to be representing growth, which indicated a sense of renewal and hope.

Nike recounted that, in her first image, she imagined herself grounded by drawing a grounding cord. She said that "the feeling of heaviness and weight in her counselling room was tangible at the end of the day, and so she drew herself as being anchored to the core of the earth; the centre of the earth." Nike indicated that she does not like clinical settings, and so her counselling room has a fireplace, pillows and comfy chairs. The dark green of the chair could symbolize healthy ego (Furth, 1988), while the second image depicts spiritual colours of purple and golden yellow, bright blue indicating health, as well as orange which could symbolize a life and death struggle (Furth, 1988).

She reported that her second image was drawn after receiving a phone call from her mother informing her that she was dying. Nike recounted that this portrait stimulated a memory of her grandmother dying, and the reversal of roles she experienced. She said,

> The one with me holding the child, I remember doing the piece when I was actually at Concordia, my grandmother had passed away and she had been quite significant in my life and we were working with clay during that process. The adult figure started out as her and the child in the art was me, and then it ended up being that she was the child and I was the adult figure. Like the roles had been reversed. I was both the child and the mother in that piece and my mother is both the child and the mother; because in some ways when we are having our conversations, when she is talking about dying, I end up in the nurturing mother role with her.

Figure 15. Self-Portraits by Nike

With the impending death of her mother, Nike indicated how, through this process, she was able to find hope. She said,

> So I think that through the process one of the gifts of doing this, the pay back for doing this is the recognition that this is devastating, but I will live through it, and I will be ok on the other side. Regardless of how hard it is now, I think that the images showed me that it will be ok. I will be ok. I don't think that I would be where I am in the process of sharing my mother's news, if I didn't have the processing of the portraits. I don't think I would quite as far on the road of acceptance as I am now.

The third image Nike described as "letting light into her heart; opening up to breathe and release." She said, she "let light and joy and wonder into her heart." The use of the golden yellow could represent life-giving energy and an emphasis on the spiritual, while the black sky could symbolize the unknown (Furth, 1988). It is interesting that the final image is both black and white which could symbolize the unknown, negative dark thoughts threat or fear, repressed feelings, and/or life's completion (Furth, 1988). Nike subsequently confirmed that the third image was about her professional self and the build-up of and the need to release negative feelings. The final image is her depiction of the release; revealing the self-expression of joy, growth, renewal and hope. The self-portraits seem similar to the developmental stage of the period of decision. In this stage, there is a need to: master a portion of one's life; feel responsible for what one is doing, express feelings and emotions with a growing concern about relationship with environment, in a period where there is very little opportunity for self-identification (Lowenfeld & Brittain, 1975).

Reflections of participants.

All of the participants indicated a sense of accomplishment with participating in and completing the process. They also felt that they gained insight as a result. For example, Alice said, "I feel great about this experience." Penny noted, "I am learning, like my kids are learning now, how to be independent and find my way in the world, to be in community and support myself." Bessie stated,

> The experience of doing my self-portrait in January lessened my anxiety and gave me clarity. It allowed me to externalize the conflict I was experiencing and make some decisions, especially about my job. I realized that I have choices.

All of the therapists related experiencing unconscious revelations and described exploring their inner and outer worlds. They observed that these experiences led to an increase in self-awareness. As previously mentioned, Alice said,

> The environment can be very negative and at times overwhelming. I found that recording the many activities including the pending feedback allowed me to take a step back from the busyness and appreciate how much was being accomplished even though several questions remain unanswered.

Salina engaged in dialogue with her image, stating,

> I really like her. There is something about her, I just really like her. She is just so not full of herself, but is so confident. She is humble and confident at the same time. She perfectly encompasses both these qualities. She is something really humble and I really like it. I just don't feel like she's simple, she may have grown up but I still see a purity to her. Her hair keeps her humble. If she had good hair, she wouldn't be so humble.

Viewing the image as the other conveyed it's meaning to the viewer (B. L. Moon, 1997).

The therapists echo B. L. Moon (1997) who contends that engaging with art reveals meaning and deepens and enriches the artist's experience of daily life. He suggests that art-making promotes awareness and self-acceptance, allows self-transcendence and brings a sense of hope and acceptance to everyday life.

In summary, one therapist described the process as having influenced her sense of self-acceptance and four therapists indicated they experienced "hope and appreciation" (de Botton & Armstrong, 2014). As B. L. Moon (1997) contends, creating art symbolizes expressing hope, adding that hopefulness is an essential component of all forms of psychotherapy.

Summary

This chapter presented the self-portraits and reflections of the art therapists, including their reflections with me. Eight themes emerged from those reflections, including: self-awareness through symbolism of environment; symbolism expressed through use of media; self-awareness through emotional, spiritual and bodily awareness; construction of self through word in art; self-awareness through engagement with inner-child; self-awareness through transformation; self-awareness of professional self; self-awareness through self-care; self-awareness of hope and appreciation; and evaluation of the tools and process. The next chapter explores the findings and implications of this research.

CHAPTER FOUR
DISCUSSION

The primary research question concerned what is the art therapist's lived-experience of drawing a full-bodied self-portrait each week for four weeks. This research project had three components: the creation of self-portraits; journaling about the participant's lived-experience when reflecting on their artwork; and exploring the four artworks as a serial with the researcher at the end of the project. Each component was very different, and designed to unearth as much about the self of the participant as possible. The research project uncovered eight themes including self-awareness through: symbolism of environment; emotional, spiritual and bodily awareness; construction of self through word in art; engagement with inner-child; transformation; awareness of professional self; self-care; and awareness of hope and appreciation. The participants found that the self-reflective practice, with the use of self-portraits and journaling, surfaced rich descriptions that facilitated their respective self-assessments, and in turn, their future direction.

This chapter offers an evaluation of process; discusses the overarching findings and implications that surfaced from this research; and points out some of the research limitations. Each is discussed in turn.

Evaluation of process

The therapists were asked to reflect on the: process of creating their weekly self-portraits; experience of the use of markers; time allotment; experience of journaling; and time discussing the portraits and reflections with me. This section discusses their responses.

All of the therapists commented on creating their weekly self-portraits. As Justin previously mentioned, "In the first drawing I took a picture of myself with the computer then copied that. In the other images I just drew without looking in the mirror." As B. L. Moon (1995) suggests, artwork is a mirror that reflects who the true nature if the artist. The artist must decide which facet of him/herself to expose and whether it is safe to expose it. This was true for at least ten therapists who recounted specifically experiencing this anxiety as they began the creative process. They had to decide what they were willing to expose, because they did not know me.

All of the therapists identified the existence of distortions within their artwork, expressing frustration with the differences between what they had expressed on paper and their experiences of themselves. For example, Mary explained, "So I didn't try to change anything and I didn't feel overly frustrated that the images didn't look like me. I just left it the way it was. I felt ok with what it was even if it wasn't a literal image of me."

Two participants made more than one portrait per week. Laura created six artworks over the four week period. She reported having created an additional portrait during the second and third week of the four week period, in addition to her weekly assignments. When asked about the additional drawings, Laura responded,

> It was a difficult month for me and maybe that is why I kept doing it, because maybe I felt there was something holding me back and I thought if I kept it up I would push past [what was holding me back].

Laura indicated that the additional work enhanced her experience of the process and increased her self-awareness. She added that the additional artworks reflected her surprise that she was actually enjoying the weekly experience.

All the therapists spoke about the art itself. They all described experiences of being able to see themselves in new ways, noting their surprise when they experienced insights stemming from how they depicted themselves. For example, Alice stated,

> The art recorded was such a tangible thing, to be able to go back and to look and to say 'Oh that's interesting', not only to be able to document things on your mind like in journaling but through the artwork, having a full picture of all the other dynamics, to be able to put things in perspective and then through reflection be able to process it.

Megan discussed the progression she could see in her art (Figure 14) stating,

> As I look at [the images] now I can see a lot of change. I think oh, wow. The first, second and third images I can see all the stress and pressure I was under. It's all me giving and giving. The fourth [image] says to me that I have to take time for me, that I have to give to myself as well. I think I decided to take a leave after the fourth picture.

Eleven therapists acknowledged the use of the media led them to experience a connection with their youthful selves. They also spoke of feeling the need to master the media which they would not normally use. These same therapists also observed that their art reflected their abilities when they were teenagers. Sandy indicated that the medium influenced the style of her drawings, noting, "I felt like I did really kid-like drawings because I felt like that is what I think of felts. I felt like that is the kind of work that teenagers would draw." Sade said,

> The journaling experience is not new to me but I know it requires time, commitment and planning, whereas doing art it can be as simple as doodling. Also, it can be done at any given moment with a pen or pencil. I like to doodle all of the time. I enjoy art process because it allows me to drift away from present stress or to get away from distractive mind. But best of all while doodling I can problem solve situations better or even see things from better angles.

All the therapists indicated that engaging in art and creative processing, made them aware of their need to maintain connections with their creativity.

All of the therapists indicated that they would have preferred to use five minutes for journaling and to have spent 55 minutes creating their self-portraits. They assumed this would have enabled them to go more deeply into the process, and/or allow them more expression, thereby encouraging further development of their artistic styles. On further reflection, they realized that, even though they wanted to make these changes, doing so would have required more time to compete the assignment. They acknowledged that, without the imposition of time limits, they would have eventually avoided their art dates which would have been problematic.

Twelve of 15 therapists reported that journaling enabled them to concretize their experiences, and helped them explore areas of concern, including: difficult work relationships; professional worries; illness; aging; and death and dying. These same therapists indicated that the creative self-reflection led to personal insight. Twelve therapists indicated that it gave them additional time for self-reflection. Nike explained that the amount of journaling time gave her more time to view her self-portrait. Nike noted, "In my self-reflection I began noticing how I represented myself, visually, and I was surprised."

All therapists compared their experience of journaling and art-making. For example, Sally said,

> I think it is easier to make excuses not to do art then it is not to do journaling. I think that journaling is more a part of our routine. I find it so much more, rich when they are combined together. I tried to do some spontaneous art making and then sit and one of the things I have been doing more is dialoguing, doing what the art said, I said, the back and forth conversation. In a written way, I find it makes a big difference to either do it in your mind or write it down.

Salina observed,

> Art has a three dimensional quality to it because whenever I do art it is situated in a context, there is space within and without, it is a piece of a larger picture. It doesn't exist on its own generally,

and even when you look at art you kind of hold it, and there's all this stuff around it, which is the environment. Writing is like a fine tuning for me, of putting connecting feelings and emotions towards a language, it's more that way. Art is special contextualizing, writing is story and stories are time.

While all participants observed that the artwork identified/brought out personal issues that needed exploration, they credited our discussion with bringing these issues into consciousness. All of the therapists indicated that having a witness present enabled them to pay attention to elements in their images which they might otherwise have missed. For example, Mary said,

> You know sometimes when you are working with people they may not say a lot, but they have had the experience of having the witness still. And, I think that both the witness and the person, who can help reflect, are both beneficial and can take you places that maybe you couldn't yourself or you didn't see that aspect or whatever, just a different journey because when I do my artwork I don't always spend reflecting on it or writing about it or thinking about it in terms of what it means or what it is saying or whatever, but I do some of that. From my experience, I have seen how it can be very helpful for people on all kinds of levels.

They also added that the conversation about their engagement in the project enabled a sense of conclusion and validated their lived-experience.

Participants reported that their overall experience of the process increased self-awareness about themselves and their contexts. They noted that this experience: deepened their relationships with themselves and about their unconscious desires; and reminded them of their need for self-care. All participants observed that the self-portraiture process had value, and reflected that they would like to integrate the self-portraiture process into their self-care routines. Their observations regarding integrating the process, however, were very general. For example, Laura indicated that she had considered integration in more specific terms, stating, "It got me thinking, it got me to work on how to integrate it."

Discussion of Findings

Four overarching findings surfaced from this phenomenological, arts-based study, including:

1. that art-making and journaling enabled art therapists to connect with their feeling and thinking states, which visually captured the artist's lived experience;
2. that self-portraiture, as a self-reflective practice, affords the artist a more direct means to focus on his/her true self;
3. the recognition of the importance of self-care, as an essential professional responsibility within their lives; and
4. that self-portraiture is a powerful tool to explore the many aspects of self.

Feeling and thinking through self-portraiture and reflection.

The first theme from this research found that art-making and journaling enabled art therapists to connect with both their feeling and thinking states. The self-portraits, using simple materials such as photocopy paper and markers, resulted in images which visually captured the artist's actual experience, in ways that words could not. The therapists reflected that being directed to use markers and photocopy paper was both the best and the worst aspect of the assignment. For instance, all therapists experienced the need to come to terms with the directed self-portraiture process in order to create their artwork. Some struggled with the directions, and a number of participants were distressed when they realized that the directions forced them to produce art that they were not used to creating. They observed that, while it was beneficial to use simple and effective media, they were unfamiliar and less competent in its use, and had wished to use media with which they were more comfortable. They noted that markers were not a typical choice of medium for artists and linked their use to youthful self-portraits. This supports the work of McNiff (1998) who contends that arts-based research needs to allow experiments with media to offer a clear structure and reliable method.

For instance, several participants found the first self-portrait drawing experience daunting. This experience seemed to evoke anxiety. This anxiety was expressed in different ways (e.g., paper too small for portrait, use of markers constraining art, time constraints, outside comfort zone, depiction of partial self-portrait or other image), and seemed connected to the focus on self, initial resistance to uncovering the nature of self, and the specific directions, including the use of media revealed anxiety and uncertainty. The participants were able to find ways to manage their anxiety (e.g., use of pencil, chalk, charcoal; initially creating a computer image), and reflected that they used these different materials in order to create a sense of comfort. They also acknowledged that they adapted to the limitations imposed by the process and indicated that their competency with the media increased over time. All of the therapists felt that their style had changed, or that they had depicted themselves differently when they reflected on their respective images. They attributed this to the specificity of directions regarding the media.

The therapists noted insights in each area of their lived experience. As they related their stories, they described triumphs, tragedies, hopes, fears, pleasures, and pain, and attributed their enhanced ability to meaningfully experience these issues to increased self-awareness. On viewing their created images, participants commented that they played out their conflicts in the creative process. A few therapists, such as Justin and Penny, made reference to the influence of the shadow, as an element of the self (McNiff, 2007). This shadow represents the parts of the self that we often do not like to acknowledge. For example, when Justin reflected on his artwork, he said, "I do have a dark side." As Penny noted when reflecting on her portraits, she felt sick most of the time that she was creating her artworks, and as such hid her face, throughout the process. She stated, "My head is not as well into work."

The creation of the self-portraits enabled the participants to release, and transform their pain, and bring identity issues to the surface. The participants' experiences concur with de Botton and Armstrong (2014) who, as previously mentioned, link seven human frailties (i.e., forgetting, pessimism, despair, disintegration, habits, comforts and taking things for granted) with seven ways in which art functions: remembering, hope, sorrow, rebalancing, self-understanding, growth, and appreciation (pp. 64-65). The experiences also harmonize with B. L. Moon (1997) and Chilton, Gerber, Bechtel, Councill, Dreyer, and Yingling (2015) who suggest that art is a means for exploring thinking and surfacing emotions enabling self-revelation and change. Further, the creation of self-portraits enabled the participants to experience a sense of increased competency in the process of creation (de Botton & Armstrong, 2014; Erikson, 1997; Lowenfeld & Brittain, 1975; B. L. Moon, 1995; Rogers, 1959).

While the majority of the participants depicted a full-bodied self-portrait at least once during the four-week process, there were a number of participants who deviated from the instructions. For example, Justin, in his depiction of his head and chest, indicated this was his avoidance of aging. For Tracey, the depiction of her head concerned her connection with clients. Megan speculated that the missing body in her first artwork was due to avoidance of pain within her body, while her third image as a tree meant that she was coming to terms with the need for self-care. Participants who did not specifically draw a full-bodied self-portrait conveyed that the resulting image concerned specific issues about self. The findings support the work of McNiff (1998) that arts-based research is unique and produces results that simply "happen" (p. 43).

The specificity of the directions allowed some flexibility. For instance, the participants were given the choice concerning the location of their self-reflective practice. This was important for two reasons: to assure engagement of participants without undo anxiety; and to enable the participants to see the value of the self-reflective process. Six participants engaged in the creative process at home while nine participants engaged in the creative process at work. Context affected the study results as each participant seemed to concentrate on their sense of self based upon the location of where they were engaging in the creative process. The findings showed that when participants engaged in the process at home they were more inclined to focus on personal issues, and when they engaged in the process at work they were more inclined to focus on work-related issues. As Erikson (1980) suggests that it is necessary to identify and work through personal issues to see clearly within the larger context, including work. While the location influenced the data it did not change the results. The participants concluded that this kind of self-reflection was important for their life.

The self-portraits enabled the therapists to explore the realm of the subconscious through the use of symbols. For example, Linda and Bessie used the symbolism of the environment which brought attention to a neglected area and provided the opportunity for healing. Alice and Tracey used words, as symbols, within their images. This enabled a dialogue with self about previously hidden information supporting the findings of Deaver and McAuliffe (2009) who contend words in art can help to make cognitive sense of the writer's created images. The images developed by Alice and Tracey conveyed a sense of being constructed. Their images and reflections affirm the findings of Johns (1995) who suggests that to become an effective practitioner involves a process of personal deconstruction and recognition within the context of who I am, and recognition to take the necessary action to change that statement into whom I need to be.

Symbols that depict self-concept were reflected within the self-portraitures supporting the work of Furth (1988) and Glaister (1996). For instance, Salina found disagreement between her inner and outer self, and resolved the conflict by the fourth portrait. The later self-portrait was firmer, clearer, stronger, centred, and symmetrical suggesting that Salina experienced congruency between inner and outer selves. Alternatively, Justin began with a self-portraiture of his head that reflected firm and clear lines and moved to images with fewer details and fainter lines. As he suggested, he was confronting himself. The findings support the work of Furth (1988) and Adams and Osgood (1973) who assert that the common interpretation of colour elicits cross-cultural similarities, and universal trends of affective meanings which are revealed to symbolize feelings, moods, tone, and amplified objects and actions within the self-portraits.

Eleven therapists acknowledged the use of the media led them to experience a connection with their inner-child and youthful selves. While engaging with their inner-child, the therapists were able to connect with their need to be generative. As Erikson (1980) notes, the psychosocial benefits of adult ego development include engagement in generative and creative activities. The participants reflected that there as a progression from youthful/childhood self, past self, to present current age self. As outlined by Spiegel, Severino and Morrison, (2000) in their support of Kohut, (1971) suggest that the goal of maturation is to differentiate within an empathic relationship. The participants amplified this positive affect that resulted from engaging with their creative self, thereby enabling empathic attunement with the "other" to facilitate maturation. The findings support the work of Lowenfeld and Brittain (1975) that the six stages of development are as relevant to the young artist as well as the adult artist. Further, the findings confirm the work of Hamblen (1984) who indicates that stage theory accounts for relationships between children's drawings and adult art with universal factors shared by both, revealing that stages can be skipped, reverted to or combined.

Participants expressed that the self-portraiture process enabled them to see themselves differently, and encouraged them to challenge their previous limits of experience and self-identity. They reported that their creativity was directed both inward and outward towards the objects and events in their contextual environments. This is consistent with the post-modern concept regarding the ability to create and reflect on self in different ways.

The true self through self-portraiture and reflection.

The second theme found that, while both the processes of art-making and journaling collect evidence, it is reasonable to suggest that self-portraiture, as a self-reflective practice, affords the artist a more direct means to focus on their true self. An artistic creation combines the opportunity to capture ideas visually with the use of imagination to reflect on life experience in order to re-imagine. This research underscored the importance for the art therapist to create art, which echoes the findings of a number of authors (Aligia, 2003; Allen, 1992; Brown, 2008). For example, Brown (2008) and Cameron (2007) contend that the artist needs to protect their inner artist suggesting that, without this inner work, a depletion or disconnection of the therapist's work-life balance may result, causing them to lack a sense of wholeness and completion. As Cameron (2007) contends, artists must recognize, nurture, and protect their inner artist in order to reveal inner truths and experience new depths of meaning.

The depiction of the body, in the self-portraits, surfaced insights into emotional, spiritual and bodily awareness. For example, self-awareness helped the therapist to: identify and modify specific behaviors; improve their reality orientation; and reduce anxiety (American Art Therapy Association, 2013). As well, findings showed that the process encouraged true self growth by identifying the pathological and graphic traits of the false body, so that a range of authentic body feelings could emerge (Machover, 1949).

Consistent with the work of Allen (1995) and Furth (1988), participants reported that they were able to bring different aspects of themselves together, as they reflected on their full-body portraits. They reported that these experiences revealed unconscious thoughts depicted within the simplicity of their projective portraits and observed that this led to a broadening of their emotional, spiritual and bodily-awareness. For example, the process encouraged a conversation with the critical self, and allowed movement between, and among; the body-self, the intellectual-self, the emotional-self and the contextual environment of the self (Machover, 1949). The self-reflection fostered self-knowing and spiritual fulfillment, as the artist first addressed their relationship with self (Allen, 2001; Cameron, 2007; Jensen, 2004; B. L. Moon, 1997).

The findings affirmed the work of Nunez (2009) who described each self-portrait as a non-verbal dialogue which enabled the artist to live through their different personae. As she noted and the therapist experienced, the non-verbal dialogue focused on what she terms interiority, and the ability to express true essence. Thus, the self-portrait is an autobiographical project that exposed underlying issues, feelings and emotions, and provided an opportunity to understand meaning. This concurs with Betensky (2001) who contends that the individual's entire body is involved in their process of self-exploration and meaning-making. In essence, the body is always in motion and intent on purpose and destination. Cameron (2007) and Sommers-Flanagan (2007) would likely agree with Betensky (2001) and add the importance for the therapist is to maintain emotional and bodily awareness, and the need to nurture, recognize and protect the inner artist.

Participants revealed the experience of connecting with their different selves which shifted and changed over time, given different self-experiences and contexts. The findings showed that the individual participants constructed their lives on the basis of these ever-changing situations and experiences that required them to make changes in what they expected of self. This concurs with Cresswell (2011), who suggests that the individual contains different kinds of selves which give rise to a dynamic self that depends upon self-experience and context.

The participants, through the creation and reflection on their self-portraits, were able to unconceal their sense of self in social encounters. This concurs with the work of Argyle (2009), who suggests, that the construction of self depends on and is influenced by feedback from others. The reflection on the self-portrait became a mirror of that feedback. This aided the way in which the participants were able to see themselves and as well how satisfied they were with themselves.

Dahl and Boss (2005) observe that the basic assumption of phenomenology is that knowledge is socially constructed. The second assumption is that knowledge is incomplete, which follows logically from the first assumption. By extension, the participants' created artwork represents the realities "from their own experience, within their own discipline and through their own mode of expression" (p. 66). Because knowledge is constructed, the creative act of art making and the situation of the art therapist give rise to a variety of meanings and, therefore, interpretations.

The addition of the written journal added another dimension which allowed the therapist to: reflect on their portrait; capture ideas; and put life experiences in perspective. As Megan said, "art is about the soul and essence whereas writing is about documenting and detailing". There was a synergistic effect when art-making was followed by journaling. For example, the self-portrait and subsequent reflection allowed each art therapist to concentrate authentically on the various aspects of self. In addition while each image of the self was motionless on a piece of paper, when the images were placed side-by-side, gradual changes from one image to the next allowed the artist to observe and identify changes in self. These gradual changes included: thinking less about environment and more about self; less about perfection; addressing and processing grief in order to come to acceptance; addressing anxiety and finding some calm; addressing life issues (i.e., retirement); and coming to terms and "full-circle" with the realization of need for self-care. This concurs with Cederboum (2009) that the interpretation of the self-portrait is a process of self-investigation which in turn leads to new meanings for the interpreter. She states that, as the story is constructed, "the interpreter is constructed with them" (Cederboum, 2009, p. 28).

Self-care as a professional responsibility.

The third theme concerns the acknowledgement by the art therapists that self-care is an important professional responsibility. The study revealed that the art therapists often avoid their artist's dates, and that they miss those experiences with art-making (Cameron, 2007). They reported that this experience re-established their inner artistic drive and desire, and enabled them to examine personal problems and opportunities, and resolve conflicts. They acknowledged the need to establish a continuing link with their own artistic process to maintain awareness of their subjective context. They added that the use of simple art materials encouraged the expression of emotions, and that this facilitated their self-awareness. Participants reported that reflecting on their artwork enabled them to connect with their creative selves within their safe, therapeutic settings, which also contributed to self-awareness. The findings support the work of Dewdney and Nicholas (2011) who contend that specific assignments create structure and safety.

Further, they expressed the need to engage in self-reflection to understand self and maintain balance in their personal and professional lives. An exercise in self-reflection increases self-awareness. The goal of increasing self-awareness is for the therapist to become more conversant with themselves. The conversation with self opens the path to listening to self, which allows for the making sense of story. By focusing on self-experience this encourages self-care. All of the participants identified an increase in self-awareness through this process. They also reported that, as their awareness increased, they connected to their past histories. For example, Bessie stated, "I have been through this before and I think that's the story. What I found in the story is that I stopped being me again." This affirms the work of Klugman (1997) concerning how movement from a problem way of being opens the way to a new way of seeing.

All participants discussed how they connected with their past, present and future selves. Leonard (1994), in describing Heidegger, adds that a person is studied within the context of their having-been-ness. Leonard (1994) contends that being, in both the past and future, is care, stating "Care, in Heidegger's sense, is having our being be an issue for us" (p. 54). This suggests that self-portraiture enables participants to be able to connect with their artistic selves as they created and re-created and connected with how creativity is fundamental to their way of being in the world, and that reflecting upon the self became care for the participants.

The research found that art therapists are exposed to a variety of demands in their work and personal life. In journaling and during interviews with me, the therapists reported that such demands overwhelm their daily schedule, which prevent them from completing self-care routines and/or engaging in their own art-making. These findings are consistent with those of Brown

(2008), Gilroy (2004) and Hocoy (2007) who note that, by decreasing their engagement with their art, the art therapist can suffer from clinification and a lack of self-awareness in their practice. The findings support the work of McNiff (1998) that arts-based research illustrates the process of inquiry that can further the effectiveness of professional practice.

Further, the findings affirm the work of Brown (2008) who suggests that when the therapist engages in self-care, their work benefits clients. For example, the experience of Nike, allowed her to reflect upon her need to grieve and place boundaries on working with clients. As B. L. Moon (1997) suggests, this process serves as a friendly messenger to the art therapist, enabling the therapist to be attentive to their effect on clients and surfacing issues that are hidden. For example, Sade indicated her portraits reflected her inner feelings she experienced at work, and stated,

> I noticed that in all four drawings I had indicated similar tense areas in all four pictures. I questioned if this is what I presented as myself to the world as being very stable on the outside but internally I am anxious on the inside.

The findings also support the work of Lessem (2005) who highlights the importance of being affirmed, recognized, accepted, appreciated and valued, contending these are crucial to cohesion of self.

Self-portraiture for art therapists

The fourth theme and finding indicates that the use of self-portraiture, as a self-reflective practice, is a powerful therapeutic technique for art therapists. Findings showed that by adding a reflective, self-portraiture practice to their weekly agenda, the therapists gain an excellent therapeutic tool for building self-awareness, facilitating self-expression of their inner reality, and rendering their feelings and experiences readily observable, to better understand self. This study emphasized the many advantages for the art therapist of scheduling a self-reflective practice at the end of their work week.

Participants, in reflecting on their four artworks, indicated they were able to connect with a need to nurture their inner artistic child-self, and that their need for self-care had been unconcealed. As explored by Cameron (2007) the artist needs to protect their inner artist suggesting that, without this inner work, a depletion or disconnection of the therapist's work-life balance may result, causing them to lack a sense of wholeness and completion. Cameron (2007) also contends that artists must recognize, nurture, and protect their inner artist in order to reveal inner truths and experience new depths of meaning. The avoidance of "artists dates" (p. 513) is also a resistance to the acknowledgment of suffering self. Each individual's subjective way of being in the world was revealed within the self-portraits as a self-manifestation (Koskela, 2012, p. 116). The resulting reflections on the artworks were a self-manifestation. As Koskela (2012) described, Heidegger's view suggests that unconcealment is an event in which truth of ones being in the world is unconvered into a unity manifesting a discourse "driven by human needs and human interests" (p. 121). The self-reflective process revealed that the mirror of the self-portrait created over time provided a clearing, in which understanding of being or essence can prevail, "while incompatible possibilities of being are concealed" (p. 124).

The connection with self, as self-reflective practice, enabled participants to identify, explore challenges, joys, create clarity, answer questions as well as explore past, present and future directions. This includes examining the media utilized and the participant's ability to use the media as significant elements linked to the participant's continuing use of his/her creativity and imagination. Bruce L. Moon (1997) observes that this activity increases an individual's self-discipline and self-regard and can thereby lead to healing. Ulman (2001) adds that this augments the individual's ability to express emotion, liberate feelings, create new self-awareness and expose deep unconscious content.

Participants also made observations regarding the benefits of reflection on the longer-term self-portraiture experience when they were able to place their four portraits side by side and reflect over the process. For many participants, the experience highlighted the differences between their weekly reflections on each individual portrait and their reflections on the series of self-images they had made over time. The process encouraged some participants to create more self-portraits, on an ongoing basis, believing that this might enable them to learn more. In their longer-term reflections on the four self-portraits, all participants specifically credited the reflective, self-portraiture practice as serving as a catalyst for self-change. The findings support the work of McNiff (1998) who contends that the goal of arts-based research is to provide the opportunity to re-experience trust in the intelligence of the creative process and the desire for relationships to develop with the images that emerge.

The therapists expressed the benefits and generative possibilities for change when engaged in self-portraiture and reflection. In this instance, exploration of self, in the image acts as a mirror reflecting the distortions and the incomplete ego-self opening the way to self-awareness (Allen, 1995). This process was a prelude to change and transformation. For example, Penny was able to release sublimated sorrow for self-transformation and self-transcendence (Jensen, 2004; Kenworthy, 1995; LeClerk, 2006; B. L. Moon, 1995, 1997; and Smith, 2008). This finding echoes the work of Cardinal (2014) who contends self-care provides an opportunity for change.

Other therapists experienced external, life-altering events during the research process. They were able to identify changes, in their artwork, that reflected these events. They were amazed that the process led to an enhanced awareness of self, the need for self-care, and by extension, hope and self-appreciation. These observations are consistent with the findings of Jensen (2004) and Steindle-Rast (1999) who suggest that the self-reflective process increases the opportunities for self-discoveries to be made and transformation to occur. It seems reasonable that the experience of self-discovery and transformation would reinforce on-going self-care through art.

In essence, this research confirmed that creating a simple projective self-portrait, at the end of the work week, provided a powerful tool for:

1. investigating the many selves on an ongoing basis;
2. an encounter of self-reflection, as both subject and object;
3. an interpretive method to enrich lived-experience that added knowledge to unearth what is both visible and invisible;
4. continued engagement in the artistic process;
5. engaging both individual elements within the self to a view of the individual's story and person as a whole;
6. assessing the working self in order to engage the agent self by unearthing symbolic, conscious, or behavioural variables;

7. a new way of viewing phenomena that individuals tend to overlook and/or disregard;
8. revealing transference/ counter-transference;
9. a significant opportunity to know and accept him/herself, perceive what the self is missing; what might be needed, and what hidden desires should be expressed; and
10. an active process of self-therapy and self-supervision.

These findings, regarding the efficacy of self-reflection, substantiate the contentions of Lowenfeld and Brittain (1975) and Oster and Crone (2004). The findings indicate that drawings provide good indications of growth, contain representations of the self and feelings, and stimulate awareness of body image and self-concept. The findings substantiate that the act of self-portraiture reflects one's ability to face oneself, to express concerns and conflict in a contained environment, and learn new strategies for problem solving. This presumes that the art therapist is ready to face self and is not clinically contraindicated (Alter-Muri, 2007).

Implications

A number of implications surface from these findings, including: the necessity for incorporating a self-reflective practice as self-care in practice, placing more emphasis on incorporating a self-reflective practice as self-care within art therapy educational programs and practice organizations, and including an art form with the self-reflective process for practitioners who engage with clients.

First as the findings indicate, there is a necessity for incorporating a self-portraiture and reflective practice as self-care for art therapists. This enables the artist to maintain their connection to their creative self and keep the artist self within alive. Journaling about the portrait enables a dialogue with selves enabling that which was hidden to surface and be addressed by the therapist. Through this self-care process there is an opportunity and implication to prevent clinification and burn-out, which could directly reduce the number of art therapists leaving the profession.

Second, consideration should be given to placing more emphasis on incorporating a self-portraiture and reflective practice, as self-care, within art therapy educational programs and practice organizations. When this self-care practice as part of training and emphasized through practice organizations, there is greater likelihood that therapists will commit the time for self-care despite competing demands.

Third, the findings suggest that there is a value for all practitioners, who work with clients, to engage in some artistic form of self-care linked to self-reflection. The inclusion of an art form enables the practitioner to connect with the creative self surfacing additional information that may not have surfaced through self-reflection alone.

Limitations

This study was limited by several factors. First, the scope of the project was small and limited to 15 participants. Second, the study included only art therapists and did not include other professional disciplines that may be using self-portraiture in their therapy practice. Third, the selection process included only art therapists from among those who held either CATA or OATA membership. Additionally, the selection process did not include representation from all provinces nor other demographic criteria (e.g., faith, ethnicity). Fourth, the resulting sample was predominantly female with only one male, which may have impacted the results. While the profession is predominantly female, there is value in exploring the impact of gender on data. Further, three of the participants were known to me through our studies in art therapy. Fifth, a further limitation concerned the limited amount of time available to engage participants; four weeks. Sixth, the three methodological frameworks (phenomenology, arts-based research and constructivism) limited the analysis to the interpretation of the internal processes and psychological states of the participants. Finally, the context for engaging participants in the creative process influenced the data but did not impact the ultimate result. For instance, the participants who selected to engage in the reflective activity at home indicated they focused more on personal issues, while those who conducted the activity at work indicted they emphasized work issues. There is a possibility that additional data could have surfaced if the location had been specified.

Conclusion

The results of this study inform the field of spiritual care and psychotherapy. For instance, the results confirmed with each participant, found that their self-portraits, using simple materials such as photocopy paper and markers, resulted in images which visually captured the artist's lived experience, in ways that words could not. Their subsequent reflections, through journaling and with viewing the images, as a serial, in discussion with this researcher, resulted in rich descriptions that facilitated their respective self-assessments, and in turn, their future directionality. The results also affirmed the importance of self-care for the art therapist through the creation of art, as a means for maintaining their inner artistic drive and desire, and balance and well-being.

This research concludes that, as a self-directed reflective practice, the self-portrait provides a means to discover the relationship between self and work, life and others. Further, it provides the professional with a means for continued engagement with artistic practice and reflection on the many selves; continuing the engagement with the creative heart, inner-child and spirit. It is my hope that this study strengthens the use of the self-portrait and journaling, as a self-reflection tool, as a means for self-supervision and for self-care within the art therapy profession. Further, that this practice be incorporated within art therapy education and practice organizations.

Recommendations for Further Study

The results of this study suggest the usefulness for additional research, including replicating this study and/or expanding its scope. For example, the study could be replicated with other art therapists or other professionals, to compare findings with those reported here. The latter choice could broaden the implications beyond art therapists to other disciplines. Future studies could also address the demographic limitations found with this project by selecting participants based on gender and/or from specific ethnicities, faiths, and communities. Studies could enable the art therapists and other professionals to select the materials and media. For instance, a future self-portrait study could allow participants to create mixed-media self-portraits. Further, it would be useful to extend this study to explore the lived-experiences of using the self-portrait, as a self-reflective practice, over a longer period of time. Exploring the cross-cultural applicability of this intervention would provide interesting findings. The exploration of the interpretation of colour as it pertains to stage theory (Hamblen, 1984) and the differences in cultural values (Adams & Osgood, 1973) could further illuminate how stage theory might benefit from modification.

Future self-portrait studies could be conducted by therapists who use art within their clinical practice, acknowledging the limitations expressed by Alter-Muri (2007). For instance arts-based therapy may be contraindicated with clients who: suffer from mental illness that leave them predisposed to suicidal tendencies which can hinder inner healing; experienced a significant change in physical appearance that leaves them unable to look at themselves; and/or who have a tendency to "obsess on their thoughts and limitations" (Alter-Muri, 2007, p. 331).

A future self-portrait body outline study could explore where individuals carry their anxiety, stress, or sorrow in their body. Recommended for further study is investigating whether art therapy programs and practicing art therapists are incorporating a self-portrait self-reflective process. Similarly, there is benefit in exploring the impact of self-portraiture, as a self-reflective practice, in retaining practicing art therapists.

CHAPTER FIVE
PERSONAL AND THEOLOGICAL REFLECTIONS

During this research study, I experienced several events of direct relevance to my investigation. The first resulted from my decision to engage in the same self-reflective process required of the participating art therapists. I began creating self-portraits on a weekly basis and continue to do so. After my initial engagement with the weekly self-reflections using the self-portrait process, I wrote an article entitled "Using Client's Creativity to Express Themselves: The Self-Portrait" (Hill, 2014). This article concerned how I, as a therapist, had incorporated the creation of a self-portrait into my work with clients. I found therapeutic value, as it allowed me to connect with my client's subconscious, while being able to identify, discover and explore areas that might be hidden to increase self-awareness and transformation. After my engagement with the self-portrait, in conjunction with working along-side my participants during my research study, I wrote another article, entitled "Art and Psychotherapy as a Self-Reflection Tool for Therapists" (Hill, 2016). In this article, I expressed learning about myself, as I reflected on my self-portraits. I explained how therapeutically connected with my subconscious, and surfaced areas that were otherwise hidden from me, so that I could explore self and increase self-awareness for self-care and transformation.

In my initial engagement with the self-portraiture process, I was aware of avoidance similar to the experiences reported by several of the participants. This avoidance led me to put off starting the process until I could become comfortable with the commitment. I needed to figure out a way to schedule precious time each week to engage in the ritual assignment, and to incorporate the ritual in a way that it could become a unified part of who I truly am.

The second event was the trip to the Art Gallery of Ontario where Suzy Lake, my fine arts mentor at the University of Guelph, was holding a retrospective show culminating years of her photography. As previously mentioned, this experience influenced the beginning of this journey and it resonates now as I finish this part of the journey. I re-write her insightful statements here as a reminder to me. In her forward to *Introducing Suzy Lake,* Gevinson (2014) quotes Lake as saying, "What is really important is that the awareness of all of this becomes a constructive thing so that we're not victims by our own hands. It's empowering to understand and overcome these gestures. Self-awareness is self-empowering" (p. 13). As well, Uhlyarik (2014) quotes Lake addressing the manner in which aging changes our perceptions of ourselves and observing that viewing her own work over time has enabled her to feel "her true self in her true space in her true rhythm" (p. 173).

My experience of reflecting upon my self-portraits enabled me to engage with a sense of integrity as a connected, healthy, whole self, as my self-awareness blossomed. This self-awareness became tangible, as I constructed my reflections of self and this book. I realized, as I reflected on my re-engagement with the work of Suzy Lake and my own self-portraits, the one thing that resonates with me is that I have been working on becoming who I truly am. When I reflect upon my images and lived-experiences of this enormous process, I realize that this is me. The questions of Who am I and What makes me, are drawn here. The drawings and the process allowed me to dig deep and explore who I think I really am. The culmination reveals what I know about myself. I find the answer peeking out at me from behind my work. I can see my true self in those moments when I take the time to reflect.

Moving from participating in classes to working on the dissertation portion of my doctorate was a challenging experience for me. First, I praised God for helping other students and me through the process of attending classes and achieving credits. Second, I prayed about the research component of this process and for those I thought I would work with. As this process unfolded, I felt increased stress and acknowledged my inexperience. During this period of anxiety, I felt God providing me with comfort in a manner that I had not previously experienced. When my Committee directed me to work with art therapists, rather than clients as my proposal had suggested, I felt a calm and peace come over me. My sense that my inner self experienced the presence of God quieted me and allowed this journey to unfold. In the unfolding, I learned that I had a new direction and a new vision which motivated and gave life to the process within counselling, as it also motivated and gave life to the therapist.

As I began to reflect upon the reason I had decided to base my research on self-portraiture, I felt overwhelmed. My heart leapt with joy when I saw that the professor, who had taught me during my undergraduate studies, was holding a retrospective exhibition of her work. As I walked around the exhibits, I began to reflect on my own blessed story, remembering how I had progressed from my undergraduate days to where I was at that time. I had not connected many elements of the journey before that day. When it was time for me to write the introduction of this book, I was filled with the Holy Spirit. I realized this journey had taken me to many places in my life, and as I reflected on its many elements, I was aware that I had been directed by God. As I reflected further, I was encouraged when I realized the presence of Jesus walking alongside me.

I became aware that I have a special talent that God wants me to use, although I did not quite know what it was. I knew that God knows I am special, and this enabled me to acknowledge and work through this research to be of help to my community. I realized from my lived-experience that the best reflection of myself is seen in the mirror that is being held up in front of me. The reflection is a friendly messenger of how it is I am perceived. This experience has shown me that I hold a belief about who it is that I am, based upon the story that I tell myself. How do I truly know who it is that I am, when aging changes my perception? How do I truly know the answer?

As I began the project, I read 2 Kings 22:1-2. Josiah became a king, having been so directed by God, and as king, he brought God's law to the people. This reminded me of the importance of being formed when we are young and of the great significance of the formation itself. I remember being appreciated for my artwork in the second grade which led to my work with art. During my undergraduate years, I followed the road towards ministry, counselling and art therapy, which led to this dissertation. Bringing my child-like self forward led to an enhancement in my spirituality, which is an important part of my work. My development has taken a long and winding road to reach this place and served as the foundation for this research.

When I began this research, I did not realize that I would engage with other art therapists in an activity that would enable them to connect meaningfully with their imaginations, their child selves, and their need for self-care. In Mark 9:36-37 (New Revised Standard Version), Jesus chose a child to stand among the disciples. Taking the child in his arms he said to them, "Whoever welcomes one of these little children in my name welcomes me; and whoever welcomes me does not welcome me but the one who sent me." It is important to acknowledge the child within, and to remain child-like in many ways. It is of equal importance for the inner child to have a voice. In the last few years, I have had to start to use reading glasses. Without them, everything is a blur. Time, space, life and work can be like that, moving at such a pace that it becomes a blur. Until the time is taken to focus in order to gain clarity, clinical aspects of work as well as endless distractions can expand to fill all time and space. To be self-aware enough to put on the glasses, to bring ourselves into sharp focus, is to begin to integrate and weave into everyday practice an engagement in creative spirit. In order to do so, each of us has to be willing to acknowledge aging and look inward in order to see.

I found that listening to the therapists' accounts of their respective journey over the four week intervention was a life-giving ministry. I was privileged to witness with them the experiences of difficulty, frustration, pain, illness, loss, grief, and disconnection that they expressed. This enabled me to understand how such experiences move people away from taking care of themselves, and in turn, pull them away from their souls. I remember how we were instructed that people who seek counselling come to us for a reason, and I reflected on this concept, as I listened to the participants' stories. During the interview process, I was amazed to hear their stories about finding themselves disconnected from their artistic self which had led them to be art therapists. They described being able to connect with their inner beings over the four week period, saying that they joined with themselves in a spiritual manner. By attending to the need for self-care, they experienced being cared for. This heightened my awareness of the importance of continuing our art and engaging in self-care so that we, as therapists, are not victims by our own hands. As I listened to the stories, it became increasing clear that it is empowering to understand and overcome what we might be avoiding. As Suzie Lake states, "Self-awareness is self-empowering" (Gevinson, 2014, p. 13).

Just like the work of this research, I am learning more about myself on a daily basis. The process of experiencing and reflecting on my self-portraits over time encouraged my re-engagement with my true self, in my true space, in my true rhythm. My sense of self was further reflected to me, as I listened to participants reflect on their mirrors of themselves. Their re-engagement and connection with their true selves affirmed their self-concept. This affirmation allowed them to experience their need to reconnect with their self-care routines and their artistic selves. It was astounding to witness what the four week intervention had accomplished. By attending to self-portrait and reflection, each participant grew closer to their sense of who they are, their sense of spirituality which allowed God to work throughout the process to soothe and repair the sense of disconnection expressed. My theological perspective on this experience was to conclude that God was trying to tell me that we are all human, and therefore, we need to take care of ourselves in order to continue to do God's work.

The following self-portraits (see Figure 16) were created as I was editing this creation. The first self-portrait is an image of me leaving my office in London, heading home late at night. The dark blue reflects the darkness of evening. My outfit is the outfit I wore that day. My rolling bag is full of files. Although my bag is not actually orange, I used this colour to reflect the work that still needs to be done. The swish is from the Holy Spirit moving with me from work to home, as I complete my tasks for the day.

Figure 16. Self-Portraits by Laurie

The next artwork depicts my state of overwhelm with all of the editing changes that need to occur. The pages surround me like the hands of a clock going around and around. At some point, the paper falls indicating that the process will end. I have drawn a big book or the dissertation, instead of what I had intended; a computer. My eyes are closed, perhaps hoping to avoid the increasing amount of work needed to finish the editing. I am somewhat standing and sitting, as if on a high stool. It looks like I have grass under my feet. Perhaps this reflects myself growing.

My next artwork depicts me taking a close look at myself. I drew a mirror on the wall to symbolize my reflection, and yet, I continued to draw myself standing in front of me. The two of us are touching one another, as if we are engaged in a dance. I realized afterward that the art on my blouse reminded me of hieroglyphics. Perhaps I am engaged in deciphering my own experience. I look larger in this picture, more solid in stature. The blackness of my skirt and boots weighing me down, looking well grounded. I also look happy in this self-portrait, like I am smiling at the viewer.

My last artwork was completed just after working with a couple in counselling. It was a difficult session. I felt that I was doing a therapeutic dance, keeping them focused and keeping them on task to end the session on time. I was happy to have accomplished what I needed. The faces reflect the clients, who appear overwhelmed with difficulties and complications. They needed more than I had to give. After I drew them, I stood back to look at the work and thought of my parents. While both have passed since I started my doctorate, they are looking down at me from above, perhaps spirits, spurning me on. I look like I am on tippy toes, trying to maintain my balance, with my eyes closed, as if reflecting within.

Through my weekly engagement with the self-portrait, I experienced a number of insights about how I see myself. I struggled with some similar insights that were mentioned by the participants. For instance, the series of self-portraits offered a mosaic of my life over a period of time which allowed me to identify and explore the daily demands of life. The process allowed me to integrate self, more fully into the different facets of my daily work, relationships and experiences. As I compare myself, even in these few portraits, I can see different selves with different interests, concerns, goals, and personality traits. I can see how it is that I have grown through the exploration of my lived experience.

As an art therapist, I learned that each of us is truly a wounded healer. The sacred message in this experience concerns the reality that God is the Creator. God allows us to grow, and when we least expect it, presents us with new circumstances to grow further. I realized that, not only in my ministry and counselling practice but also in my educational journey, God was calling me to stretch and grow. I can see within my portraits and through the versions of this dissertation how I have grown. I can only imagine how I will continue to grow, change and evolve beyond this experience.

The writing part of the research process required me to reflect deeply, as I quickly realized that I am not a natural writer, and I struggled with the process of writing. The Bible says that "weeping may endure for a night, but joy comes in the morning" (King James Version, Psalm 30.5). I had to remind myself to turn to my support system for help and to remember that difficulties do not last forever; there will be joy. As a result of my participation in the process, with every conversation, I was aware of myself growing in empathy for myself and others.

I saw God at work in this process. Previously I wrote a thesis, but I was never required to be as diligent or work as hard as I have for this research project. I believe that God was asking me to learn, to work hard and not to give up. I also believe that God used me to enable the participants to connect with the heart of what deeply matters to them and to have hope. The hope for me is that I have provided an awareness of the need for all of us to take the time and look in the mirror for the self-awareness needed to not to be victims at our own hands, and confidently see the reflection of our true selves. The inner fire that first started the drive to become an art therapist should be cherished and utilized. For me, it is a favorite aspect of my personality. I hope that it fiercely burns, as I continue the connection with my creative inner self. I hope that the work that I have undertaken in this process helps others to surface feelings, build on experience, and learn more about what fosters connection with self.

I find my purpose in seeking deeper understanding in the therapeutic experience, as therapist. I never want to lose that or my creative self. To be aware of what constitutes self is integral to our self-construction and our authenticity. To appreciate who I am, a constructive enterprise, an authentic me.

The work undertaken in this research and intervention process was God's work. The participants were able to see themselves in a new way, revealing Christ within the mirror. I had the opportunity to see the same when I looked in the mirror.

EPILOGUE

You have finished this book. What have you learned?

Simply a practical and workable technique for attaining a successful practice of self-supervision. Examples have been shown of participants who have applied this self-supervision technique. These stories have been told to demonstrate that through these same methods you can obtain a self-supervisory process to be better able to give precise self-feedback, conduct your own search of assets, skills and resources, create change, help answer questions, provide corrective feed-back, as a means for self-monitoring, and to self-learn. But reading is not enough. Please apply and practice this technique and see how you can obtain increased self-understanding.

I wrote this book out of a sincere desire to help professionals maintain their self-care. It will give me great pleasure to know that this technique has helped you. I have absolute confidence that it will. Please see my website www.thecounsellinghouse.ca for more information about the author, workshops, supervision, and educational opportunities.

REFERENCES

Adams, F. & Osgood, C. (1973). A Cross Cultural Study of the Affective Meanings of Color. *Journal of Cross-Cultural Psychology,* 4(2), 135-156.

Aliaga, M. (2003). *The neophyte art therapist: A crushed spirit or a flourished soul?* (Unpublished master's thesis). C.W. Post, Long Island University, Brookville, NY.

Allen, P. B. (1992). Artist-in-Residence: An alternative to "clinification" for art therapists. *Art Therapy Journal of American Art Therapy Association,* 9(1), 22-29.

Allen, P. B. (1995). *Art is a way of knowing: A guide to self-knowledge and spiritual fulfillment through creativity.* Boston, MA: Shambhala Publication Inc.

Allen, P. B. (2001). Art making as spiritual path: The open studio. In J. A. Rubin (Ed.), *Approaches to art therapy: Theory and technique* (pp. 178-188). New York, NY: Routledge, Taylor & Francis Group.

Allen, K. R. & Piercy, F. P. (2005). Feminist autoethnography. In D. H. Sprenkle & F. P. Piercy (Eds.), *Research methods in family therapy* (2nd ed.) (pp. 63-84). New York, NY: The Guilford Press.

Alter-Muri, S. (2007). Beyond the face: Art therapy and self-portraiture. *The Arts in Psychotherapy,* 34, 331-339.

American Art Therapy Association, (2013). *What is art therapy?* Alexandria, Virginia: American Art Therapy Association. Retrieved from http://www.arttherapy.org/upload/whatisarttherapy.pdf

American Psychological Association (2002). Ethical principles and code of conduct. *American Psychologist, 57,* 1060-1073.

Anderson, L. R. (1982). The aesthetic preference: Overcoming the pragmatic error. *Family Process, 21,* 43-56.

Argyle, M. (2009). *Social Interaction.* (2nd ed.). Piscataway, NJ: Transaction Publishers.

Backos, A. (1997). *Self-portraits with rape survivors in Feminist-Rogerian art therapy.* (Doctoral dissertation). Retrieved from Primo by Ex Libris. (ISNB: 9780591329896)

Ball, B. (2002). Moments of change in the art therapy process. *The Arts in Psychotherapy, 29,* 79-92.

Baumeister, R., & Bushman, B. (2007). *Social psychology and human nature.* Belmont, CA: Wadsworth International Edition.

Becerra, L. (2018). *The power of art: The emotional and physiological impact of creating self-portraits using mandalas and human figure drawings.* (Doctoral dissertation). Retrieved from ProQuest Information and Learning. (ISNB: 978-0355087529)

Benz, E. (2005). Imago Dei: Man as the image of God. (A. F. Keele, Trans.) *Review of Books on the Book of Mormon 1989-2011.* 17(1), 223-54.

Berger, P. L., & Luckmann, T. (1966). *The social construction of reality: A treatise in the sociology of knowledge.* Garden City, NY: Anchor Books.

Betensky, M. (2001). Phenomenological art therapy. In J. A. Rubin (Ed.), *Approaches to art therapy: Theory and technique* (pp. 121-133). New York, NY: Routledge, Taylor & Francis Group.

Betts, D. J. (2006). Art therapy assessments and rating instruments: Do they measure up? *The Arts in Psychotherapy, 33,* 422-434.

Blumenfeld-Jones, D. (2016). *Ethics, aesthetics, and education: A Levinasian Approach.* New York, NY. Palgrave Macmillan.

Boy, A. & Pine, G. (1980). Avoiding counselor burnout through role renewal. *The Personal Guidance Journal,* 59(3), 161-163.

Breunlin, D. C. (1999). Toward a theory of constraints. *Journal of Marital and Family Therapy,* 25(3), 365-382.

Brown, C. (2008). The importance of making art for the creative arts therapist: An artistic inquiry. *The Arts in Psychotherapy, 35,* 201-208.

Bryce-Smith, D. (1992). *The self-portrait: Its history and types* (Doctoral dissertation). Retrieved from ProQuest Dissertations and Theses Global. (Thesis No. U040700)

Burns, R. C. (2009). *Kinetic-House-Tree-Person drawings (K-H-T-P): An interpretive manual.* New York, NY: Routledge.

Cameron, J. (2007). *The complete artist's way: Creativity as a spiritual practice.* New York, NY: Penguin Books.

Cardinal, K. (2014). The personality tea pot: The effects and future application in art therapy. *Canadian Art Therapy Association Journal, 27*(2), 13-30.

Carr, S. (2017). *Portrait Therapy.* London, UK: Jessica Kingsley Publishers

Carr, S. & Hancock, S. (2017). Healing the inner child through portrait therapy: Illness, identity and childhood trauma. *International Journal of Art Therapy, 22*(1), 8-21.

Cederboum, N. (2009). *"Self-Portrait"–a study of the 'self': A quest for the creation and the development of the 'self' through a 'chain of observations'* (Doctoral dissertation, Anglia Ruskin University). Retrieved rom http://in.bgu.ac.il/icqm/DocLib1/%D7%A0%D7%95%D7%A8%D7%99%D7%AA-%D7%A6%D7%93%D7%A8%D7%91%D7%90%D7%95%D7%9D.pdf

Chenail, R. J. (2005). The use of phenomenology for family therapy research: The search for meaning. In D. H. Sprenkle & F. P. Piercy (Eds.). *Research methods in family therapy* (2nd ed.) (pp. 63-84). New York, NY: The Guilford Press.

Chilton, G., Gerber, N., Bechtel, A., Councill, T., Dreyer, M., & Yingling, E. (2015). The art of positive emotions: Expressing positive emotions within the intersubjective art making process. *Canadian Art Therapy Association Journal, 28*(1-2), 12-25.

Chilvers, I. & Beam, R. (2003). *The artist revealed: Artists and their self-portraits.* San Diego, CA: Thunder Bay Press.

Cox, E., & Lothstein, L. M. (1989). Video self-portraits: A novel approach to group psychotherapy with young adults. *International Journal of Group Psychotherapy, 39*(2), 237-253.

Craddick, R. A. (1963). The self image in the Draw A Person test and self-portrait drawings. *Journal of Projective Techniques & Personality Assessment, 27*(3), 288-291.

Cresswell, J. W. (2011). Being faithful: Bakhtim and a potential postmodern psychology of self. *Culture and Psychology,* 17(4), 473-490.

Cresswell, J. W. (2014). *Research design: Qualitative, quantitative, and mixed methods approaches* (4th ed.). Thousand Oaks, CA: SAGE Publications Inc.

Cumming, L. (2010). *A face to the world: on self-portraits.* Hammersmith, London: William Collins.

Dahl, C. M., & Boss, P. (2005). The use of phenomenology for family therapy research: The search for meaning. In D. H. Sprenkle & F. P. Piercy (Eds.), *Research methods in family therapy* (2nd ed.) (pp. 63-84). New York, NY: The Guilford Press.

Dalley, T., Rifkind, G., & Terry, K. (1993). *Three voices of art therapy: Image, client, therapist.* London and New York: Routledge.

Darewych, O. H. (2014). *The bridge drawing with path art-based assessment: Measuring meaningful life pathways in higher education students* (Doctoral dissertation). Retrieved from ProQuest Dissertations and Theses Global. (Thesis No. 3615961)

David, T. (2016). Portrait of self and other: Developing a mentalization-focused approach to art therapy within a personality disorder service. In R. Hughes (Ed.), *Time-limited art psychotherapy: Developments in theory and practice* (pp. 92-118). New York, NY: Routledge/Taylor & Francis Group.

Deaver, S. P., & McAuliffe, G. (2009). Reflective visual journaling during art therapy and counselling internships: A qualitative study. *Reflective Practice,* 10(5), 615-632.

de Botton, A., & Armstrong, J. (2013). *Art as therapy.* New York, NY: Phaidon Press.

Dewdney, I., & Nicholas, L. (2011). *Drawing out the self: The objective approach in art therapy.* London, Ontario: The Ontario Art Therapy Association.

DiLeo, J. H. (1983). *Interpreting children's drawings.* New York, NY: Brunner/Mazel Publishers.

Duncan, B., Parks, B., & Rush, G. (1990). Eclectic strategies practice: A process constructive perspective. *Journal of marital and family therapy,* 16, 165-179.

Duncan, B. L., Miller, S. D., Wampold, B. E., & Hubble, M. A. (2010). *The Heart and soul of change: Delivering what works in therapy* (2nd ed.). Washington, DC: American Psychological Association.

Emery, L. F., Walsh, C., & Slotter, E. B. (2015). Knowing who you are and adding to it: Reduced self-concept clarity predicts reduced self-expansion. *Social Psychological and Personality Science, 6*(3), 259-266.

Erikson, E. H. (1980). *Identity and the life cycle.* New York, NY: W.W. Norton & Company.

Erikson, E. H., & Erikson, J. M. (1997). *The life cycle completed: Extended version with new chapters on the ninth stage of development.* New York, NY: W.W. Norton & Company.

Erikson, E. H. (2009). On the generational cycle: An address. *International Journal of Psycho-Analitical, 61*, 213-220.

Esteban-Guitart, M., Monreal-Bosch, P., Perara, S., & Bastiani, J. (2017). Schooling and identity: A qualitative analysis of self-portrait drawings of young indigenous people from Chiapas, Mexico. *Frontiers in Psychology, 7*(2083). Retrieved from https://doi.org/10.3389/fpsyg.2016.02083

Farrar, S., Stopa, L., & Turner, H. (2015). Self-imagery in individuals with high body dissatisfaction: The effect of positive and negative self-imagery on aspects of the self-concept. *Journal of Behavior Therapy and Experimental Psychiatry, 46*, 8-13.

Findigart. (2013, March 13). *Self portrait of spiritual awareness.* Retrieved from http://findigart.com/gallery/assorted/self-portrait-of-spiritual-awareness/

Finlay, L. (2005). "Reflexive embodied empathy": A phenomenology of participant-researcher intersubjectivity. *The Humanistic Psychologist, 33*(4), 271-292.

Fisher, M. A. (2008). Clarifying confidentiality with the ethical practice model. *American Psychologist, 63*(7), 624-625.

Freud, S. (2010). *The ego and the id.* Middletown, DE: Pacific Publishing Studio.

Furth, G. M. (1988). *The secret world of drawings: Healing through art.* Boston, MA: Sigo Press.

Ganim, B., & Fox, S. (1999). *Visual journaling: Going deeper than words.* Wheaton, IL: Quest Books.

Gaze. (1979). In *Coles concise English dictionary.* Toronto, Canada: Coles Publishing Company Limited.

Gemin, J. (1999). The dissolution of the self in unsettled times: Postmodernism and the creative process. *Journal of Creative Behavior,* 33(1), 45-61.

Gevinson, T. (2014). On Suzy Lake. In G. Uhlyarik (Ed.), *Introducing Suzie Lake* (p. 13). London, UK: Black Dog Publishing.

Ghaye, T., & Lillyman, S. (1997). *Learning journals and critical incidents: Reflective practice for health care professionals.* Dinton, Wiltshire: Quay Books.

Gilbert, M., Lydiatt, W., Aita, V., Robbins, R., McNeilly, D., & Desmarais, M. (2016). Portrait of a process: Arts-based research in a head and neck cancer clinic. *Medical Humanities,* 42(1), 57-62.

Gilroy, A. (1992). *Art therapists and their art: A study of occupational choice and career development, from the origins of an interest in art to occasionally being able to paint* (Unpublished doctoral dissertation). University of Sussex, Falmer, Brighton.

Gilroy, A. (2004). On occasionally being able to paint revisited. *International Journal of Art Therapy,* 9(2), 69-71.

Gilroy, A., Tipple, R., & Brown, C. (Ed.) (2012). *Assessment in art therapy.* New York, NY: Routledge.

Giorgi A. (1985a). Sketch of a Psychological Phenomenological Method. In A. Giorgi, (Ed.). *Phenomenology and psychological research* (pp. 8-22). Pittsburgh, PA: Duquesne University Press.

Giorgi A. (1985b). The phenomenological psychology of learning and the verbal learning tradition. In A. Giorgi (Ed.), *Phenomenology and psychological research* (pp. 23-85). Pittsburgh, PA: Duquesne University Press.

Giorgi, A. (1997). The theory, practice, and evaluation of the phenomenological method as a qualitative research procedure. *Journal of Phenomenological Method as a Qualitative Research Procedure,* 28(2), 235-260.

Giorgi, A. (2012). An affirmation of the phenomenological psychological descriptive method: A response to Rennie. *Psychological Methods,* 19(4), 542-551.

Glaister, J. A. (1996). Serial self-portrait: A technique to monitor changes in self-concept. *Archives of Psychiatric Nursing,* 10(5), 311-318.

Glass, C. R., Arnkoff, D. B., & Shapiro, S. J. (2001). Expectations and preferences. *Psychotherapy,* 38(4), 455-461.

Groenewald, T. (2004). A phenomenological research design illustrated. *International Journal of Qualitative Methods,* 3(1), 42-55.

Gross, E., & Stone, G. (1964). Embarrassment and the analysis of role requirements. In M. Argyle (Ed.), *Social encounters: Contributions to social interaction* (pp. 355-368). Chicago, IL: Aldine Publishing Company

Hamblen, K. (1984). Artistic development as a process of universal-relative selection possibilities. (Doctoral dissertation). Retrieved from https://files.eric.ed.gov/fulltext/ED252457.pdf

Hammer, E. (1967). *The clinical application of projective drawings.* Springfield, IL: Charles C. Thomas.

Handelzalts, J. E., & Ben-Artzy-Cohen, Y. (2014). The Draw-A-Person test and body image. *Rorschachiana,* 35, 3-22.

Hanes, M. J. (2007). "Face-to-face" with addiction: The spontaneous production of self-portraits in art therapy. *Art Therapy: Journal of the American Art Therapy Association,* 24(1), 33-36.

Hanson, W. E., & Poston, J. M. (2011). Building confidence in psychological assessment as a therapeutic intervention: An empirically based reply to Lilienfeld, Garb, and Wood. *Psychological Assessment,* 23(4), 1056-1062.

Hanson, J. M., & Poston, W. E. (2010). Meta-Analysis of psychological assessment as a therapeutic intervention. *Psychological Assessment,* 22(2), 203-212.

Hendrixson, B. (1986). A self-portrait project for a client with short-term memory dysfunction. *American Journal of Art Therapy,* 25(1), 15-24.

Hill, L. (2014). Art and psychotherapy. *Psychologica,* 36(1), 27-31.

Hill, L. (2016). Art and Psychotherapy as a Self-Reflection Tool for Therapists.

Psychologica, 40(1), 19-21.

Hocoy, D. (2007). Art therapy as a tool for social change: A conceptual model. In F. Kaplan (Ed.), *Art therapy and social action* (pp. 21-39). Philadelphia, PA: Jessica Kingsley Publishers.

Hoffman, L. (1990). Constructing realities: An art of lenses. *Family Process,* 29, 1-12.

Hood, A. B., & Johnson, R. W. (2007). *Assessment in counseling: A guide to the use of psychological assessment procedures* (4th ed.). Alexandria, VA: American Counseling Association.

Hoy, A. (1987). *Fabrications: Staged, altered, and appropriated photographs.* New York, NY: Cross River Press.

Husserl, E. (2012). *Husserl: Ideas.* New York, NY: Routledge.

Identity (1979). In *Coles concise English dictionary.* Toronto, Canada: Coles Publishing Company Limited.

Janson, H. W. (1986). *History of art.* (Vol. 2, 2nd ed.), Revised and expanded by A. Janson, Harry N. New York, NY: Abrams Incorporated.

Jensen, R. M. (2004). *The substance of things seen: Art, faith and the Christian community.* United Kingdom: William B. Eerdmans Publishing Company.

Johns, C. (1995). Framing learning through reflection within Carper's fundamental ways of knowing in nursing. *Journal in Advanced Nursing Practice,* 22, 226-234.

Kaufman, B., & Wohl, A. (1992). *Casualties of Childhood.* Springfield, IL: Brunner/Mazel Publishers.

Keeling, M., & Bermudez, M. (2006). Externalizing problems through art and writing: experience of process and helpfulness. *Journal Marital and Family Therapy,* 32(4), 405-419.

Kellog, R., & O'Dell, S. (1970). *The psychology of children's art.* New York, NY: Random House.

Kenworthy, W. (1995). *A study of personal interrelationships through the self-portrait* (Doctoral dissertation). Retrieved from ProQuest Dissertations and Theses Global. (Thesis No. 1377612)

Klugman, D. (1997). Existentialism and constructivism: A bi-polar model of subjectivity. *Clinical Social Work Journal,* 25(3), 297-313.

Kohut, H. (1971). *The analysis of the self: A systematic approach to the psychoanalytic treatment of narcissistic personality disorders.* New York, NY: International Universities Press.

Kohut, H. (1984). *How does analysis cure?* Chicago, IL: University of Chicago Press.

Kolb, L. C. (1975). Disturbances of the body image. In S. Arieti (Ed.), *American handbook of psychiatry* (2nd ed.) (p. 4). New York, NY: Basic Books.

Koskela, J. (2012). Truth as Unconcealment in Heidegger's being and time. *Minerva – An Internet Journal of Philosophy,* 16, 116-128.

Koufer, H., Arbel, H., & Barak. F. (2004). Diagnosis of anxiety expression using self-portrait drawn by patients during chemotherapy. *Journal of Clinical Oncology,* 22(14_suppl), 8244.

Kroger, J. (2005). [Review of the book Erikson on development in adulthood: New insights from the unpublished papers by C. H. Hoare]. *Identity: An international Journal of Theory and Research,* 5(1), 91-94.

Kroll, L., Mikhailova, E., & Serdiouk, E. (1995). Taking turns before the mirror I: Theory and setting. *Group Analysis,* 28, 281-289.

Kroon, N. (1999). Historical overview of projective testing. In N. Kroon, *The thematic apperception test for children: An investigation into the validity of the thematic apperception test for child assessment through an evaluation of the tasks of emotional development test* (pp. 6-53). Portland, OR: Veronique Kroon, Singing Song Books.

Landgarten, J. (2001). Art therapists who are artists. *American Journal of Art Therapy,* 39(3), 81-83.

LeClerc, J. (2006). The unconscious as paradox: Impact on the epistemological stance of the art psychotherapist. *The Arts in Psychotherapy,* 33(2), 130-134.

Leibowitz, M. (1999). *Interpreting projective drawings: A self psychological approach.* Ann Arbor, MI: Taylor and Francis.

Leonard, V. (1994). A Heideggerian phenomenological perspective on the concept of person. In P. Benner (Ed.), *Interpretive phenomenology: Embodiment, caring and ethics in health and illness* (pp. 43-63). Thousand Oaks, CA: Sage Publications Inc.

Lessem, P. A. (2005). *Self psychology: An introduction.* New York, NY: Jason Aronson.

Levick, M. (2012). The Levick Emotional and Cognitive Art Therapy Assessment (LECATA). In A. Gilroy, R.Tipple, & C. Brown, *Assessment in art therapy* (pp. 169-188). New York, NY: Routledge.

Levine, S. (1992). *Poiesis: The language of psychology and the speech of the soul.* London, UK: Jessica Kingsley Publishers.

Lichtenburg, J. D. (1989). *Psychoanalysis and motivation.* Hillsdale, NJ: Analytic Press.

Lichtenburg, J. D. (1992). *Self and motivational systems: Toward a theory of psychoanalytic technique.* Hillsdale, NJ: Analytic Press Inc.

Lieberman, J. S. (2000). *Body talk: Looking and being looked at in psychotherapy.* Northvale, NJ: Jason Aronson Inc.

Lincoln, Y., & Guba, E. (1985). *Naturalistic inquiry.* CA: SAGE Publications Inc.

Loven, A. (2003). The paradigm shift – rhetoric or reality? *International Journal for Educational and Vocational Guidance,* (3), 123-135.

Lowenfeld, V., & Brittain, W. L. (1975). *Creative and mental growth* (6th ed.). New York, NY: Macmillan Publishing, Co. Inc.

Lum, W. (2002). The use of self of the therapist. *Contemporary Family Therapy,* 24(1), 181-197.

Machover, K. (1949). *Personality projection in the drawing of a human figure: A method of personality investigation.* Springfield, IL: Charles, C. Thomas Publisher.

Malchiodi, C. A. (1998). *Understanding children's drawings.* New York, NY: The Guilford Press.

Malchiodi, C. A. (2007). *The art therapy sourcebook.* New York, NY: MacGraw-Hill.

Merstein, B. (1965). *Handbook of projective techniques.* New York, NY: Basic Books, Inc.

McNiff, S. (1981). *The arts and psychotherapy.* Sringfield, IL: Charles, C. Thomas.

McNiff, S. (1998). *Art based research.* Philadelphia, PA: Jessica Kingsley Publishers.

McNiff, S. (2004). *Art heals: How creativity heals the soul.* Boston, MA: Shambala.

McNiff, S. (2007). Empathy with the shadow: Engaging and transforming difficulties through art. *Journal of Humanistic Psychology,* 47(3), 392-399.

McNiff, S. (2012). Art-based methods for art therapy assessment. In A. Gilroy, R. Tipple & C. Brown (Ed.), *Assessment in art therapy* (pp. 66-80). New York, NY: Routledge.

Merry, T. (1997). Counselling and creativity: An interview with Natalie Rogers. *British Journal of Guidance and Counselling*, 25(2), 263-273.

Miller, C. (2014). *Assessment and outcome in the arts therapies: A person-centred approach*. UK: Jessica Kingsley Publishers.

Moon, B. L. (1995). *Existential art therapy: The canvas mirror* (2nd ed.). Springfield, IL: Charles C. Thomas Publisher.

Moon, B. L. (1997). *Art and soul: Reflections on an artistic psychology*. Springfield, IL: Charles C. Thomas Publisher.

Moon, C. H. (2002). *Studio art therapy: Cultivating the artist identity in the art therapist*. Philadelphia, PA: Jessica Kingsley Publishers.

Moon, J. A. (1999). *Learning journals: A handbook of academics, students and professional development*. New York, NY: SAGE Publications Inc.

Morin, C., & Bensalah, Y. (1998). The self-portrait in adulthood and aging. *The International Journal of Aging and Human Development*, 46(1), 45-70.

Morin, C., Pradat-Diehl, P., Robain, G., Bensalah, Y., & Perrigot, M. (2003). Stroke hemiplegia and specular image: Lessons from self-portraits. *International Journal of Aging and Human Development*, 56(1), 1-41.

Moustakas, C. (1994). *Phenomenological research methods*. California, USA: SAGE Publications Inc.

Murphy, H. (1997). *Canetti and Nietzsche: Theories of humor in Die Blendung*. New York, NY: State University of New York Press.

Murstein, B. I. (1965). *Handbook of projective techniques*. New York, NY: Basic Books Inc.

Nasinovskaya, E. E., & Shalina, O. S. (2008). The self-portrait as a means of mastering the realm of personal experiences. *Voprosy Psychologii*, 1, 77-88.

Nouwen, H. (1979). *The wounded healer: Ministry in contemporary society*. New York: Image Books.

Nunez, C. (2009). The self-portrait, a powerful tool for self-therapy. *European Journal of Psychotherapy and Counselling*, 11(1), 51-61.

Orbach, S. (2009). *Bodies*. London, UK: Profile Books.

Oster, G. & Crone, P. G. (2004). *Using drawings in assessment and therapy* (2nd ed.). New York: Routledge.

Otero-Pailos, J. (2010). *Architectures historical turn: Phenomenology and the rise of the postmodern.* Minneapolis, MN: Regents of the University of Minnesota.

Palacios, E. G., Echaniz, I. E., Fernandez, A. R., & Camino Ortiz de Barron, I. (2015). Personal self-concept and satisfaction with life in adolescence, youth and adulthood. *Psicothema, 27*(1), 52-58.

Platzman, S. (2001). *Cezanne: The self-portrait.* California: University of California Press.

Polley, D. L. (2003). *Exploring autophotography as a complementary therapy for female rape survivors* (Unpublished doctoral dissertation). Alliant International University, California.

Portrait. (1979). In *Coles concise English dictionary.* Toronto, Canada: Coles Publishing Company Limited.

Price, A. (2004). Encouraging reflection and critical thinking in practice: By reading this article and writing a practice profile, you can gain a certificate of learning. *Nursing Standard* 18(47), 46.

Riley, S. (1994). *Integrative approaches to family art therapy.* Philadelphia, PA: Jessica Kingsley Publishers.

Riley, S. (2004). *Integrative approaches to family art therapy* (2nd Ed.). Chicago, IL: Magnolia Street Publishers.

Robb, C. (2006). *This changes everything: The relational revolution in psychology.* New York, NY: Picador.

Rogers, C. (1959). A theory of therapy, personality, and interpersonal relationships, as developed in the client-centred framework. In S. Koch (Ed.), *Psychology: A study of a science (Study 1, Volume 3: Formulations of the person and the social context),* pp. 184-256). York, PA: McGraw-Hill.

Rosen, H. (1977). *Pathway to Piaget.* Cherry Hill, NJ: Postgraduate International.

Santrock, J. W., MacKenzie-Rivers, A., Malcomson, T., & Leung, H. K. (2011). *Life-span development* (4th ed.). China: MacGraw-Hill Ryerson.

Satir, V., Banmen, J., Gerber, J., & Gomari, M. (1991). *The Satir model: Family therapy and beyond.* Palo Alto, CA: Science and Behaviour Books, Inc.

Schaverien, J. (1990). The scapegoat and the talisman: Transference in art therapy. In T. Dalley, C. Case, J. Schaverien, F. Weir, D. Halliday, P. Hall, & D. Waller (Eds.), *Images of art therapy: New developments in theory and practice* (2nd ed.) (pp. 74-108). New York, NY: Tavistock Publications/Routledge.

Schaverien, J. (1995). *Desire and the female therapist: Engendered gazes in psychotherapy and art therapy*. New York, NY: Routledge.

Schildkraut, J. J. (1999). Rembrandt by himself. *The American Journal of Psychiatry,* 156(12), 2009-2010.

Schön, D. A. (1983). *The reflective practitioner: How professionals think in action*. New York, NY: Basic Books.

Scotti, V. (2016). *Beyond words: Making meaning of transitioning to motherhood using portraiture: An arts-based study* (Doctoral dissertation). Retrieved from ProQuest Dissertations and Theses Global. (Thesis No. 10099587)

Self. (1997). In *Coles concise English dictionary*. Toronto, Canada: Coles Publishing Company Limited.

Self-concept. (2017). In *Oxford English Dictionary*. Retrieved from https://en.oxforddictionaries.com/definition/self-concept

Self-portrait. (1997). In *Coles concise English dictionary*. Toronto, Canada: Coles Publishing Company Limited.

Smith, F. (2008). *Seeing and being seen: Self-portraiture in art therapy*. Montreal, Quebec: Concordia University.

Sommers-Flanagan, J. (2007). The development and evolution of a person-centred expressive art therapy: A conversation with Natalie Rogers. *Journal of Counseling and Development,* 85, 120-125.

Sprenkle, D. H., & Piercy, F. P. (Eds.) (2005). *Research methods in family therapy* (2nd ed.). New York, NY: The Guilford Press.

Spiegel, J., Severino, S., & Morrison, N. (2000). The role of attachment functions in psychotherapy. *The Journal of Psychotherapy Practice and Research,* 9(1): 25-32.

Steindl-Rast, D. (1999). *A listening heart: The spirituality of sacred sensuousness*. New York: A Crossroad Publishing Company.

Stiles, W. B. (1993). Quality control in qualitative research. *Clinical Psychology Review,* 13, 593-618.

Stolorow, R. D., Atwood, G. E., & Brandschraft, B. (1994). *The intersubjective perspective.* Northvale, NJ: The Analytic Press.

Stolorow, R. D., Brandschraft, B., & Atwood, G. E. (1987). *Psychoanalytic treatment: An intersubjective approach.* Hillsdale, NJ: The Analytic Press.

Stuckey, H., & Nobel, J. (2010). The connection between art, healing, and public health: A review of current literature. *American Journal of Public Health,* 100(2), 254-263.

Sutton, L., Townend, M., & Wright, J. (2007). The experiences of reflective learning journals by cognitive behavioural psychotherapy students. *Reflective Practice,* 8(3), 387-404.

Thompson, A. (2013). *The self-portrait, narcissism, and the other* (Doctoral dissertation). Retrieved from ProQuest Dissertations and Theses Global. (Thesis No. 1543098)

Topolovčan, T. (2016). Art-based researching of constructivist teaching. *Croatian Journal of Education,* 18(4), 1141-1172.

Tuber, S. (2008). *Attachment, play, and authenticity: A Winnicott primer.* New York, NY: Jason Aronson.

Uhlyarik, G. (2014). Home in Toronto. In G. Uhlyarik (Ed.), *Introducing Suzie Lake* (pp. 127-173). London, UK: Black Dog Publishing.

Ulman, E. (2001). Art therapy: Problems of definition. *American Journal of Art Therapy,* 44(1), 16-26.

Van Lith, T. (2008). A phenomenological investigation of art therapy to assist transition to a psychosocial residential setting. *Art Therapy: Journal of the American Art Therapy Association,* 25(1), 24-31.

VanKatwyk, P. L. (2003). *Spiritual care and therapy: Integrative perspectives.* Waterloo, Ontario: Wilfrid Laurier Press.

Walker, D. (1985). Writing and reflection. In R. Boud, R. Keogh, & D. Walker (Eds.), *Reflection: Turning experience into learning.* New York, NY: Nichols Publishing Company.

Wang, C. (2015, April 3). *Symbolism of Colors and Color Meanings Around the World.* Retrieved from https://www.shutterstock.com/blog/color-symbolism-and-meanings-around-the-world

Watzlawick, P. (1984). *The invented reality.* New York, NY: W.W. Norton Incorporated.

Webb, A. (2015). Everything man. *ROM Magazine,* 2015(4), 20-28.

Weiser, J. (1999). *Phototherapy techniques: exploring the secrets of snapshots in family albums.* Vancouver, BC: PhotoTherapy Centre.

Weiser, J. (2008). *Phototherapy techniques: Exploring the secrets of personal snapshots and family albums.* Vancouver, BC: PhotoTherapy Centre.

Weisz, J. R., Chorpita, B. F., Frye, A., Ng, M. Y., Lau, N., Bearman, S. K., & Hoagwood, K. E. (2011). Youth top problems: Using idiographic, consumer-guided assessment to identify treatment needs and to track change during psychotherapy. *Journal of Consulting and Clinical Psychology,* 79(3), 369-380.

Welkener, M., & Magolda, M. (2014). Better understanding students' self-authorship via self-portraits. *Journal of College Student Development,* 55(6), 580-585.

Williams, T. O., Fall, A, Eaves, R. C., & Woods-Groves, S. (2006). The reliability of scores for the Draw-A-Person intellectual ability test for children, adolescents, and adults. *Journal of Psychoeducational Assessment,* 24(2), 137-144.

Willis, P. (2001). The "things themselves" in phenomenology. *Indo-Pacific Journal of Phenomenology,* 1, 1-14.

Winnicott, D. W. (1953). Transitional objects and transitional phenomena. *International Journal of Psychoanalysis,* 34, 89-97.

Winnicott, D. W. (1960). The theory of parent-infant relationship. *International Journal of Psychoanalysis,* 41, 585-595.

Winnicott, D. W. (1965). *The maturational processes and facilitating environment: Studies in the theory of emotional development.* New York, NY: The Hogarth Press and the Institute of Psycho-Analysis.

Wright, K. (2009). *Mirroring and attunement: Self-realization and psychoanalysis in art.* New York, NY: Routledge.

APPENDIX A
ADVERTISEMENT

Registered and/or Professional members of either the Canadian Art Therapy Association or the Ontario Art Therapy Association who are currently working in the field of art therapy are invited to participate in a doctoral thesis research project by Laurie Ponsford-Hill. Laurie is currently looking to recruit no more than 15 art therapists to engage in a self-reflective process for the period of one month requiring an anticipated time allotment of 5.5 hours total. Laurie is looking for a wide range of therapists that reflect the membership of both associations. The purpose of this study is to explore the impact upon the therapeutic process of utilizing self-portraiture for the therapist in order to reflect on process and lived-experience, and to explore if the therapist will then integrate this into therapy with their clients and how or if the experience will thus inform their work. This research project has been reviewed and approved by the University Research Ethics Board of Wilfrid Laurier University. Please contact Laurie Ponsford-Hill @ 519-421-2845 or help@thecounsellinghouse.ca for more information and your participation package.

APPENDIX B
WEEKLY REFLECTION PROCESS

Set aside one hour at the end of your work week each week for a total of 4 weeks. Make sure that you have on hand colour markers, photocopy paper 8.5 x11 inches and a journal. Take 5 minutes and draw a full-bodies self-portrait. Take the remaining one hour and reflect upon yourself, your week, your self-portrait and what you see contained within or missing from your portrait as you journal and reflect upon your experience.

At the end of the 4 week process photograph your artwork and email the artwork to the researcher. Once the researcher has the artwork in hand the researcher will contact the participant for a time to be interviewed about the process. The researcher will ask a list of questions about the process and the participant will be recorded for data dissemination.

Survey Questions for Therapist:

How often do you use art in your practice?
How many years have you been in practice?
Do you use art as a subjective assessment tool in practice?
How many years of practice as an art therapist?
What are the populations that you normally work with?
Do you use a self-reflective process as an art therapist?
Have you used self-portraiture with clients?

APPENDIX C
QUESTIONS FOR THE TELEPHONE SCRIPT

1. Describe the experience of drawing the four self-portraits?
2. What did you experience as you repeated the exercise over the four weeks?
3. As you reflect on the four self-portraits, how has the self-portrait changed or did they change?
4. As you look at the four images what did you notice, was there a story that emerges for you?
5. Are there any themes that you might see emerging in your work as you look at the four images?
6. Describe your experience of the creative process over the four weeks?
7. What was the experience of the identification of a constraint as you were reflecting on your portrait(s)?
8. If you did identify a constraint, what was that experience like for you?
9. When reflecting on the four self-portraits what do you notice about your self-concept?
10. What was the experience like looking at your portrait as you were reflecting upon the experience?
11. What was the experience like for you as the portrait looked back at you?
12. When you reflect on the experience of the self-portrait and journaling over the past four weeks, and your work over that period of time, how did you integrate the experience?
13. How would you integrate self-portraiture into your work or your self-reflection process?

ABOUT LAURIE PONSFORD-HILL PHD

Like many therapists, Laurie Ponsford-Hill began as a newly graduated therapist feeling like she could provide her services all day, every day. She realized at a certain point in her career that this was simply not true, and this fueled her determination to understand everything about the need to maintain balance in her life.

Laurie earned a Master of Divinity degree, and directed her work towards pastoral care, later earning a Master of Counselling Psychology degree and furthering her Registrations to that of Psychotherapist, Marriage and Family Therapist, Social Worker, and Art Therapist. Her career led her to a greater understanding about herself and her relationships. Laurie continued to broaden her education and went on to complete a doctoral program in Human Relationships at Wilfrid Laurier University, Waterloo Lutheran Seminary.

Laurie feels fortunate to have attained balance in her work and home life and empathizes with many others engaged in their own personal struggles to attain balance. She has dedicated her career towards helping others on that journey, designing the Self-Supervision program, which was meticulously tested in this clinical research study. The Art of Self-Supervision: Studying the link between self-supervision and self-care chronicles the remarkable findings of this study: that professionals can overcome burnout and improve their health and life balance by focusing on their self-portrait.

Laurie is currently the Clinical Director and Supervisor at The Counselling House, in both London and Woodstock Ontario, an agency that focuses on the supervision of counselling interns and newly graduated therapists, and their development of self-supervision. Laurie maintains a private consulting practice specializing in the development of maintaining healthy relationships with self, work, home, others, God, and the world.